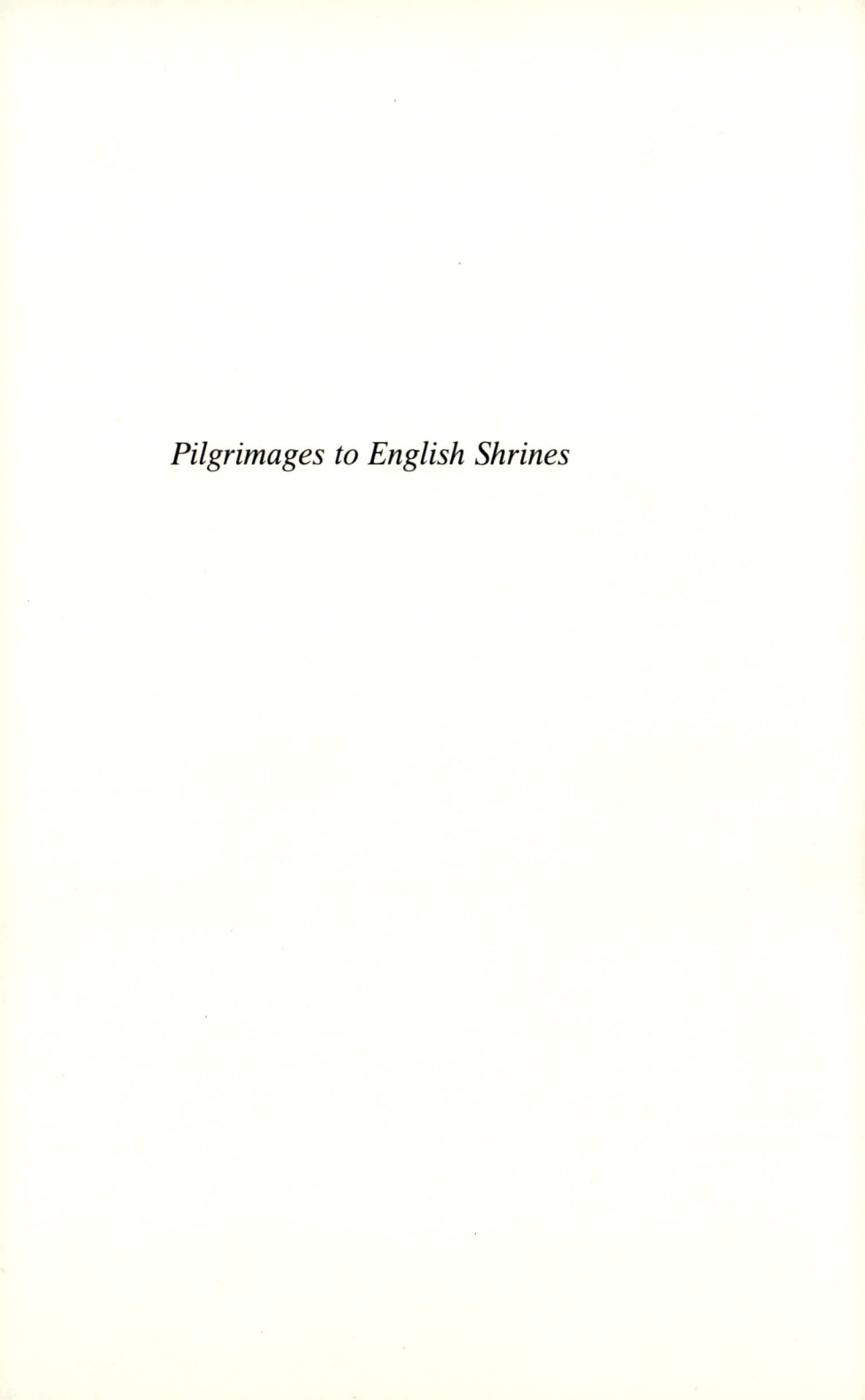

Pilgrimages to English Shrines

PILGRIMAGES

TO

ENGLISH SHRINES

By Mrs S. C. Hall.

With notes and illustrations by

F. W. Fairholt, f.s.a.

Bardon Enterprises
Portsmouth

This collection of essays was originally published in the
Art Journal between the years of 1849-1852.

First published in parts by George Virtue, London, 1849-1852.

ISBN : 1-902222-07-5

Typeset and printed in England
by Bardon Enterprises.
Bound in England by Ronarteuro.

Portsmouth, Hampshire, England.

CONTENTS

The Birth-Place of Thomas Chatterton.

HATTERTON—poor Chatterton! We had been brooding sadly over his fragment of a life, ending at seventeen—and turning page after page of Horace Walpole's literary fooleries, to find his explanations and apologies for want of feeling and sympathy, which his flippant style and heartless commentaries, illustrate to perfection ; and we closed, with an aching heart, the volumes of both the parasite of genius, and him who was its mightiest creation and most miserable victim :—

'The marvellous boy who perished in his pride

It was only natural for us to recall the many instances we have ourselves known, during the past twenty years, or more, of sorrow and distress among those who sought distinction in the thorny labyrinths of literature :—those who

————'waged with Fortune an eternal war,
Checked by the scoff of Pride, by Envy's frown,
And Poverty's unconquerable bar ;'

and those who, after a brief struggle with untoward fate, left the battle-field, to die, 'unpitied and unknown!'

We have seen the career of a young literary man commenced with the first grand requisite of all excellence worth achieving—ENTHUSIASM ; high notions of moral honour, and a warm devotedness to that 'calling' which lifts units to a pinnacle formed of the dry bones of hundreds slain. We have seen that enthusiasm frozen by disappointment—that honour corrupted by the contamination of dissipated men—that devotedness to THE CAUSE fade away before the great want of nature—want of bread—which it had failed to bestow. We have seen, ay, in one little year, the flashing eye dimmed—the round cheek flattened—the bright, hopeful creature, who went forth into the world—rejoicing like

1

the sun to run his course—dragged from the waters of our leaden Thames, a discoloured remnant of mortality—recognised only by the mother who looked to him for all the world could give!

This is horrible—but it is a tragedy soon played out. There are hundreds at this moment possessed of the *consciousness* of power without the *strength* to use it. To such, a little help might lead to a life of successful toil—perhaps the happiest life a man can lead. A heritage of usefulness is one of peace to the last. We knew another youth, of a more patient nature than he of whom we have just spoken. He seemed never weary. We have witnessed his nightly toil ; his daily labour ; the smiling patience with which he endured the sneers levelled, *only* in English society, against '*mere* literary men.' We remember when, on the first day of every month, he used to haunt the booksellers' shops to look over the magazines, cast his eyes down the table of contents, just to see if 'his poem' or 'his paper' had been inserted—then lay them down one after another with a pale sickly smile, expressive of disappointment, and turn away with a look of gentle endurance. The insertion of a sonnet, for which perhaps he might receive seven shillings, would set him dreaming again of literary immortality ; and at last the dream was realised by an accident, or rather, to speak advisedly, by a good Providence. He became known—known at once—blazed forth : something he had written attracted the town's attention, and ladies in crowded drawing-rooms stood upon chairs to see that poor, worn, pale man of letters : and magazines, and grave reviews, and gaily-bound albums, all waited for his contributions—charge what he pleased ; and flushed with fame, and weighed down with money—money paid for the very articles that had been rejected without one civil line of courtesy—the great sustaining hope of his life was realised ; he married one as worn and pale with the world's toil, as himself—married—and died within a month! The tide was too tardy in turning!

Who shall say how many men of genius have walked, like unhappy Chatterton, through the valley of the shadow of death, and found no guide, no consolation—no hope ; if, the one GREAT HOPE had not been most mercifully planted early in their hearts and minds.

It was with melancholy pleasure that, during the past summer, our Pilgrimage was made to the places connected with the boy's memory, in

Bristol ; first to Colston's school, in which he was educated ;[1] next to
the dull district in which he was either born or passed his boyhood ; then
to the Institution, where his 'Will,' a mad document, and other memo-
randa connected with his memory, are preserved with a degree of care,
that seems—or is—a mockery, when contrasted with the worse than
indifference of the city to all that concerned him when alive ; next to the
house of Master Canynge, and next to the monument (Redcliffe Church)
with which his name will be associated as long as one of its stones remains upon another : chewing the cud of sweet and bitter fancies
through its long-drawn aisles ; pondering sadly in the muniment-room,
where the cofres that suggested the forgeries, still lie rotting ; and gazing
with mingled sorrow and surprise on the 'Cenotaph to Chatterton,'
which now, taken to pieces, occupies the corner of a damp vault—

> 'A solemn cenotaph to thee,
> Sweet Harper of time-shrouded minstrelsy!'

Ah! such books as we have been reading, and such memories as we
have been recalling, are, after all, unprofitable—a darkness without
light. We closed our eyes upon the world, which, in our momentary
bitterness, we likened to one great charnel-house, entombing all things
glorious and bright. We walked to the window ; the rain was descending in torrents—pour, pour ; pattens clattered in the areas, and a solitary
post-man made the street echo with his impatient knocks. A poor organ-
boy, whom we have long known, was moving, rather than walking, in
the centre : his hat flapped over his eyes by the rain, yet still he turned
the handle, and the damp music crawled forth : he paused opposite our
door, turned up the leaf of his hat, and looked upwards : we missed the
family of white mice which usually crawled on the top of his organ :

---

[1] Of Edward Colston, well and beautifully has William Hewitt said, 'You cannot help
feeling the grand beneficence of those wealthy merchants, who, like Edward Colston,
make their riches do their generous will for ever ; who become thereby the actual fathers
of their native cities to all generations ; who roll off, every year of the world's progress,
some huge stone of anxiety from the hearts of poor widows ; who clear the way before the
unfriended, but active and worthy lad ; who put forth their invisible hands from the heaven
of their rest, and become the genuine guardian angels of the orphan race for ever and
ever : raising from those who would otherwise have been outcasts and ignorant labourers,
aspiring and useful men ; tradesmen of substance ; merchants the true enrichers of their
country, and fathers of happy families. How glorious is such a lot! how noble is such an
appropriation of wealth! how enviable is such a fame! And amongst such men there were
few more truly admirable than Edward Colston! He was worthy to have been lifted by
Chatterton to the side of the magnificent Canynge, and one cannot help wondering that he
says so little about this great benefactor of his city.'

poor child, he had sheltered them in his bosom ; it was nothing more than natural that he should do so, and the act was common-place enough—but it pleased us—it diminished our gloom. And we thought, if the great ones of the land would but foster the talent that needs, and deserves, protection from the storms of life, as that lonely boy sheltered the creatures entrusted to his care, the world would be all the better. We do not mean to insult the memory of such a genius as Chatterton by saying that he required a PATRON—the very sound is linked with a servility that degrades a noble nature : but we do say he sadly wanted a FRIEND—someone who could have understood and appreciated his wonderful intellectual gifts ; and whose strength of mind and position in society would have given power to direct and control the overleaping and indomitable pride which ultimately destroyed 'the Boy.' His career teaches a lesson of such rare value to all who seek distinction in any sphere of life that we would have it considered well—as a beacon to warn from ruin.

> 'Oh! what a tangled web we weave,
> When first we practise to deceive!'

Despite his marvellous talents, his industry, his knowledge, his magnitude of mind, his glorious imagination, his bold satire, his independence, his devotional love of his mother and sister—if he had lived through a long age of prosperity, Chatterton could never have been trusted, nor esteemed, *from his total went of truth.* His is the most striking example upon record of the necessity for uprightness in word and deed. Where a great end is to be achieved—there must be consistency, a union between noble daring and noble deeds—there must be Truth! No man has ever deviated from it without losing not only the respect of the thinking, but even the confidence of the unwise. Chatterton's earliest idea seems to have been how to deceive ; and, were it possible to laugh at youthful fraud, there would be something irresistibly ludicrous in the lad bewildering the old pewterer, Burgun. Imagine the fair-haired rosy boy, the brightness of his extraordinary eyes increased by the covert mischief which urged him forward—fancy his presenting himself to Master Burgum, who, dull as his own pewter, had the ambition, which the cunning youth fostered, of being thought of an 'ancient family'—fancy Chatterton in his poor-school dress presenting himself to this man, whose business, Chatterton's biographer, Mr. Dix, tells us, was carried on in the house now occupied by Messrs. Sanders, Bristol

Bridge,[2] and informing him that he had made a discovery—presenting to him various documents, with a parchment painting of the De Burgham arms, in proof of his royal descent from the Conqueror.

BRISTOL BRIDGE.

Mr. Dix assures us, 'that never once doubting the validity of the record, in which his own honours were so deeply implicated, he presented the poor bluecoat-boy, who had been so fortunate in *finding* so much, and so assiduous in his endeavours to collect the remainder, with *five shillings!*' Blush, Bristol, blush at this record of a citizen's meanness ; the paltry remuneration could have hardly tempted even so poor a lad as Thomas Chatterton to continue his labours for the love of gain ; yet he furnished Burgum with further information, loving the indulgence of his mystifying powers, and secretly satirising the folly he duped.

---

[2] Our engraving shows this house, and Bristol Bridge, both memorable as being connected with the earliest of Chatterton's fabrications. Bristol Bridge was finished in September, 1768, and in the October following, Chatterton sent to 'Felix Farley's Bristol Journal,' the curiously detailed account of the ceremonial observances on opening the ancient bridge at Bristol, 'taken from an Old Manuscript,' and which, being his first printed forgery, led, by the attention it excited to the production of other works, and among them the Rowley Poems. At this time he was in his 16th year ; but some years before he had fabricated Burgum's pedigree, and some poetry by a pretended ancestor of his, of the alleged date of 1320, called 'The Romaunte of the Cnyghte.' The house where Burgum lived, and where Chatterton first tried his powers of deception, is the central one of the three seen above the bridge in our Cut.

BIRTH-PLACE OF CHATTERTON.

It is quite impossible to trace back any circumstance which could, to speak advisedly, have led to such a course of deception as was practised by this boy ; born of obscure parents, his father, a man of dissolute habits, was sub-chanter of the Cathedral, and also master of the free school in Pyle-street ; this clever, but harsh and dissolute man died in August, 1752, and the poet was born on the 20th of the following November.[3] Such a parent could not be a loss ; he would have been, in all

[3] The place of Chatterton's birth has been variously stated ; Mr. Dix, in his 'Life of Chatterton,' has mentioned *three*. His first being that 'he was born on the 20th of November, in the year 1752 in a house situated on Redcliff Hill, behind the shop now (1837) occupied by Mr. Hasell, grocer,' and which has since been destroyed. But in the appendix to his volume is a communication stating that Mrs. Newton (Chatterton's married sister) left a daughter who 'died in 1807, in the house where Chatterton was born ; I believe in the arch at Cathay,' a street leading from the church-yard to the river-side. But the most certain account seems to be that of Mrs. Edkins (also printed by Dix) who 'went to school to Chatterton's father, and was present when the son was born, at the Pyle School.' Now, as Chatterton was born about three months after his father's death, and he had been for some years master of the school, it is unlikely that his wife would be removed from the house she inhabited until after her confinement, 'when,' says Mrs. Edkins, 'she went to a house opposite the upper gate on Redcliff Hill.' The house appropriated to the master of Pyle Street School is shown in our engraving, it is at the back of the school, which faces the street, and is approached by an open passage on one side of it leading into a small court-yard, beyond which is a little garden. Over the door is inserted a stone, inscribed, 'This house was erected by Giles Malpas, of St. Thomas Parish, Gent., for the use of the master of this School, A.D. 1749.' The house has but two sitting-rooms, one on each side of the door, that to the right being the kitchen ; and in one of them the dissolute father of

human probability, as careless of his son as he was of his wife ; and, at all events, Chatterton had not the misery of early cruelty to complain of, for he had a mother, tender and affectionate, although totally unfit to guide and manage his wayward nature. Her first grief with him arose, strange as it may seem, from his inaptitude for learning—as a child he disdained A B C, and indulged himself with his own thoughts. When nearly seven years old he 'fell in love,' to use his mother's phrase, 'with an illuminated French manuscript,' and thus learned his letters from the very sort of thing he spent his early days in counterfeiting. His progress was wonderful, both as to rapidity and extent, and his pride kept pace therewith. A friend, wishing to give the boy and his sister a present of china ware, asked him what device he would choose to ornament his with. 'Paint me,' he said, 'an angel with wings and a trumpet, to trumpet my name over the world.' Here was a proof of innate ambition ; if his mother had had an understanding mind, this observation would have taught her to read his character. Such ambition could have been directed,—and directed to noble deeds.

He was admitted into the Blue Coat School, commonly called 'Colston's School,'[4] before he was eight years old, and his enthusiastic joy at the prospect of learning so much, was damped by finding that, to quench his thirst for knowledge, 'there were not books enough.' When he took in rotation the post of doorkeeper at the school, he used to indulge himself in making verses ;[5] and his sister, who loved him tenderly, pre-

---

the Poet is said by Dix to have 'often passed the whole night roaring out catches, with some of the lowest rabble of the parish.' He was succeeded in the office of Schoolmaster by Edmond Chard, who held it for five years ; and he was followed in 1757 by Stephen Love, who was master twenty-one years, and to whom Mrs. Chatterton first sent her son for education ; and who, 'after exhausting the patience of his schoolmaster, was sent back to his mother with the character of a stupid boy, and one who was absolutely incapable of receiving instruction.'

[4] This school, founded in 1708 by Edward Colston, Esq., is situated in a street called St. Augustine's Back behind the houses facing the drawbridge. It is the mansion in which Queen Elizabeth was entertained when she visited the city ; and was purchased by Colston, because of its applicability to his charitable purposes. Here the scholars are boarded, lodged, and clothed, and are never permitted to be absent—except on Saturdays and Saints' days, from one till seven. They are simply taught reading, writing, and arithmetic. The school-room is on the first floor, and runs along the entire front of the building ; the bedrooms are the large airy rooms above. Behind the house is a paved yard for exercise. Chatterton remained here about seven years.

[5] The gate seen at the side of Colston's School in our cut, is that by which the school is entered ; a narrow paved passage beside the house conducts to the angle of the building, when you turn to the left, and so reach the house by an open court-yard. In a corner of

CHATTERTON AS DOORKEEPER.

sented him with a pocket-book, in which he wrote verses, and gave it back to her the following year. There was nothing in this species of tuition or companionship to create or foster either the imitations or the satire he indulge in, he had neither correction nor assistance from any one. Even before his apprenticeship to Mr. John Lambert he felt he was not appreciated or understood ; perhaps no one ever *acted* a greater satire upon his own profession than this harsh attorney, who deemed his apprentice on a level with his footboy. He must have been a man utterly devoid of perception and feeling ; his insulting contempt of what he could not understand added considerably to the sarcastic bitterness of Chatterton's nature, and it is easy to picture the boy's feelings when his productions were torn by this tyrant and scattered on the office floor! He has his reward John Lambert, the scrivener, is only remembered as the insulter of Thomas Chatterton![6]

this angle, commanding a view of the entrance to the school, and also of the outer gate, is placed the doorkeeper's lodge delineated in our cut. It is a small building of brick, covered with lead, about six feet in height. It has within an iron seat, and an iron ledge for books. The windows are unglazed ; and in winter it must be singularly uncomfortable, particularly as the occupant must traverse the length of the yard in all weathers. It is said to be the intention of the authorities to remove this little building : this is to be regretted as it is almost the only unchanged memorial of her boy-poet which Bristol possesses. It was customary for the boys to take the office of doorkeeper in rotation for the term of one week ; and it was in Chatterton's twelfth year, when he was doorkeeper, that he wrote here his first poem 'on the Last Epiphany, or Christ coming to Judgment.'

[6] Lambert's first office was on St. John's Steps ; but the unceasing spirit of change, which has more or lass destroyed all the Bristol localities connected with Chatterton, has swept this one away ; 'the Steps' have now been turned into a sloping ascent, and the old houses removed or renovated. Shortly after he had entered Lambert's service, his office was removed to Corn Street, and here, from the house delineated in our cut, he dated his first communication to Horace Walpole. It is immediately in front of the Exchange, and although the lower part has been altered frequently within remembrance, the upper part remains as when Lambert rented it. It may be noted, that the upper floors of the adjacent houses are still devoted to lawyers' and merchants' offices.

It is impossible not to pause at every page of this boy's brief but eventful life, and lament that he had no friend ; reading, as we do, by the light of other days, we can see so many passages where judicious counsel, given with the intelligent affection that would at once have opened his heart, *must* have saved him ; his heart, once laid bare to friendship, would have been purified by the air of truth ; it was its *closeness* which infected his nature. And yet the scrivener considered him a good apprentice. His industry was amazing ; his frequent employment was to copy precedents, and one volume, in his hand-writing, which is still extant, consists of three hundred and forty-four closely-written folio pages. There was in that gloomy office an

LAMBERT'S OFFICE.

TOMB OF CANYNGE.

edition of Camden's 'Britannia,' and, having borrowed from Mr. Green, a bookseller, Speight's 'Chaucer,' he compiled therefrom an ingenious glossary, for his own use, in two parts. 'The first,' Mr. Dix says, 'contained old words, with the modern English—the second, the modern English, with the old words ; this enabled him to turn modern English into old, as an English and Latin dictionary enables the student to turn English into Latin.' How miserable it is, amongst those evidences of his industry and genius, to find that all his ingenuity turned to the furtherance of a fraud. He seems to have been morally dead to everything like the disgrace attending falsehood ; for, when struggling afterwards in London to appear prosperous while starving, he wrote home to Mr. Catcott, and concludes his letter by stating that he intended going abroad as a *surgeon*, adding, 'Mr. Barrett has it in his power to assist me greatly, by *his giving me a physical character* ; I hope he will.' He seems to have had no idea that he was asking Mr. Barrett to do a dishonest action.

MUNIMENT ROOM.

But the grand fraud of his short life was boldly dared by this boy in his sixteenth year. Why he should have ever descended to forge when he felt the high pressure of genius so strong within him, is inexplicable. Why, with his daring pride, he should have submitted to be considered a transcriber, where he originated, is more than marvellous. The spell of a benighting antiquity seemed around him : it might lead one to a belief in 'Gramarie—that some false spirit had issued forth from the 'cofre of

Mr. Canynge,[7] so long preserved in the room over the north porch of this Bristol church of Redcliffe—a '*cofre*,' secured by six keys, all of which being lost or mislaid, the vestry ordered the '*cofre*' to be opened ; and not only 'Canynge's *cofre*' but all the '*cofres*' in the mysterious chamber ; not from any love of antiquity, but because of the hope of obtaining certain title-deeds supposed to be contained therein.   Well, these intelligent worthies, having found what concerned themselves, took them away, leaving behind, end open, parchments and documents which might have enriched our antiquarian literature beyond all calculation.[8] Chatterton's father used to carry these parchments away wholesale, and covered with the precious relics, bibles and school-books : most likely other officers of the church did the same. After his death, his widow conveyed many of them, with her children and furniture, to her new residence, and, woman-like, formed them into dolls and thread-papers. In process of time, the child's attention being aroused by the illuminated manuscripts, he conveyed every bit of parchment he could find to a small den of a room in his mother's house, which he called his own ; and, when he grew a little older, set forth, with considerable tact, in

---

[7] The great Bristol merchant, William Canynge, jun., is buried in Redcliffe Church, which he was a great benefactor, as he was to the city of Bristol generally. He entered the church to avoid a second marriage, and was made Dean of the College of Westbury, which he had rebuilt.   There are two monuments to his memory in Redcliffe Church, both of which are seen in our engraving. One is a raised altar tomb with an enriched canopy ; and upon the tomb lie the effigies of Canynge and his wife in the costume of the fifteenth century. The other tomb is of similar construction, and is believed to have been brought here from Westbury College ; it represents Canynge in his clerical robes, his head supported by angels, and resting his feet on the figure of a Saracen. Here Chatterton frequently ruminated ; indeed, the whole church abounds with memorials which call to mind the sources of his inspiration ; near the door is an effigy inscribed 'Johannes Lamyngton,' which gave name to one of his forgeries. He was never weary of rambling in and about the church, and all his early works originated here.

[8] The muniment-room is a large low-roofed apartment over the beautiful north porch of Redcliffe Church, which was constructed by Canynge. It is hexagonal, and lighted by narrow unglazed windows.   The floor rests on the groined stones of the porch, strong beams of oak forming its roof. It is secured by two massive doors in the narrow passage leading from the stairs into it. Here were preserved several large chests, and among them *Canynge's cofre ;* from which Chatterton assured the world he had obtained the Rowley MSS.; and from which MSS. were carried away and destroyed, but the old chests still remain. There are seven in all, and they bear traces of great antiquity. Many have been strongly bound with iron, but all are now in a state of decay. This lonely cheerless room, strewn with antique fragments and suggestive of the boy-poet's day-dreams, is certainly the most interesting relic in Bristol. Its comfortless neglect is a true epitome of the life of him who first shaped his course from his reveries within it.

answer to all questions asked of him as to how he obtained the poems and information, that he himself had searched the old *'cofres'*[9] and

CANYNGE'S HOUSE

discovered the poems of the Monk Rowley. Certainly he could not have had a better person to trumpet his discovery than 'a talkative fool' like Burgum, who was so proud of his pedigree as to torment the officers of the Heralds' College about his ancestors ; and he was not the only one imposed on by Chatterton's talent.   His simple-minded mother bore testimony to his joy at discovering those 'written parchments upon the covered books ;' and, of course, each discovery added to his antiquarian knowledge ; for, though no trace exists of the Monk Rowley's originals, there is little doubt that on some of those parchments he found enough to set him thinking, and with him to think and act was the same thing ; indeed, there is one passage in his poems bearing so fully upon the fraud, that we transcribe it.   He is writing of having discharged all his obligations to Mr. Catcott :—

---

[9] The house said to be that of Canynge is situated in Redcliffe Street, not very far from the church.   It is now occupied by a bookseller, who uses the fine hall seen in our cut, as a storehouse for his volumes.   Chatterton frequently mentions this 'house nempte the rodde lodge ;' and in Skelton's 'Etchings of Bristol Antiquities' is an engraving of this building, there called 'Canynge's chapel or Masonic Hall,' showing the painting in the arch at the back, representing the first person of the Trinity, supporting the crucified Saviour, angels at each side censing, and others bearing shields.   This was 'the Rood' with which Chatterton was familiar, and which induced him to give the name to Canynge's house in his fabrications.   This painting is now destroyed, but we have restored it from Skelton's plate in our engraving.

'If ever obligated to thy purse,
Rowley discharges all, my first chief curse!
For had I never known the antique lore,
I ne'er had ventured from my peaceful shore ;
But, happy in my humble sphere, had moved
Untroubled, unsuspected, unbeloved.'[10]

A Mr. Rudhall[11] said that, when Chatterton wrote on a parchment, he held it over a candle to give it the appearance of antiquity ; and a Mr. Gardener has recorded, that he once saw Chatterton rub a parchment over with ochre, and afterwards rub it on the ground, saying, 'that was the way to antiquate it.' This *exposé* of Chatterton's craft is so at variance with his usual caution that we can hardly credit it. A humble woman, Mrs. Edkins, speaks of his spending all his holidays in the little den of a room we have mentioned, where he *locked* himself in, and would remain the entire day without meals, returning with his hands and

---

[10] The monk Rowley was altogether an imaginary person conjured up by Chatterton as a vehicle for his wonderful forgeries. He was described by him as the intimate friend of Canynge, his constant companion, and a collector of books and drawings for him. It has been well remarked, that although it was *extraordinary* for a lad to have written them in the 18th century, it was *impossible* for a monk to have written them in the 15th. Indeed, it seems now both curious and amusing that his forgeries should have deceived the learned. When Rowley talks of purchasing his house 'on a repayring lease for ninety-nine years,' we at once smile, and remember his fellow-forger Ireland's Shaksperian *Promissory* note, before such things were invented. Our fac-simile of the pretended Rowley's writing is obtained from the very curious collection of Chatterton's Manuscripts in the British Museum. It is written at the bottom of some drawings of monumental slabs and notes, stated to have been 'collected ande gotten for Mr. William Canynge, by mee, Thomas Rowley.' There are, however, other autographs of Rowley in the collection, so entirely dissimilar in the formation of the letters, that it might be expected to have induced a conviction of forgery. Many of the manuscripts too are still more dissimilar ; and the construction of the letters totally unlike any of the period. Some are written on little fragments not more than three inches square, the writing sometimes neat and clean, at other times bad, rambling, and unintelligible. The best is the account of Canynge's feast, which has been engraved in fac-simile by Strutt, to the edition of Rowley's Poems, 1777. The writing is generally bolder than Barrett's fac-simile ; and that gentleman, in endeavouring to revive the faded ink, has greatly injured the originals, which are now in some cases almost undistinguishable. The drawings of pretended ancient coins and heraldry are absurdly inventive ; and the representations of buildings exactly such as a boy without knowledge of drawing or architecture would fabricate ; yet they imposed on Barrett who engraved them for his history of Bristol. Many of his transcripts show the shifts the poor boy was put to for paper : torn fragments and backs of law-bills are frequently employed. Among the rest is a collection of extracts from Chaucer to aid him in the fabrication of his MSS. The whole is exceedingly instructive and curious.

[11] This gentleman was the proprietor of the 'Bristol Journal,' to which Chatterton sent his first forgery ; and with whom he afterwards became intimate.

face completely begrimed with dirt and charcoal ; and she well remembers his having a charcoal pounce-bag and parchment and letters on a little deal table, and all over the ground was a litter of parchments ; and she and his mother at one time fancied he intended to discolour himself and run away to the gipsies ; but afterwards Mrs. Edkins believed that he was labouring at the Rowley manuscripts, and she thought he got himself bound to a lawyer that he might get at old law books. The testimony she bears to his affectionate tenderness towards his mother and sister is touching : while his pride led him to seek for notoriety for himself, it was only to render his mother and sister comfortable that he coveted wealth.

It is not our province to enter into the controversy as to whether the MS. were originals or forgeries : it would seem to be as undecided today as it was three quarters of a century ago : the boy 'died and made no sign :' and the world has not been put in possession of any additional facts by which the question might be determined : the balance of proof appears in favour of those who contend they were the sole offspring of his mind, suggested merely by ancient documents from which he could have borrowed no idea except that of rude spelling ; yet it is by no means impossible that poems did actually exist, and came into his hands, which he altered and interpolated, but which he did not create.

FAC-SIMILE OF MSS.

In aid of his plans, Chatterton first addressed himself to Dodsley, the Pall Mall bookseller, once with smaller poems, and afterwards on behalf of the greatest production of his genius—the tragedy of 'Ælla ;' but the booksellers of those days were not more intellectual than those at the present : they devoured the small forgery of the great Horace Walpole, 'The Castle of Otranto,' and rejected the magnificence of a nameless composition. This man's neglect drove the young poet to the 'Autocrat of Strawberry Hill.' In reply he at first received a polished letter. The literary trifler was not aware of the poverty and low station of his correspondent, and so was courteous ; he is 'grateful' and 'singularly obliged ;' bowing, and perfumed, and polite. Other communications followed. Walpole inquired—discovered the poet's situation ; and *then* he changed! The poor fond boy! how hard and bitter was the rebuff.

How little had he imagined that *the* Walpole's soul was not, *by five shil-lings*, as large as the Bristol pewterer's!—that he who was an adept at literary imposition could have been so harsh to a fellow-sinner! This volume of his works containing 'Miscellanies of Chatterton' is now be-fore us. Hear to his indignant honesty! He declares that 'all the house of forgery are relations ; and that though it be but just to Chatterton's memory to say his poverty never made him claim kindred with the rich-est, or more enriching branches, yet that his ingenuity in counterfeiting styles, and I believe hands, might easily have led him to those more fac-ile imitations of prose—promissory notes.' The literal meaning of this paragraph stamps the littleness of the man's mind. A slight—a very slight effort on his part might have turned the current of the boy's thoughts, and saved him from misery and death. We do not call Chat-terton 'his victim,' because we do not think him so ; but he, or any one in his position, might have turned him from the love of an unworthy notoriety to the pursuit of a laudable ambition.

Following in the world's track (which he was ever careful not to outstep), when the boy was dead, Walpole bore eloquent testimony to his genius. The words of praise he gives his memory are like golden grains amid the chaffy *verbiage* with which he defends himself. If he perceived this at first, why not have come forward hand and heart, and shouted him on to honest fortune? But, like all *clique kings,* he made no general cause with literature ; he only smiled on his individual worship-pers, who could applaud when he said, with cruel playfulness, 'that singing birds should not be too well fed!'

His master, Lambert, dismissed the youth from his service, be-cause he had reason to suppose he meditated self-destruction ; and then he proceeded to London. How buoyant and full of hope he was during his probationary days there, his letters to his mother and sister testify ; his gifts, also, extracted from his necessities, are evidences of the bent of his mind—fans and china—luxuries rather than necessaries ; but in this, it must be remembered his judgment was in fault, not his affec-tions. In all things he was swayed, and guided by his pride,—his in-domitable pride. The period, brief as it was, of his sojourn in the great Metropolis proved that Walpole, while he neglected him so cruelly, un-derstood him perfectly, when he said that 'nothing in Chatterton could be separated from Chatterton—that all he did was the effervescence of ungovernable impulse, which, cameleon like, imbibed the colours of all it looked on ; it was Ossian, or a Saxon monk, or Gray, or Smollett, or

Junius.' His first letter to his mother is dated, April the 26th, 1770. He terminated his own existence on the 24th of August in the same year. He battled with the crowded world of London, and, what was in his case a more dire enemy than the world, his over-whelming pride, for nearly four months. Alas! how terrible are the reflections which these few weeks suggest! Now borne aloft upon the billows of hope, sparkling in the fitful brightness of a feverish sun, and then plunged into the slough of despair, his proud, dark soul disdaining all human participation in a misery exaggerated by his own unbending pride. Let us not talk of denying sympathy to persons who create their own miseries ; they endure agonies thrice told. The paltry remuneration he received for his productions is recorded by himself. Among the items is one as extraordinary as the indignant emotion it excites :—

> Received from Mr. Hamilton, for 16 songs, 10s. 6d.
> Of Mr. Hamilton, for 'Candidus' and Foreign
> Journal... 2s. !!

We are wearied for him of the world's dark sight : yet in the same book is recorded that the same publisher owed him £10 19s. 6d.! This sum might have saved him, but he was too proud to ask for money ; too proud to complain ; too proud to accept the invitation of his acquaintances, or his landlady, to dine or sup with them ; and all too proud to hint, even to his mother and sister, that he was anything but prosperous. Ardent as if he had been a son of the hot south, he had learned nothing of patience or expediency. His first residence was at Mrs. Walmsley's, in Shoreditch, but, doubtless, finding the lodging too expensive, he removed to a Mrs. Angell's, sac-(or dress) maker, 4, Brook Street, Holborn. This woman, who seems to have been of a gentle nature, finding that for two days he had confined himself to his room, and gone without sustenance, invited him to dine with her ; but he was offended, and assured her he was not hungry. It is quite impossible to account for this uncalled-for pride. It was his nature. Lord Byron said he was mad : according to *his* view of the case, all eccentricity is madness ; but in the case of unhappy Chatterton, that madness which arises from 'hope deferred,' was unquestionably endured. Three days before his death, pursuing, with a friend, the melancholy and speculative employment of reading epitaphs in the churchyard of St. Pancras, absorbed by his own reflections, he fell into a new-made grave. There was something akin to the raven's croak, the death-fetch, the fading spectre, in this foreboding accident ; he smiled at it, and told his friend he felt the sting of speedy dissolution :—

'Then black despair,
The shadow of a starless night, was thrown
Over the earth on which he moved alone.'

At the age of seventeen years and nine months, his career ended ; it was shown that he had swallowed arsenic in water, and so—

'perished in his pride!'

An inquest was held, and yet though English-men—men who could read and write, and hear—who must have heard of the boy's talents, either as a poet, a satirist, or a political writer—though these men were guided by a coroner, one, of course, in a more elevated sphere than those who usually determine the intentions of the departed soul—yet was there not one—NOT ONE of them all—with sufficient veneration for the casket that had contained the diamond—not one with enough of sympathy for the widow's son—to wrap his body in a decent shroud, and kneel in Christian piety by his grave!—not one to pause and think that, between genius and madness,

'What thin partitions do the bounds divide!'

In a letter from Southey to Mr. Britton (dated in 1810, to which we have already referred, and which Mr. Britton kindly submitted to us with various other correspondence on the subject), he says, 'there can now be no impropriety in mentioning what could not be said when the collected edition of Chatterton's works was published,—that there was a taint of insanity in his family. His sister was once confined ; and this is a key to the eccentricities of his life, and the deplorable rashness of his death.' Of this unhappy predisposition, indeed, he seems to have been himself conscious, for 'in his last will and testament,' written in April 1770, before he quitted Bristol, when he seems to have meditated suicide—although, from the mock-heroic style of the document his serious design may be questioned,—he writes, 'If I do a mad action it is conformable to every action of my life, which all savoured of insanity. His 'sudden fits of weeping, for which no reason could be assigned, when a mere child, were but the preludes to those gloomy forebodings which haunted him when a boy. His mother had said, 'she was often apprehensive of his going mad.'

And so,—the verdict having been pronounced,—he was cast into the burying-ground of Shoe Lane workhouse—the paupers' burying-ground,—the end, as far as his clayey tabernacle was concerned, of all his dreamy greatness. When the ear was deaf to the voice of the

CHATTERTON'S CENOTAPH.

charmer he received his meed of posthumous praise. Malone, Croft, Dr. Knox, Wharton, Sherwin, Pye, Mrs. Cowley, Walter Scott, Hayley, Coleridge, Dermody, Wordsworth, Shelley, William Howitt, Keats, who dedicated his 'Endymion' to the memory of his fellow-genius ; the burly Johnson, whose praise seemed unintentional ; the gentle and most Christian poet, James Montgomery,—have each and all offered tributes to his memory. Robert Southey, whose polished, strong, and long unclouded mind was a treasure-house of noble thoughts, assisted Mr. Cottle in providing for the poet's family by a collection of his works ; and, though last, not least, excellent John Britten has laboured all his long life to render justice to the poor boy's memory. To him, indeed, it was mainly owing, that the cenotaph to which we have referred (and which now lies mouldering in the Church vault), was erected in the graveyard of Redcliffe Church, by subscription, of which the contributions of Bristol were very small.[12]

Chatterton was another warning, not only that

'Against self-slaughter
There is a prohibition so divine—'

but that no mortal should ever abandon Hope! for a reverend gentleman,—who was, in all things, what, unhappily, Horace Walpole was not,—had actually visited Bristol, to seek out and aid the boy, while he lay dead in London.

---

[12] The cenotaph erected to Chatterton, in 1838, from a design by S. C. Fripp, has now been removed : it stood close to the north porch, beside the steps leading into it. One of the inscriptions, which he directs in his will to be placed on his tomb, has been adopted. 'To the Memory of Thomas Chatterton. Reader, judge not, if thou art a Christian. Believe that he shall be judged by a superior Power. To that Power alone is he now answerable.'

'Beware of desperate steps ; the darkest day,
Live till to-morrow, will have passed away.'

The knowledge of these facts cheered us as we set forth to the neighbourhood of Shoe-lane to see the spot where he had been laid. Alas! it is very hard to keep pace with the progress of London changes. After various inquiries we were told that Mr. Bentley's printing-office stands upon the ground of Shoe Lane Workhouse. We ascended the steps leading to this shifting emporium of letters, and found ourselves face to face with a kind gentleman, who told us all he knew upon the subject, which was, that the printing-office stands—not upon the burying-ground of Shoe Lane Workhouse, where he had always understood Chatterton was buried—but upon the church burial-ground. He showed us a very curious basso-relieve, in cut stone, of the Resurrection, which he assured us had been 'time out of mind' above the entrance to the Shoe Lane burying-place 'over the way,' and which is now the site of Farringdon Market. This, when 'all the bones' were moved to the old graveyard in Gray's Inn Road, had come 'somehow' into Mr. Bentley's possession.

We were told also that Mr. Taylor, another printer, had lived, before the workhouse was pulled down, where his office-window looked upon the spot pointed out as the grave of Chatterton, and that a stone, 'a rough white stone,' was remembered to have been 'set in a wall' near the grave, with 'Thomas Chatterton' and something else 'scratched' into it.

We strayed back through the damp chill of the city's evening fog to the marketplace, hoping, even unconsciously, to stand beside the pit into which the marvellous boy had been thrust ; but we grew bewildered. And as we stood upon the steps looking down upon the market—alone in feeling, and unconscious of everything but our own thoughts—St. Paul's bell struck, full, loud, and clear ; and, casting our eyes upward, we saw its mighty dome through the murky atmosphere. We became still more 'mazed,' and fancied we were gazing upon the monument of Thomas Chatterton!

The Tomb of Thomas Gray.

HE view from the Royal Terrace at Windsor is one of such surpassing beauty, that the longer we gaze the more we appreciate its variety, its luxurious richness, and its vast extent. It is in truth a glorious landscape, unrivalled in Europe. Well may the Sovereign who, day by day, looks over such a scene, be proud thereof! The smiling villages, the spired churches, the embowered dwellings of 'knight and squire,' the stately mansions, the wide spreading lawns, the variegated parks, the noble forest sheltering beneath its foliage the tributary strangers of distant lands—the stately avenue, the noble river upon whose banks the

> 'antique towers
> That crown the wat'ry glade,'

nurture, within time-honoured walls, the future leaders of the senate and the field—under the very shadows of the Royal pile they thus learn to reverence with all the deep devotion of English hearts, and to defend as much by wisdom as by the dauntless bravery that carries Englishmen triumphant through the world :—

> 'From the stately brow
> Of Windsor's heights, th' expanse below
> Of grove, of lawn, of mead, survey!'

No foreigner should be permitted to leave England without spending a long day at Windsor, and it should not be the first, but the last, of his Island excursions, inasmuch as it is the radiant crown of our English sights. It is, indeed, delicious to stand upon that noble terrace, to lift our eyes to the horizon and carry the sight over the intervening space,—resting it midway upon the quaint points and pinnacles of Eton, to which we may thence descend by 'the hundred steps.' From this exalted position it is impossible to imagine anything in nature more surpassingly beautiful than the wide range of country within ken ; and if read (as who is not?) in the history of the past, how peopled it becomes with glorious

20

memories—with pageants and tournays, with accidents and incidents, with great struggles too between arbitrary power and a people who would be, and are, free—the only really free people at this time of writing, in broad Europe. But it is not well to withdraw from the terrace and believe you have seen Windsor. You must leave the stately apartments, the carvings, the paintings, the sculpture, the tapestry, the corridor, the chambers—where, in the sanctity of private life, the Lady whom we honour both from duty and affection, reigns paramount as woman, as fully as queen :—you must turn from the cups of Benvenuto Cellini, and forget the vase that graced the Spanish Armada, and the golden salvers, and relics of old times ;—you must look your last at the banners in St. George's Chapel, while you remember that the pavement you have trod covers the mouldering dust of kings ;—you must not, if your time be limited, listen a moment longer to the tones of that unrivalled organ, pealing to the fretted roof : but away—not direct to the Long Walk—but through the ugly and straggling Clewer Green—not gazing back until after passing the pretty lodge gate at St. Leonard's, and entering the domain, you look up at the stately castle from the lowland you are about to leave. The foreground is such as Cuyp has painted, and as Sidney Cooper can paint still, especially if the sun is preparing to set, and

'the lowing herd winds slowly o'er the lea ;'

the meadows have that soft green 'plashy' look which refreshes eyes aching from the effects of the rich and gorgeous palace ; they are as a prairie to groups of beautiful cattle ; each a study—the whole a picture. Above sits the castle the fine grey stonework standing out against the sky, whose deep blue is fading, so as to harmonise all the better with the colour of the noble pile ; and from this point of view the objectionable parts of the town, which sometimes interfere with the dignity of the palace, are not visible ; yet you must not tarry there, but proceed—still on—still refreshing your eyes with the shady dells of deep copses that stretch to the right and left of your wooded way. Pause again a moment on the brow of St. Leonard's Hill before you are in sight of the entrance to the dwelling, and fail not to look down upon the valley, with Maidenhead in the distance. Keep the high road, which either ancient right, or the liberality of the proprietor, permits you to do, until you reach the Queen's highway, leading, past Forest Hill and Prince Albert's farm, to Wingfield ; cross it and pass through a gate, and then, for the time being, you are as free of Windsor Forest, as the red deer, or the white goats, or the wild buffalo's who enjoy its full freedom with you. For some time your road conducts you through a copse of young oaks, stretching on both sides as far as you can see over ever waving ferns, affording cover rather than food to the pheasants, who gaze at you with starry eyes, and hardly deign to rise at your approach. Here and there, fitting respect has been shown to some ancient oaks that have withstood the storms of centuries :—space has been cleared around them ; several are perfectly hollow, others gnarled and rugged ;—such fine studies for the pencil, that we expected to see an artist, instead of a satyr, start from the wood, fully equipped for service. Presently you perceive to the left an open prairie., always spotted with deer, and then leaving the close wood behind, you pass another royal lodge, on lofty ground ; then on to Queen Anne's green drive ; there pause, and see how the castle bursts upon you in full magnificence. We know nothing more glorious than to view it when the sun is setting, the heavens flooded with tints of amber and of rose : the castle, from its commanding seat, looking the more cold, and grand, and dark, when contrasted with the brightness of the sky, while here and there some tree or mound seems adopted by the heavens, and steeped in its own splendour. The road leads gallantly on to where a group of noble beeches overshadows the way ; the forest land breaks down into a glade, and, far beyond it again rises the castle. But that is not all ; you must pause at the statue of the third George, and look along the three mile drive, terminated by the castle entrance ; this view gives you only the entrance, seeming more like the erection of a fairy tale, than a reality ; but it is a wonderful lesson in perspective. It is matter of regret that the double row of trees at either side are elm ; they will not last as long as the oak or the ash, but there is no tree better adapted to receive grand masses of light :—nor is its foliage heavy ; its leaves are small, it hangs loosely, and is, in general very picturesque ; it is the first tree to salute the spring, with its light and cheerful green ; and, in autumn, its yellow leaf harmonises with the orange of the beech, and the ochrey tint of the royal oak. These elms are at present in high perfection, and 'the long drive,' during which the castle grows in magnitude at every step, is never tedious. Nothing is more contemplative than a long avenue ; its monotony is so suggestive. How much such a circuit as that we have endeavoured to describe, fills the mind! how much is taken in by the eye, to prompt the imagination!

GRAY'S HOUSE AT STOKE[13].

---

[13] The manor house of Stoke Pogis, where Gray resided with his mother and his aunt, was a solitary house suited to the retiring character of the Poet. When he lived in it it was then in the possession of Viscountess Cobham. Its architecture was of the Elizabethan era, and Gray himself has happily described it in his *Long Story :* —

'In Britain's Isle —no matter where —
    An ancient pile of building stands :
The Huntingdons and Hattons there,
    Employed the power of fairy hands

To raise the ceiling's fretted height,
    Each panel in achievements clothing,
Rich windows that exclude the light,
    And passages that lead to nothing.

Full oft within these spacious walls,
    When he had fifty winters o'er him
My grave Lord Keeper led the brawls ;
    The seals and maces danced before him.'

The house originally belonged to the Earls of Huntingdon and the family of Hatton. It was here that Gray lived when he wrote the *Elegy ;* it had been handed about in MS. previous to its publication and had met with many admirers ; among them was Lady Cobham. She felt a strong desire to become acquainted with the author, and Lady Schaub and Miss Speed, then at Stoke Pogis, undertook to introduce her to the Poet. They called on the author at his aunt's solitary residence, and not finding him at home left their cards. The Poet surprised at such a compliment returned the visit ; and in commemoration of so unexpected and peculiar an introduction, immortalised the adventure in his *Long Story.* After Gray's death, when the estate fell into the hands of Mr. Penn, that gentleman pulled down

And if there be yet time, how well it may be employed in visiting the resting-place of the poet Gray, which is but two miles from Slough.

STOKE POGIS CHURCH.

The steeple of his 'country church' is one of the most remarkable of the objects seen from the Terrace. Without knowing it to be the one hallowed by 'the Elegy,' the stranger could not fail to inquire concerning its name and whereabouts. A visit to this church and its 'lap of earth' will be repaid amply.

It was a lovely Sabbath morning, before summer had quite finished her sojourn among us, and when autumn had barely touched the topmost branches of the trees with her golden wand, that we determined on a pilgrimage to Stoke Pogis, and left the pretty hill of Clewer at an early hour to go to church,[14] at the place rendered immortal by the Poet who wrote so little, and yet so much. We passed through the ugly,

---

the greater part of the mansion, but left the portion we have engraved, as a memento of his favourite poet.

[14] The altar-tomb seen near the church, beside which two figures stand, covers the grave of Gray's aunt and mother ; it was erected by him, and the concluding words of the epitaph simply, but most touchingly, record his sense of that most melancholy bereavement, for which the world can offer no substitute —a mother's love. It reads thus : —

scrambling town, hanging on the skirts of royalty, as a tattered parasite around a lordly tree ; and over the bridge, which Eton youths may not cross, into the town of the *boy-college,* where the Poet was educated with his friend West : and though West went to Oxford, and Gray to Cambridge, their friendship only terminated with their lives.

Eton lies so very low that it is well the lads have long vacations, though all look happy and full of life, and in the very spirit of health. The previous day we had seen scores of them playing foot-ball in the meadows appropriated to their amusement—recalling one of the most finished poems of our most finished poet—

> 'Say, Father Thames, for thou hast seen
> Full many a sprightly race
> Disporting on thy margent green,
>   The paths of pleasure trace ;
> Who foremost now delight to cleave,
> With pliant arm thy glassy wave?
> The captive linnet which enthrall?
>   What idle progeny succeed
>   To chase the rolling circle's speed,
> Or urge the flying ball?'

IN THE VAULT BENEATH ARE DEPOSITED,
IN HOPE OF A JOYFUL RESURRECTION,
THE REMAINS OF
MARY ANTROBUS.
SHE DIED NOVEMBER 5, 1749,
AGED 66
IN THE SAME PIOUS CONFIDENCE
BESIDE HER FRIEND AND SISTER,
HERE SLEEP THE REMAINS OF
DOROTHY GRAY,
WIDOW, THE CAREFUL AND TENDER MOTHER
OF MANY CHILDREN, ONE OF WHOM ALONE
HAD THE MISFORTUNE TO SURVIVE HER.
SHE DIED MARCH 11, 1753,
AGED 67 YEARS.

The Poet's name is not upon the tomb, but he also lies with them in their grave, and it is recorded on a tablet fixed in the church wall :—'Opposite to this stone in the same tomb upon which he has so feelingly recorded his grief at the loss of a beloved parent, are deposited the remains of Thomas Gray, the author of the Elegy written in a country churchyard, &c. &c. He was buried August 6, 1771.

But now on the Sabbath, all was still! the dew, unmarked by a single footstep ; the shadows,—shadows, which are to the eye what echoes are to the ear—lying heavily upon the grass! We passed too (though somewhat out of our road) 'the ivy mantled tower' of Upton Church.[15]

"THE IVY MANTLED TOWER"

It added to our enjoyment to visit the scenes of the Poet's early days on our way to his favourite village ; to look upon the old walls within whose sanctuary he imbibed that classic taste, perfected at Oxford, and the fruit of which seemed the chief solace of his life. It is impossible to read his few poems and letters and journals without feeling that his affections were circumscribed within a very small compass—and all under his control. We could not imagine him betrayed into an emotion, or shaken by a sympathy. And yet he was so thoroughly right, so elevated and ennobled by genius, that while you doubt the possibility of his reviving or exciting enthusiasm or affection, you venerate and admire him as a true poet and an admirable man.

---

[15] Our cut is engraved from a sketch by Alfred Montague. Upton Tower is very old, and bears traces of Norman workmanship. It is very near Eton, and is believed by many to have been the one the Poet had in mind when writing. It certainly accords better than that at Stoke Pogis with his description ; Upton was one of his early haunts. The gloomy character of the church and neighbourhood in twilight must well have been suited to one so 'unlike a boy,' as he is described to have been.

His friend Mason, at the commencement of the collected edition of his poems and letters, makes the trite observation,—that the lives of men of letters seldom abound with incidents ; and perhaps, no life ever afforded fewer than that of the Poet to whose grave our pilgrimage is made—that is to say, of what people of the world consider 'incidents,' but to the poetic temperament, things having neither name nor habitation, yet existing,—shadows of thoughts and feelings, revivals of past times, or the creations of the imagination, supply not only 'incidents,' but become *events ;* so that often a life has been full to overflowing of such as cannot be recorded ; or if it were possible to record them, they could not be understood.   Mason may most justly describe Gray as a 'virtuous, a friendly, and an amiable man ;' indeed his truth uprightness, and sincerity, rendered him peculiarly adapted for the highest friendship : it was the atmosphere in which he lived—

> 'Neither too hot nor too cold

for his moral constitution.   There is in the volume we have read, one letter to his friend West, who was evidently an erratic genius, fond of change of scene, and the luxury of no employment, or who perhaps called his day-dreams occupation : the letter is to be found on the 187th page of Rivington's little edition, with a frontispiece and vignette by Mr Uwins, designed before the accomplished Painter went to Italy and returned to delight all who look upon his pictures—the letter is, as we have said, on the 187th page, and is a model of refined feeling, practical sense, and earnest, hardy, disinterested friendship, evincing the extent of his discretion and the soundness of his judgment at the age of four-and-twenty.   It is much more philosophic than poetic, and proves that the excitement of foreign travel (he dates from Florence) did not in the least throw his mind off its well-poised balance.   Indeed, nothing can be more matter-of-fact than Mr. Gray's account of his lengthened stay abroad. 'We went there, and saw that, and then visited the other :' there is little more in his descriptions ; and yet he is so clear, that you see all he wishes you to see.   He is rarely, if ever, roused into enthusiasm ; his warmth is that of a Greek statue ; his eye is of stone rather than of fire. At Rome he met 'The Pretender' and his two sons ; the peculiar character of Gray prevented his giving any sympathy to this crushed branch of the House of Stuart (a circumstance much to be deplored), and his account of Charles Edward in age, singularly contrasts with that of the Charles Edward either of history or imagination, when, in his young days, he held court at Holyrood, and enlisted the warm sympathies of many a high-hearted man, and pure-souled woman. The fallen fortunes of the Prince might have excited the enthusiasm of the poet ; but Gray was a remarkable example of poetry without enthusiasm.

The letters and journals are, however, full of interest and models of a close and yet graceful style ; of rare value now-a-days, when writers elaborate words rather than thoughts. His *morale* also was of the highest. He honoured Art, and his classics were worthy of old Rome ; he was, certainly, of a musing, melancholy turn, not likely to move the affections of any except those who knew him in his earlier years, when the yielding heart readily receives strong impress from light matters ; for in one of his letters he complains bitterly of living for a month in the house with three women, who did little but laugh from morning to night, and would concede nothing to the sullenness of his disposition. Again, and in another, he says seriously, 'Cambridge is a delight of a place, *now there is nobody* in it. I do believe you would like it if you knew what it was without inhabitants.'

As we drove along we talked ever what we had read, until we remembered that the calm dignified classic poet, who loved Cambridge only when it was without inhabitants, was born amid the bustle of Cornhill, and even in midlife rebuilt his house there ; so that his theory and practice by no means harmonised. He was born on the 26th of December, 1716, and was educated at Eton under the care of his mother's brother Mr. Antrobus, who was at that time one of the assistant-masters, and also a Follow of St. Peter's College, Cambridge, to which Mr. Gray removed, and was admitted as a pensioner in the year 1734. He contracted a friendship while there with Horace Walpole, who was fond of asserting, in his keen epigrammatic way, what seems to be very true, that 'Gray never was a boy.' Gray's correspondence with this trifler in great things, is very interesting. He accompanied Mr. Walpole abroad, and though their acquaintance was dissevered, Mr. Mason says Mr. Walpole laid the blame on himself. The Poet had all the sensitiveness and mistrust of self which accompanies true genius ; and there is something to excite a smile in his nervous anxiety touching his 'misfortune,' as he expresses it, 'of receiving a communication from the "Magazine of Magazines"[16] for the time being—saying that an *ingenious* poem, called

---

[16] This journal was originated by a speculative bookseller, and it was intended to combine in its pages the pith of its various monthly contemporaries, in the same way that the 'Gentleman's Magazine' had first done by the newspapers. The success of the last-named miscellany, which was begun by Cave, in 1731, soon led to the establishment of the 'Lon-

"Reflections in a Country Churchyard" has been communicated to the editor, which the editor is printing ; and begging, not only the writer's confidence, but the honour of his *correspondence.*' Like all persons of narrow views, the proprietors of the 'Magazine of Magazines' thought they conferred an honour on the author of the Elegy by bringing him into *notice!* as our generous-hearted injudicious neighbours the Americans do to this day, when they scrape together the rakings of literature, and describe the minutiæ of our habits and dwellings—thinking the notoriety, which to our English habits is the most painful of all things—fame! Gray so instinctively shrunk from this, that he wrote a most simple and earnest letter to Mr. Walpole, entreating him to get Dodsley to print the 'Elegy' forthwith anonymously, *and to print it without any interval between the stanzas,* giving as a reason, that the sense is in some places continued beyond them![17] Being thus relieved from his nervousness, he continued tolerably tranquil until informed that it was in contemplation to publish his portrait with his poems. This threw him into a fresh agony. He again wrote to Mr. Walpole, saying, 'Sure you are not out of your wits ; this I know, if you suffer my head to be printed, you will infallibly put me out of mine. I conjure you immediately to put a stop to any such design. Who is at the expense of engraving it I know not, but if it be Dodsley, I will make up the loss to him. The thing as it was I know will make me ridiculous enough ; but to appear in proper person, at the head of my works, consisting of half-a-dozen ballads in thirty pages, would be worse than the pillory. I do assure you, if I had received such a book, with such a frontispiece,

---

don Magazine ;' and the success of both to a host of imitators : and their number led to the establishment of this 'Magazine of Magazines,' which was to condense the best articles from all.

[17] Gray's 'Elegy,' like all his other poems, appears to have been much elaborated in thought, and subject to great supervision. At the sale of his books and papers, at the end of the year 1845, the original manuscript was sold for 100*l.*, and Mr. Penn, of Stoke Pogis, was believed to have been the purchaser. There was a curious instance of this supervision of the lines which now stand—

Some mute inglorious *Milton* here may rest,
Some *Cromwell* guiltless of his country's blood'

They had originally been—

Some mute inglorious *Tully* here may rest,
Some *Cæsar* guiltless of his country's blood.'

The alteration is curious, as it shows Gray's love of classicality ; ultimately overruled by the dictates of a sound criticism, which would make such allusions out of place in a poem so eminently full of pure English simplicity.

ceived such a book, with such a frontispiece, without any warning, *I believe it would have given me a palsy!'*

We had thought of visiting Burnham, where the poet's uncle resided, if it were only in memory of the description, half serious, half absurd, which he gives of a spot famous for its beauty and its beeches ; but the summer had passed without our putting our design into action. Much as Gray loved and venerated his mother, and respected the aunt (Miss Antrobus) who, to remedy his father's extravagance, joined with her in the establishment of a species of India warehouse at Cornhill, there is a tone of well-bred mannerism and respect in his letters to his mother, rather than the outpouring of warm affection. In all his memoirs there is no trace of his having formed an attachment, or, as it is called, 'fallen in love' with anything less mortal than a classic Muse ; and while we loitered through the beautiful drive which, as we approached Stoke Green, became perfectly umbrageous, we could not recall a single line of Gray's that bore evidence of inspiration by the 'tender passion.'

The repose of a Sabbath morning was over the country ; we passed, and met, groups of persons, and hordes of little children 'dressed for church ;' the bells had not yet commenced sending forth their summons ; and the elders of the people were standing beneath the shadows of their homesteads, or looking after the 'young men and maidens,' the heritors of their toil, and their dwellings, with as much pride as pleasure. There had been a long continuance of rain previous to our excursion ; so that the sunshine made this Sabbath one of more than ordinary beauty and happiness ; the leaves clung to their parent trees, and the verdure was more bright and fresh than usual for the season ; the swallows 'hawked' rapidly through the air ; the cattle stood sleepily in the ponds fringed by graceful willows ; many hard-working horses felt that this, even to them, was a day of rest, and looked, we fancied, with pitying eyes on those who experienced no freedom from labour ; the dogs winked in the sunbeams, and the dignified hen stalked triumphantly at the head of her full grown brood. Few spots in England can boast of anything more lovely than the park and lane scenery immediately in the neighbourhood of Stoke Pogis ; the church,—in its intense retirement, forming a portion, and a most beautiful and hallowed portion of the domain—rendered even more interesting by associations with the venerated name of Penn—does not stand like ordinary churches, by the way-side or in a village, but like the church at Great Hampden, amid time-

honoured trees, shedding a halo on the residence which has lately found
a new proprietor—one who is entitled to all respect,—and who is worthy
to be its occupant—but who can never be entirely at home among these

> 'Brown o'er-arching groves
> That Contemplation loves.'

All matters at Stoke Pogis are better cared for than at Great Hampden ; you drive through a pretty gate-way guarded on the left by a lodge
covered with climbers ; on the right, an embowered path leads to the
monument, and the parterre which surrounds this memento of respect
and admiration is kept in as perfect order as any flower-garden can be :
it is separated from the meadow, through which the carriage-road continues after passing the lodge by a sunk fence, and you see, to great advantage, the church, with

> 'Those rugged elms, that yew-tree's shade,'

'THAT YEW TREE'S SHADE.'[18]

---

[18] The reason which induced our ancestors so constantly to plant yew trees in churchyards have been variously stated. Some affirm that it was to insure a supply of yew-bows
that the young men of the parish might practise archery, when enjoined by law. But Brady
in his *Clavis Calendaria*, says, 'Among our superstitious forefathers, the palm-tree or its
substitute box and yew, were solemnly blessed on Palm-Sunday, and some of their
branches burnt to ashes and used on Ash-Wednesday in the following year ; while other
boughs were gathered and distributed among the pious who bore them about in their numerous processions, a practice which was continued in this country until the second year of
Edward VI.' Caxton, in his Directory for keeping the festivals in 1483, also shows that the

backed by ancient plantations. We have never visited a more *meditative* scene ; and this feeling was increased by the winning voice of the church-bell, fraught with its divine message, swelling above the landscape ; the mingled congregation moving on noiselessly, the rich and poor, the old and young, might have been imagined an array of pilgrims, bound for the sacred temple. 'Imagined!' Were they not so? are we not all pilgrims, toiling onward ; working our way through anxieties and

THE PORCH OF STOKE POGIS CHURCH.

tribulations, now led forward by hope, now driven back by disappointment,—all pilgrims!—all troubled—all unsafe—all uncertain of success ; whose ears hear the church-bells, though their promise may not strike upon the heart. Pilgrims, and weary and profitless pilgrims are we all, to out selves and others, until we find the right path ; and keeping our eyes fixed upon the bright star of salvation hold out both hands to help onwards our fellow-men ; knowing and believing that, despite the hardest the world can do unto us, there is a living and eternal hope which never fails! Oh what glad tidings of great joy are brought to

---

yew was substituted for the palm in England : —'but for that we have non olyve that beareth grained leaf, therefore we take yew instead of palm olyve.' The melancholy shade and evergreen tint of the yew afford a good type of immortality which may have also been another reason for their constant appearance in our churchyards, many of which contain yews of many centuries growth.

every faithful heart by these musical church bells!—In groups, or one by one, the congregation entered the porch which Mr. Fairholt's little wood cut so faithfully pourtrays.[19] And yet the scene had so inspired us with meditation, that we still lingered within the enclosure. We thought how strongly it must have acted on the mind of the poet (Robert Montgomery) when he visited Stoke Pogis, and was there inspired by one of his sweetest and most tender poems—

'Memories bright and deep pervade
The quiet scene, where once a bard hath thought.
    *   *   *   *   *
How many a foot, where pensive Gray hath rov'd,
Will love to linger! 'Tis the spell of Mind
That consecrates the ground a poet trod ;
The air is eloquent with living thoughts,
And fine impressions of his favour'd muse ;
While Inspiration, like a god of Song,
Wakes the deep echoes of his deathless lyre!'

We cannot recall the poem stanza by stanza ; like a strain of music heard long since, it comes in broken fragments to our memory.

'But lo!—the churchyard!—Mark those "rugged elms,"
That "yew-tree shade,"—"yon ivy-mantled tower,"
And thread the path where heaves the mouldering heap ;
Then stranger, thou art soulless earth indeed,
If the lone bard beside thee does not stand,
Formed into life by Fancy's moulding spell!
'Twas here he mused,—here Poetry and Thought,
And Silence, their enamour'd sister, came ;
And Taste and Truth their kindred magic blent,
And proud Attempt, and pure Conception rose,
While Melody each chord of mind attun'd,

---

[19] The porch of Stoke Pogis is a very fine example of an ornamental structure of the kind ; the open tracery at the sides is boldly and tastefully executed, and there are few of our country churches which can boast a more beautiful specimen. In the olden time the church porch was the gathering-place for the villagers ; and here marriages were solemnised. The reader of Chaucer will remember the Wife of Bath's declaration : —

'Husbands at chirche-door have I had five.'

At that time stone porches were usual, which, with the room over them, termed *the Parvise*, became a sort of little chapel, having a Piscina. Fire-places are frequently found in them, showing that they were dwelt in. In these rooms it was not uncommon to keep the church chests, within which the various writings and other valuable properties of the church were kept. Some few of these still remain ; as at Newport Church, Essex, where a very remarkable one exists.

'Till soft Religion, like an angel, smiled,
And bade his genius make the grave sublime.'

The bell ceased,—the only living creature lingering on the path, was a pretty, gentle-looking girl of ten or eleven years old, using every possible art to tranquillise a child whose thin wailing voice seemed strangely at variance with the quiet beauty of the scene.

The accompanying sketch of the Poet's monument was made before the ground immediately around the testimonial was arranged as a parterre ;[20] upon our page it appears broken, uncultivated, whereas, in reality, it is exquisitely arranged, and contains numberless flowers,— breathing incense to the Poet's memory,—nor do we think the perspective quite correct, it seems to us that the church is much nearer the monument than it here appears. The monument, however, is fidelity itself ; and is seen to great advantage from various points of the surrounding country.

THE MONUMENT OF GRAY.

---

[20] The monument was erected by the Mr. Penn who purchased the house and estate of the Poet, and was repaired, and the flowers planted around it in 1831; when it was inclosed with a fence. The sketch shows it in its original condition. It bears appropriate inscriptions on each side—passages from the Poet.

Before we entered the church (whither the little girl, having won the child to tranquillity by her caresses, had gone before us, and as if fearing the renewal of a disturbance, to which she was most likely accustomed, had crouched down just inside the door) we turned for a moment to look at the tomb, or rather tombs, the one consecrated by the Poet to the memory of his mother, the other marking his own resting-place—

'Upon the lap of earth.'

We could hear the *tone* of the minister's voice, and almost fancy we could distinguish the words ; but there was no mistaking the 'Amen' of the congregation, so earnest, so solemn, rolling round the building ; the fervent 'So be it, of a Christian church, not shouted forth in ecstasy, or with fanatic exultation, but a deep-hearted solemn aspiration that thrilled the very heart, inspiring resignation and hope, and all the meek yet mighty virtues of our exalted faith. Those country churches are wonderful landmarks of history and religion ; the aged and low bending trees that have stood the storms of centuries, the massive ivy, the grey, stern, steady walls, tell a State's history as well as one of a higher and holier origin : it will indeed be long before the neat, new, trim 'Ebenezers' show such time-honoured marks as dear 'Mother Church ;' for ourselves we feel strangely moved when we see the spire of the village church pointing to the heavens, or hear the faintest sound of the distant church bells float above the landscape.

We passed the little maid and her infant charge as we entered ; it would have been difficult for an artist to catch the anxious yet most lovely expression of the young girl's face ; her 'divided duty' well performed, yet most unsatisfactorily to herself ; her uplifted finger arrested the child's attention, while her eyes were for a moment fixed upon the fine intelligent head of the clergyman, eager not to lose a syllable of those time-honoured and most faithful and touching petitions to the throne of mercy which abound in our Church service, and yet chained back to the worldly duty of restraining the temper and tears of her fretful charge, whose wandering eyes and sharp, pale, pinched-up features, denoted a precocious intelligence and the acid temper of a fragile or diseased body.

The interior of the church is picturesque and well cared for, and after service, which was performed throughout with dignified simplicity, and completed by a sermon sufficiently plain to be comprehended by the unlettered, while its graceful language and unaffected piety carried the listener beyond this world to the happiness rather than the terrors of the next ; we were shown the entrance-porch to the house of Stoke, and the pew appropriated to the use of the family—the old seats, the richly stained glass, the subdued light, the beautiful domain beyond, the over-hanging trees, the full bosomed melody of the birds, the murmurs of the half-whispered greetings and retreating footsteps of the congregation as they passed out of the public porch, the manner of our guide, whose attention increased in proportion to the expression of our sympathy with the scene—are all vividly impressed upon our memory.

'The churchyard was full, very full,' our guide had said, 'and a wonderful quantity of persons visited it and read the epitaphs, and even *scratched* their names on the church walls, though it was forbidden, and took away bits of the yew and wild flowers. It was,' he thought 'a pleasant churchyard to be buried in. Not too full, but not lonely ;' and indeed he said truly, for in those country churchyards—once at least each, week—the children's children of the silent dead pass beside their graves ; the modest head-stone and the light waving grass seem more akin to humanity and human feelings than the dungeon like vaults, or huge 'slabs,' pressing so heavily upon what we loved so well in the churches or church-yards of our towns. Again we stood beside the Poet's grave, read the epitaph on his mother, and cast many a longing, lingering look behind, while leaving the churchyard immortalised by the most perfect Elegy in our language.

The locality is, indeed, full of objects of deep interest ; there are, in the immediate neighbourhood, many shrines worthy of pilgrimage ; but there is one which in its pure and unadorned simplicity, in the abun-dant thoughts to which it cannot fail to give birth, and in its close asso-ciation with incidents which have since become a history, goes far be-yond all the rest—we mean the GRAVE OF WILLIAM PENN, the founder, or—as he is styled upon the grave-stone of his son, in a village-church not far distant—the *Proprietor* of Pennsylvania. The remains of this truly great man lie in the little Quakers' grave-yard of "Jordans," near to the village of Chalfont St. Giles, some four or five miles from Stoke Pogis.

The House of Andrew Marvel.

FEW months ago we had been strolling about Palace-yard, and instinctively paused at No. 19, York-street Westminster. It was evening ; the lamplighters were running from post to post, but we could still see that the house was a plain house to look at, differing little from its associate dwellings ; a common house, a house you would pass without a thought, unless the remembrance of thoughts that had been given to you from within the shelter of those plain, ordinary, walls, caused you to reflect ; aye, and to thank God, who has left with you the memories and sympathies which elevate human nature. Here, while Latin secretary to the Protector, was JOHN MILTON to be found when 'at home ;' and in his society, at times, were met, all the men who with their great originator Cromwell, astonished Europe. Just think of those who entered that portal ; think of them all if you can—statesmen and warriors ; or, if you are really of a gentle spirit, think of two—but two ; either of whom has left enough to engross your thoughts and fill your hearts. Think of JOHN MILTON and ANDREW MARVEL! think of the Protector of England, with two such secretaries!

Evening had deepened into night ; busy hands were closing shutters, and drawing curtains, to exclude the dense fog, that crept slowly and silently, like an assassin, through the streets ; the pavement was clammy, and the carriages rushing through the mist, like huge eyed misshapen spectres, proved how eager even the poor horses were to find shelter ; yet for a long while, we stood on the steps of this building, and at length retraced our steps homeward. Our train of thought, although checked, was not changed, when seated by a comfortable fire. We took down a volume of Milton ; but 'Paradise Lost' was too sublime for the mood of the moment, and we 'got to thinking' of Andrew Marvel, and displaced a volume of Captain Edward Thompson's edition of his works ; and then it occurred to us to walk to Highgate and once again enjoy the sight of his quaint old cottage on the side of the hill just facing,

37

'Cromwell House,' and next to that which once owned for its master the great Earl of Lauderdale.

We know nothing more invigorating than to breast the breeze up a hill, with a bright clear sky above, and the crisp ground under foot. The wind of March is as pure champagne to a healthy constitution ; and let mountain men laugh as they will at Highgate-hill, it is no ordinary labour to go and look down upon London from its height.

Here then we are, once more, opposite the house where lived the satirist, the poet, the INCORRUPTIBLE PATRIOT.

It is, as you will see presently, a peculiar-looking dwelling, just such a one as you might well suppose the chosen of Andrew Marvel— exquisitely situated, enjoying abundant natural advantages ; and yet altogether devoid of pretension ; sufficiently beautiful for a poet, sufficiently humble for a patriot.

MARVEL'S HOUSE. FRONT VIEW.

It is an unostentatious home, with simple gables and plain windows, and is but a story high. In front are some old trees, and a convenient porch to the door, in which to sit and look forth upon the road, a few paces in advance of it. The front is of plaster, but the windows are modernised, and there are other alterations which the exigencies of tenancy have made necessary since Marvel's days.

The dwelling was evidently inhabited ;—the curtains in the deep windows as white as they were when we visited it some years previous to the visit concerning which we now write, and the garden as neat as when in those days we asked permission to see the house, and was answered by an elderly servant, who took in our message ; and an old gentleman came into the hall, invited us in, and presented us to his wife, a lady of more than middle age, and of that species of beauty depending upon expression, which it is not in the power of time to wither, because it is of the spirit rather than the flesh ; and we also remembered a green parrot, in a fine cage, that talked a great deal, and was the only thing which seemed out of place in the house. We had been treated with much courtesy ; and, emboldened by the memory of that kindness, we now ascended the stone steps, unlatched the little gate, and knocked.

Again we were received courteously and kindly by the lady we had formerly seen ; and again she blandly offered to show us the house. We went up a little winding stair, and into several neat, clean bed-rooms, where everything was so old-fashioned, that you could fancy Andrew Marvel himself was still its master.

'Look out here,' said the old lady ; 'here's a view! They say this was Andrew Marvel's writing closet when he wrote *sense ;* but when he wrote *poetry*, he used to sit below in his garden. I have heard there is a private way under the road to Cromwell House, opposite ;—but surely that could not be necessary. So good a man would not want to work in the dark ; for he was a true lover of his country, and a brave man. My husband used to say, the patriots of those times were not like the patriots now ;—that then, they acted for their country,—now they talk about it! Alas! the days are passed when you could tell an Englishman from every other man, even by his gait, keeping the middle of the road, and straight on, as one who knew himself and made others know him. I am sure a party of roundheads, in their sober coats, high hats, and heavy boots, would have walked up Highgate Hill to visit Master Andrew Marvel, with a different air from the young men of our own time,—or of their own time, I should say,—for *my* time is past, and *yours* is passing.'

That was quite true ; but there is no reason, we thought, why we should not look cheerfully towards the future, and pray that it may be a bright world for others, if not for ourselves ;—the greater our enjoyment in the contemplation of the happiness of our fellow-creatures, the nearer we approach God.

MARVEL'S HOUSE. BACK VIEW.

It was too damp for the old lady to venture into the garden ; and sweet and gentle as she was, both in mind and manner, we were glad to be alone. How pretty and peaceful the house looks from this spot. The snowdrops were quite up, and the yellow and purple tips of the crocuses bursting through the ground in all directions. This, then, was the garden the poet loved so well, and to which he alludes so charmingly in his poem, where the nymph complains of the death of her fawn—

> 'I have a garden of my own,
> But so with roses overgrown,
> And lilies, that you would it guess,
> To be a little wilderness.'

The garden seems in nothing changed ; in fact, the entire appearance of the place is what it was in those glorious days, when inhabited by the truest genius and the most unflinching patriot that ever sprung from the sterling stuff that Englishmen were made of in those wonder-working times. The genius of Andrew Marvel was as varied as it was remarkable ;—not only was he a tender and exquisite poet, but entitled to stand *facile princeps* as an incorruptible patriot, the best of controversialists, and the leading prose wit of England. We have always considered his as the first of the 'sprightly runnings' of that brilliant stream of wit, which will carry with it to the latest posterity the names of Swift, Steele, and Addison. Before Marvel's time to be witty was to be strained, forced, and conceited ; from him—whose memory consecrates that cottage—wit came sparkling forth, untouched by baser matter. It was worthy of him ; its main feature was an open clearness. Detraction or jealousy cast no stain upon it ; he turned aside, in the midst of an exalted panegyric to Oliver Cromwell, to say the finest things that ever were said of Charles I.

CROMWELL HOUSE.

The Patriot was the son of Mr. Andrew Marvel, minister and schoolmaster of Kingston-upon-Hull, where he was born in 1620; his father was also the lecturer of Trinity Church in that town, and was celebrated as a learned and pious man. The son's abilities at an early age were remarkable, and his progress so great that at the age of thirteen, he was entered as a student of Trinity College, Cambridge ; and it is said that the corporation of his natal town furnished him with the means of entering the college and prosecuting his studies there. His shrewd and inquiring mind attracted the attention of some of the Jesuit emissaries who were at this time lurking about the Universities, and sparing no pains to make proselytes. Marvel entered into disputations with them, and ultimately fell so far into their power, that he consented to abandon the University and follow one of them to London. Like many other clever youths he was inattentive to the mere drudgery of university attendance, and had been reprimanded in consequence ; this and the news of his escape from college, reached his father's ears at Hull. That good and anxious parent followed him to London ; and, after a considerable search, at last met with him in a bookseller's shop ; he argued with his son as a prudent and sensible man should do, and prevailed on him to retrace his steps and return with him to college, where he applied to his studies with such good-will and continued assiduity, that he obtained the degree of Bachelor of Arts in 1638. His father lived to see the fruits of his wise advice, but was only spared thus long ; for he was unfortunately drowned in crossing the Humber, as he was attending the daughter of an intimate female friend, who, by this event becoming childless, sent for young Marvel, and by way of making all the return in her power, added considerably to his fortune.

This accession of wealth gave him an opportunity of travelling, and he journeyed through Holland, France, and Italy. While at Rome he wrote the first of those satirical poems which obtained him so much celebrity ; it was a satire on an English priest there, a wretched poetaster named Flecknoe. From an early period of life Marvel appears to have despised conceit, or impertinence, and he found another chance to exhibit his powers of satire in the person of an ecclesiastic of Paris, one Joseph de Maniban, an abbot who pretended to understand the characters of those he had never seen ; and to prognosticate their good or bad fortune from an inspection of their hand-writing. Marvel addressed a poem to him which, if it did not effectually silence his pretensions, at all events exposed them fully to the thinking portions of the community.

Beneath Italian skies his immortal friendship with Milton seems to have commenced ; it was of rapid growth but was soon firmly established ; they were, in many ways, kindred spirits, and their hopes for the after destinies of England were alike. In 1653 Marvel returned to England, and during the eventful years that followed, we can find no record of his strong and earnest thoughts, as they worked upwards into the arena of public life. One glorious fact we know, and all who honour virtue must feel its force,—that in an age when wealth was never wanting to the unscrupulous, Marvel, a member of the popular and successful party, continued POOR. Many of those year's he is certain to have passed—

> 'Under the destiny severe
> Of Fairfax, and the starry Vere—'

in the humble capacity of tutor of languages to their daughters. It was most likely, during this period, that he inhabited the cottage at Highgate, opposite to the house in which lived part of the family of Cromwell, a house upon which we shall remark presently. In 1657 he was introduced by Milton, to Bradshaw. The precise words of the introduction run thus, 'I present to you Mr. Marvel, laying aside those jealousies and that emulation which mine own condition might suggest to me, by bringing in such a coadjutor.' His connection with the State took place in 1657, when he became assistant secretary with Milton in the service of the Protector. 'I never had,' says Marvel, 'any, not the remotest relation to public matters, nor correspondence with the persons then predominant until the year 1657.'

After he had been some time fellow-secretary with Milton, even the thick-sighted burgesses of Hull perceived the merits of their townsman, and sent him as their representative into the House of Commons. We can imagine the delight he felt at escaping from the crowded and stormy Commons to breathe the invigorating air of his favourite hill, to enjoy the society of his former pupils, now his friends ; and to gather, in

'——a garden of his own,'

the flowers that had solaced his leisure hours when he was comparatively unknown. But Cromwell died, Charles returned, and Marvel's energies sprung into aims at acts which, in accordance with his principles, he considered base, and derogatory to his country. His whole efforts were directed to the preservation of civil and religious liberty.

It was but a short time previous to the Restoration, that Marvel had been chosen by his native town to sit as its representative in Parliament. The Session began at Westminster in April 1660, and he acquitted himself so honourably that he was again chosen for the one which began in May 1661. Whether under Cromwell or Charles, he acted with such thorough honesty of purpose, and gave such satisfaction to his constituents that they allowed him a handsome pension all the time he continued to represent them, which was till the day of his death. This was probably the last borough in England that paid a representative.[21] He seldom

---

[21] The custom of paying members of the house of Commons for the loss of time and travelling expenses, was common in the seventeenth century ; constituencies believed such equivalents necessary for the attention to their interests and wishes, which a Parliamentary agent was expected to give. In the old Corporation books of provincial towns are many entries for payments to members of Parliament, and in some instances we find them peti-

spoke in Parliament, but had much influence with the members of both Houses ; the spirited Earl of Devonshire called him friend, and Prince Rupert particularly paid the greatest regard to his councils ; and whenever he voted according to the sentiments of Marvel, winch he often did, it used to be said by the opposite party, that 'he had been with his tutor' Such certainly was the intimacy between the Prince and Marvel, that when he was obliged to abscond, to avoid falling a sacrifice to the indignation of those enemies among the governing party whom his satirical pen had irritated, the Prince frequently went to see him, disguised as a private person.

The noted Doctor Samuel Parker published Bishop Bramhall's work, setting forth the rights of kings over the consciences of their subjects, and then came forth Marvel's witty and sarcastic poem, 'The Rehearsal Transposed.'[22] And yet how brightly did the generosity of his noble nature shine forth at this very time, when he forsook his own wit in that very poem to praise the wit of Butler, his rival and political enemy. Fortune seems about this period to have dealt hardly with him. Even while his political satires rang through the very halls of the pampered and impure Charles, when they were roared forth in every tavern, shouted in the public streets, and attracted the most envied attention throughout England, their author was obliged to exchange the free air, apt type of the freedom which he loved, for a lodging in a court off the Strand, where, enduring unutterable temptations, flattered and threatened, he more than realised the stories of Roman virtue.

The Poet Mason has made Marvel the hero of his 'Ode to Independence,' and thus alludes to his incorruptible integrity :—

'In awful Poverty his honest Muse
    Walks forth Vindictive through a venal land ;

---

tioning to Government for disfranchisement, because they could not afford to pay the expanses of a Member.

[22] Marvel's first *exposé* of Parker's false logic was in 1672, in the poem named above, which was immediately answered by Parker, and re-answered by Marvel, who appears to have had some private threat sent him, as he says his pamphlet is occasioned by two letters ; one the published 'Reproof' of him by Parker in answer to his first attack ; 'the second, left for me at a friend's house, dated November 3rd, 1673, subscribed J.G., and concluding with these words—If thou derest to print any lie or libel against Dr. Parker, by the Eternal—I will cut thy throat.' This last reply of Marvel's, however, effectually silenced Parker : 'It not only humbled Parker, but the whole party,' says Burnet, for, 'from the king dawn to the tradesman, the book was read with pleasure.'

In vain Corruption sheds her golden dews,
In vain Oppression lifts her iron hand ;
He scorns them both, and arm'd with Truth alone,
Bids Lust and Folly tremble 'on the throne.'

Marvel, by opposing the ministry and its measures, created himself
many enemies,[23] and made himself very obnoxious to the government,
yet Charles II. took great delight in his conversation, and tried all means
to win him over to his side, but in vain ; nothing being ever able to
shake his resolution. There were many instances of his firmness in re-
sisting the offers of the Court, in which he showed himself proof against
all temptations.

We close our eyes upon this peaceful dwelling of the heroic sena-
tor, and imagine ourselves in the reign of the second Charles, threading
our way into that 'court off the Strand' where Marvel ended his days.
We enter the house, and climbing the stairs even to the second floor,
perceive the object of our warmest admiration. He is not alone though
there is no possibility of confounding the poet with the courtier. Andrew Marvel is plainly dressed, his figure is strong, and about the middle size his countenance open, and his complexion of a ruddy cast ; his
eyes are of a soft hazel colour, mild and steady ; his eyebrows straight
and so flexible as to mould without an effort into a satirical curve, if
such be the mind's desire ; his mouth is close, and indicative of firmness
and his brown hair falls gracefully back from a full and noble forehead.
He sits in an upright and determined manner upon an uneasy-looking
high-backed chair. A somewhat long table intervenes between him and
his visitor ; one end of it is covered with a white cloth, and a dish of
cold meat is flanked by a loaf of bread and a dark earthenware jug. On
the opposite end is placed a bag of gold, beside which lies the richly-

---

[23] No stronger satire could he penned than that descriptive of the Court of Charles, in
the poem called 'Britannia and Raleigh :' —

'A colony of French possess the Court,
Pimps, priests, buffoons, in privy chambers Sport ;
such slimy monsters ne'er approach'd a throne
Since Pharaoh's days, nor so defil'd a crown ;
In sacred ears tyrannick arts they croak,
Pervert his mind, and good intentions choak.'

But not only do the courtiers feel the lash, for when Raleigh implores Britannia to urge
his duty on the king, and save him from the bad who surround him, she interrupts him
with —

'Raleigh, no more! for long in vain I've try'd
The Stuart from the tyrant to divide.'

embroidered glove which the cavalier with whom he is conversing has flung off. There is strange contrast in the attitude of the two men. Lord Danby lounges with the ease of a courtier and the grace of a gentleman upon a chair of as stiff and uncomfortable an appearance as that which is occupied after so upright a fashion by Andrew Marvel.

'I have answered you, my lord,' said the patriot, 'already. Methinks there need be no further parley on the subject ; it is not my first temptation, though I most fervently desire it may be the last.'

The nobleman took up his glove and drew it on. 'I again pray you to consider,' he said, 'whether if with us, the very usefulness you so much prize would not have a more extensive sphere. You would have larger means of being useful.'

'My lord, I should certainly have the means of tempting usefulness to forsake duty.'

The cavalier rose, but the displeasure that flushed his countenance soon faded before the serene and holy expression of Milton's friend.

'And are you so determined?' said his lordship, sorrowfully. 'Are you really so determined? A thousand English pounds are there, and thrice the sum—nay, anything you ask—'

'My lord! my lord!' interrupted Marvel, indignantly, 'this perseverance borders upon insult. Nay, my good lord, you do not so intend it, but your master does not understand me. Pray you, note this : two days ago that meat was hot ; it has remained cold since, and there is enough still for to-morrow ; and I am well content. A man so easily satisfied is not likely to exchange an approving conscience for dross like that!'

We pray God that the sin of Marvel's death did not rest with the great ones of those times ; but it was strange and sudden.[24] He did not leave wherewith to bury the sheath of such a noble spirit but his constituents furnished forth a decent funeral, and would have erected a monument to his memory in the church of St. Giles-in-the-Fields, where he was interred ; but the rector, blinded by the dust of royalty to the

---

[24] 'Marvel died in 1678, in his fifty-eighth year, not without the strongest suspicions of having been poisoned ; for he was always very temperate, and of an healthful and strong constitution to the last.'

merits of the man, refused the necessary permission. Marvel's name is remembered, though the rector's has been long forgotten.[25]

Wood tells us, that Marvel was in his conversation very modest, and of few words ; and Cooke, the writer of his life, observes that he was very reserved among those whom he did not know, but a most delightful and improving companion among his friends. John Aubrey, who knew him personally, thus describes him : 'He was of a middling stature, pretty strong set, roundish cherry-cheeked, hazel-eyed, brown-haired.' He was (as Wood also says) in conversation very modest, and of a very few words. He was wont to say, that he would not drink high or freely with any one with whom he would not trust his life.

Marvel lived among friends at Highgate ; exactly opposite to his door was the residence of General Ireton and his wife Bridget, the eldest daughter of Oliver Cromwell ; and which house still bears his name, and is described in 'Prickett's History of Highgate,' one of those local topographical works which deserve encouragement :—'Cromwell House is supposed to have been built by the Protector whose name it bears, about the year 1630, as a residence for General Ireton, who married his daughter and was one of the commanders of his army ; it is, however, said to have been the residence of Oliver Cromwell himself, but no mention is made, either in history or in his biography, of his having ever lived at Highgate. Tradition states, there was a subterraneous passage from this house to the mansion house which stood where the New Church now stands, but of its reality no proof has hitherto been adduced. Cromwell House was evidently built and internally ornamented in accordance with the taste of its military occupant. The staircase, which is of handsome proportions, is richly decorated with oaken carved figures, supposed to have been of persons in the general's army, in their costume ; and the balustrades filled in with devices emblematical of warfare. On the ceilings of the drawing-room are the arms of General Ireton ; this and the ceilings of the other principal apartments are enriched in conformity with the fashion of those days. The proportion of the noble rooms, as well as the brick-work in front, well deserves the notice and study of the antiquarian and the architect. From the platform on the top of the mansion may be seen a perfect panorama of the surrounding country.'

---

[25] On the death of this rector, however, the monument and inscription was placed on the north wall of the church, near the spot where he is supposed to lie.

STAIRCASE.

The staircase above described is here engraved. It is a remarkably striking and elegant specimen of internal decoration, of broad and noble proportion, and of a solid and grand construction suitable to the time of its erection ; the wood-work of the house is everywhere equally bold and massive ; the door-cases of simple but good design. There are some ceilings in the first story which are in rich plaster work, ornamented with the arms of Ireton ; and mouldings of fruit and flowers, of a sumptuous and bold enrichment.

The series of figures which stand upon the newels of the staircase are all engraved below.

There are ten remaining out of twelve, the original number : the missing two are said to have been figures of Cromwell and Ireton, destroyed at the Restoration. They stand about a foot in height, and represent the different soldiers of the army, from the fifer and drummer to the captain, and originally, to the commanders. They are curious for more reasons than one ; their locality, their truthfulness, their history, and the picture they help us to realise of the army of Cromwell are all so many claims on our attention.

The Church of St. Andrew Undershaft, the Tomb of John Stow.

ARE OLD LONDON! We pass with a gaze of chilled astonishment along the interminable lines of nearly reddened or stuccoed houses which like the web of the spider, cross, and fret, and disturb at every step. Truly, those who dwell in modern tenements must put great trust in Providence, for they can have none in brick and mortar. Such things! Puff! We fancy we could blow them down ; they will never live long enough to tell a story ; they grow *green*, not *grey*, with age ; and when in a humour for 'substantials,' it is indeed a pleasure to get away from them into the city, where the dwellings of old times were built to endure, and where enduring memories hang around them. Of all the time-honoured names associated with the antiquities of London, there is none in which we so much delight as that of JOHN STOW ; and we feel grateful for the hours passed with so much profit and pleasure in his society, in traversing with him the lanes, and streets, and alleys—visiting the old churches (least changed of all) and contemplating the beauty of the monuments contained therein. Much as we owe him for the storehouse of antiquarian riches he bequeathed to such as desire to learn from the past what may be expected from the future, we owe still more to the earnest and honest *example* of the simple and single-minded old pilgrim, who was entirely devoid of all love of display—without ostentation, without an aim to achieve aught but TRUTH—which, next to his GOD, he worshipped ; humble-minded as to himself and desirous of means, not for the indulgence of luxury, but that he might finish what he had begun, in the fear of God, and to the glory of the city of London.

OLD LONDON BRIDGE.

The days we have spent in turning over his interesting survey of his favourite City[26] and Westminster, until the shades of evening reminded

---

[26] The general aspect of the City of London from the bridge eastward to the Tower, may be seen in the above engraving, as it appeared in the year 1589. The principal feature is old London Bridge, the only roadway at this time over the Thames between London and Southwark. This bridge was the especial glory of Londoners ; and all the older writers speak of it in the most rapturous terms. In the edition of Abraham Ortelius's *Epitome of The Theatre of the Worlde,* published in London by James Shaw in 1603, its praises conclude the sum total of Great Britain's glories, when speaking of the 'Ancient and flourishing famous cittie of London, which, as wel for beautie, riches, and trade, is not inferior but equal with the beste citties of Europe. The river of Thames is beautefied with statelye pallaces built on the side thereof, moreover a sumptuous bridge sustayned upon nineteen arches with excellent and beauteous housen built thereon.' Times have indeed changed since this was written ; when the nineteen arches were gloried in, which formed the strongest argument in our own time for its demolition. The fortified gate seen on the Southwark side of the bridge, was known as the Traitor's Gate ; and above it were exhibited the heads of those who had suffered for treason : the reader will perceive several stuck upon poles above the eastern tower. Here it was that the head of Sir Thomas More was placed ; and afterwards when about to be cast in the Thames, was purchased by his daughter Margaret Roper, and piously buried in a leaden case in the family vault in St. Dunstan's Church Canterbury, where it still reposes. This entrance to London was defended by a portcullis and a draw-bridge beyond. The stack of houses beyond that formed a second Southwark gate and tower, which was finished in 1579, and it consisted of four circular turrets, connected by curtains and surmounted by battlements, containing a great number of transom casements ; beneath was a broad covered passage, the building projecting considerably over each side of the bridge. It was a noble and ornamental structure, but the most splendid and curious building which adorned London Bridge at this time, was the famous Nonesuch house, so called, because it was constructed in Holland, entirely of

us that we had been, with (despite its present living multitudes), what might be called a city of the dead! None of those senseless ones who sneered at his occupation are abroad now, nor of those, near to him in blood, but far from him in heart, who disturbed him day and night with unfounded accusations—nor of those young buoyant spirits who cried aloud in the streets, or made rare sport, which joyed the old man's heart to hear, though it might disturb his meditations. Did we not say, truly, that we were wandering through a city of the dead? How have we gone over, thought by thought, the traits given in these cumbrous volumes of the olden time! The curious memory of Smithfield, originally Smoothe-field, 'both in name and deed' 'where, save on holy Fridays,' earls, bar-ons, knights, and citizens repaired to see or buy ambling horses, pacing it delicately ; or trotters, fit for men at arms, riding more hardly ; or boys racing one horse against another, with a desire of victory, or a hope of praise. And old Stow loved well to quote whatever redounded to the honour of his glorious city. Thus, from old Fitz-Stephen, he gives his eulogy thereon—'*Ancienter* than Rome, built by the ancient Trojans and by Brute, before that was built by Romulus and Remus, and, there-fore, useth the ancient customs of Rome. This city, even as Rome, is divided into wards. It hath,' he continues glowing with enthusiasm, 'it hath yearly sheriffs, instead of consuls ; it hath the dignity of senators in aldermen ; it hath under-officers ; common sewers and conduits in streets : according to the quality of causes, it hath general courts, and assemblies upon appointed days. I do not think there is any city wherein are better customs.'[27] And then, after enumerating their customs, he continues, 'The only plagues of London are immoderate quaffing among

---

wood, and being brought over in pieces, was erected in this place with wooden pegs only, not a single nail being used in the whole fabric. It is the next building seen in our view with central and side towers, and was most elaborately carved and painted. For further information on this structure, we must refer the reader to Mr. Thomson's learned and curious volume, *The Chronicles of London Bridge.*

[27] The elder London antiquaries were true men, hearty lovers of their city, proud of it as the focus of England's greatness. Their enthusiasm is pleasant to read. Stow never let slip a chance of lauding his London ; and William Camden, in his *Remaines,* did the same by his native country generally. His hearty, sterling English feeling makes him speak of his countrymen as 'this warlike, victorious, stiff, stout and vigorous nation ;' of his coun-try as 'walled and guarded by the sea, with safe havens, so that it may be termed *the lady of the Sea ;*' of the air as 'most temperate and wholesome,' and of the language as a selec-tion of the best qualities of all others, 'gathering the honey of their good qualities, and leaving the dregs to themselves. How then can the language, which consisteth of all these, sound other than full of sweetness?'

the foolish sort, and often casualties by fire.' How pleasantly does Stow enumerate the changes which had taken place since the Chronicle was written, and which he considers improvements.   He tells us how 'the skinners dwell in Budge Row, instead of in St. Mary Pollipers ;' how 'the vintners have moved from the Vine Tree into divers places ;' but that 'the brewers, for the most part, remain near to the friendly waters of the Thames ;' how 'the poulterers have gone from the Poultry, between the stocks and the great conduit in the Cheap,[28] into Grass Street and St. Nicholas' Shambles ;' and 'the Paternoster bead-makers and text-writers are gone out of Paternoster Row, and are called stationers of Paul's Churchyard ;' he also says that 'the patten-makers of St.

CHEAPSIDE CROSS.

Margaret's, Patten's Lane, are clean worn out.'   And after much more information of the same sort, he comments upon the charge of 'immoderate quaffing' and 'fire casualties,' and mourneth that quaffing is mightily increased, but adds that great preventatives are used against

[28] The Cheapside Cross and Conduit are exhibited above, from Le Serre's engraving representing the entry into London of the queen mother Mary de Medicis to visit her daughter Henrietta Maria, the queen of Charles I. The cross was destroyed on the 2nd of May 1643, under the pretence of its being papistical, by the fanatics who had begun their reign of gloom. A troop of horse and two companies of foot waited to guard those who demolished it, 'and at the fall of the top-cross drums beat, trumpets blew, and multitudes of caps were thrown in the air, and a great shout of people with joy. The 2nd of May the Almanack sayeth was the Invention of the Cross, and the sixth day at night was the leaden pope's burnt in the place where it stood, with ringing of bells and great acclamations, and no hurt done in all these actions.' The Conduit of West-cheap was built by John Wells, grocer, mayor in 1433, who caused fresh water to be conveyed from Tyburn to the conduit here for the service of the city. Water at this time was procured for home consumption at these conduits, to which apprentices and others were sent ; and the large water-pots in which it was carried home form a curious feature in some of the old views surrounding the various conduits.

fires ; of himself he complaineth of various faults, which excite a smile when the present state of the streets is considered, how that a number of cars and drays, carts and coaches, *inconvenience* the streets,[29] and 'the coachman rides behind his horses' tails, and looketh not behind himself ;' and the drayman sleeps, and suffers his horse to carry him home, although, except on royal service, 'no *shod*' carts should enter the precincts of the city.

We often close our eyes after the perusal of a particular passage, and recall the scenes so simply yet so graphically pictured by this most patient of historical antiquaries. We conjure up the gay presence of Richard Nevill, Earl of Warwick, who 'lodged' with his six hundred men (whose red jackets were embroidered with ragged staffs before and behind), in Warwick-lane. *Beefeaters* they might well be called devouring 'six oxen at breakfast!' merry men! ready to roister in the city, and prank gaily through the streets, to the great annoyance of the city fathers, and the great delight of the mild and fair city maids, who, however mild and fair, were, and are, ever more ready to prefer such scarlet-jacketed knaves to the more grave apprentices.[30] Or, in the reign of the Seventh Henry, we hear the bells of the nearest steeple ringing a sort of half joyous, half solemn peal, giving notice to the poor, that Richard Redman, the Bishop of Ely, was about to go forward ; a man of holy and unbounded charity, maintaining great housekeeping, an *alms-dish*, and scores of those who could do no work, and yet caused the bells to tell of his progress, so that the

---

[29] Nothing could exceed the virulence with which they were hated by the vulgar, who termed them hell *carts*, and abused all who rode in them.

[30] The city apprentice of the days of Stow is delineated in our cut above, with his water-jug as he would go to the conduit on service of his master. The peculiarity of civic costume at this time was its plainness ; the elders dressed in long furred gowns over their doublet and hose, the younger ones and apprentices were gownless ; but all were distinguished by 'the city flat cap,' of which a cut is given above. These flat caps are the 'statute caps' alluded to by Shakspeare in *Love's Labour's Lost*, and they were so termed because they were enjoined by the statute of the fifteenth of Queen Elizabeth to be worn 'by all persons above the age of six years (except the nobility and same others) on sabbath days and holidays' upon penalty of ten groats. This was done 'in behalfe of the trade of cappers,' for it was also enjoined that each cap should be made of wool, 'knit, thicked, and drest in England.'

poor might come forth and receive each his largess at his hand, given with a sweetening and preserving blessing. And truly the people did pour forth abundantly to taste his charity. Our religious ancestors certainly excelled in this 'most excellent gift ;' and it is no small merit to our City Historian that at the very name of charity, his heart seemed to open widely, as the rose opens its beauty to the sun. He quotes the statement of Venerable Bede, 'how that the prelates of his time, having peradventure but wooden churches, had, notwithstanding, on their board at meals one *alms-dish,* into which was carved some good portion of meat out of every other dish brought on their table ; all which was given to the poor, *besides the fragments left. '* The rare lesson thus conveyed being, not that the *'fragments'* only were given to the poor—we are all ready enough to cast the 'fragments' when our hunger or our taste is satisfied, to the poor or to the dogs, caring little which, inasmuch as being no longer needed, they become unpleasant—but the lesson was to have, as Christ said we must have, *'the poor always with us,'* and thus to provide for them, carving into the alms-dish, in the first instance, a portion of whatever was provide for ourselves. To our mind this was a noble custom, a lesson of piety and Christian charity, a text, and a sermon. Surely this was rendering our feasts 'a bond of love.' But much as the Church was given to deeds of charity, there is ample proof in our chronicles that a love of feasting was time out of mind a characteristic of the worthy citizens of London. Their inordinate desire after the good things of this life was deemed necessary of retrenchment by an act of council, reprinted in 1680, that no 'maior or sheriff should have at there table any more than courses one, not to consist of more than six dishes!' and no banquet after dinner save 'ipocras and wafers!' It would be curious to know if this act of council *hath been repealed.* We should suppose it has, to judge from the long bills of dainty fare which we see announced in the daily journals on the annual accession of each city monarch.

His intense love of the city makes old John Stow an enthusiast in all that concerns it ; each drop of the Thames glitters like a diamond in his eyes, and every pebble is a jewel ; and yet much as he honoured relics of all kinds, he honoured them only as types of greater things—as data to go from, as texts to preach upon. As we have said, the beauty of his character was truth, and in truth only was his strength ; it was the care of his life to think, to act, to speak to gather truth. He was neither an abstract historian, dealing only with principal events, nor was he a hunter after mere dust and ashes, bits and scraps, but a thinker and

COMBINER, being himself the rare combination of an historian and an antiquary ; minute in all small things that tended to the illustration of great things, and, knowing that the universe is made up of atoms, deeming no atom of that universe beneath his notice. Every little detail of the Christmas and Easter pageants is given in his 'Survey,' with a zest of enjoyment at innocent pastimes ; and the few words of introduction to his description of the May-games, is redolent of the perfume of the hawthorn and wood-violet. No cold, dry, chipping antiquary, not even Jonathan Oldbuck, could write thus :—'In the month of May, namely, on May-day, in the morning, every man (except impediment) would walk into the sweet meadows and green woods, there to rejoice their spirits with the beauty and savour of sweet flowers, and with the harmony of birds—*praising God in their kind!'*

All through the history we note the same holy feeling, not thrust in, but the spontaneous growth of the good man's mind, even as fair flowers spring up amid the ruins of old Rome ; for instance, in the chapter concerning the Sports and Exercises, we have been delighted with picturing the bonfires according to his description :—'The wealthier sort, at Midsummer, setting out tables before their doors, illumed by the blaze of those sacred fires, and upon the tables placing stores of sweet bread and good drink, whereunto they would invite their neighbours and passengers also to sit and be merry with them, in great familiarity, *praising God for his benefits bestowed on them.* These were called *bonfires*, as well of good amity amongst neighbours, that, being before at controversie, were there, by the labour of others, reconciled, *and made of bitter enemies loving friends.'* But good Master Stow writes as if hearty reconciliation were the work of a moment. Such freedom of trust is sure evidence of a foolish or a noble mind ; and, of a truth, there was no folly in that of JOHN STOW.

Charles Knight calls Stow a 'trudger and trencher' in the field of London antiquities, and so he was ; but he did not confine himself —as we have already shown—to *mere* 'trudging and trenching :' while he investigated, he elevated, and his veneration for all that was ancient, fully accounts for the affection which there is no doubt he bore to the things and forms of a religion—whatever he might feel as to its spirit— which he lived to see overthrown and insulted by Henry and Elizabeth. John Stow was born, according to his biographer Strype, in 1525 a 'citizen of the citizens'—tradesmen of respectability dwelling upon Cornhill[31]—where it is fair to suppose John was born, though he is afterwards found residing near the pump at Aldgate and finally in Lime-street ward, St Andrew's parish. Strype quotes his *grand-father's* will which is curi-

CORNHILL. NORTH-EAST VIEW.

ous from its elaborate weakness and verbosity, particularly when contrasted with that of his mother, as remarkable for its concentration and strength. After noting that his body is to be buried an the little green churchyard of the parish church at St. Michael's in Cornhill, and calling himself 'citizen and tallow-chandler,' he bequeaths to the high altar of

---

[31] The old view above exhibits a north-east view of Cornhill in the reign of Elizabeth, with the pump or conduit formerly situated at the intersection of Gracechurch Street, Cornhill, Bishopsgate Street, and Leadenhall Street. To the spectator's right appear the walls of the church of St. Peter on Cornhill. The building with the double row of pointed windows to the left is the ancient Leaden hall, built by Sir Simon Eyre, who was Lord Mayor in 1445, having been originally purchased by Sir Richard Whittington, and presented to the city. In 1534 it was designed to have been made a bourse or exchange but the idea was abandoned. As early as 1523 there was a market for fish here ; and in 1533 another for butcher's meat, with the understanding that the charges for such sold there was not to exceed 'one halfpenny a pound for beef, and one farthing extra for mutton.' Leadenhall itself was considered as the chief garner for corn in the city under the management of the mayor. Stow says that Roger Acheley, mayor in 1512, kept the market so well, that he would be at the Leaden Hall by four o'clock in the summer's mornings ; and from thence he went to the other markets, to the great comfort of the citizens.'

the aforesaid church, for *'forgotten tithes* twelve pence, to Jesus' brotherhood twelve pence, to St. Christopher and St. George twelve pence,
also to the seven altars in the church aforesaid, in the worship of the
seven sacraments every year ; during three years, twenty pence ; five
shillings, to have on every altar a watching candle—burning from six of
the clock till it be past seven—in worship of the seven sacraments, and
this candle shall begin to burn and to be set upon the altar from all Hal-
lowe'en day, 'till it be Candlemas day following, and *it shall be watching candle of eight in the pound.'* The tallow-chandler would have good
weight! He also bequeaths twenty pence to the brotherhood of clerks 'to
drink,' and his charity to the poor is by no means disinterested, for
though he gives to a poor man and woman, every Sunday in one year,
'the sum of one penny,' it is to say 'five paternosters and aves, and a
creed,' for the repose of his soul, so that he had more of a trader's spirit
than descended to his grandson : the whole of the items are in accordance with his belief that the prayers of the living can rescue the souls of
the dead ; and the wonder hath always been, not that the Church, we
mean the priesthood of the Roman Catholic church, receive so much
from their flocks, but that they receive so little ; for who with such belief would not give all their worldly goods to secure their own salvation.
Either John Stow's mother was of a different faith from her husband's
father ; or she had imbibed the spirit that was purifying the sacrifice ;
she bequeathed her body to be buried by her husband's, in the same
parish, allowing a proportion to bury her decently, 'ten shillings, to
drink withal, after her funeral,' an unconditional and unrequited gift to
the poor of 'five shillings,' and these pious and trusting words of the
belief in free redemption :—

'I bequeath my soul unto Almighty God, my Maker and Creator ; and to
his only Son, our Lord Jesus Christ, my only Saviour and Redeemer ; with the
Holy Ghost, and into the fellowship of the holy host of heaven.'

TAILORS' HALL.

Whether he followed his family's occupation or not, has been matter of grave debate. It is now ascertained that he pursued the trade of a tailor,[32] which it is very clear he exercised in the early part of his life,

---

[32] Grindall in his report to the Privy Council, after they ordered his house to be topsy-turvied to search for treasonable books, calls him 'Stow, the tailor.' The old hall of the Tailors' Company is engraved above, from a drawing made by William Goodman in 1599. Pennant says, 'At the extremity of Threadneedle Street appears the origin of its name in Merchant Taylor's Hall, at the period when they were called "Taylors, and Linen Armourers," under which title they were incorporated in 1280; and by Henry VII. by that of the "Art and Mystery of Merchant Taylers." To the right is seen the hall with its louvre, some time belonging to "a worshipful gentleman, named Edmond Creping." The lower buildings in the centre are the alms-houses belonging to the company. The building, occupied a considerable space, with gardens behind reaching to Cornhill. The interior of the hall was adorned with costly tapestry, or arras, representing the life of the patron saint of the company, "St John the Baptist ; it had also a screen supporting a silver image of that saint, in a tabernacle of carved work. The windows were painted with the armorial bearings belonging to the chief members of the company ; it was decorated also with flags and streamers, and, when filled with tables, the floor strewn with rushes, and the board covered on festive occasions must have been "a glorious scene." The company had much plate of a valuable kind, and after the great fire of London had destroyed their hall, the melted metal of this kind alone weighed 200 pounds. The company was especially honoured by the great number of the nobility enrolled as members ; and they possessed a chamber expressly devoted to the king when he visited the city, which was furnished in a costly manner, having a gallery over it, and bow-windows looking in the gardens. Rushes

from the record of a quarrel he had with a certain man named Ditcher, whose wife appears to have deserved the ducking-school as an arrant shrew. Imagine her coming in her fly cap, her hair (it must have been of shrewish red) combed back, her elbows stuck out from her grey jacket that was pinched in over her thin waist, her lips tremulous with passion, her voice 'cutting keen'—there she stands, over against the stall, which Stow, mild and gentle, and prudent, had very wisely, hearing the clangor of her approach, deserted—there she stands, railing and abusing the worthy citizen, his wife and daughters ; and the longer she rails the fiercer she becomes, not on account of the irritation caused by reply, but the more stinging irritation produced by silence ; and then home she goes, and, with much railing and wicked tears, excites her husband to a breach of the peace. Now her husband, William Ditcher, was, we take it, a small man ; and John Stow was 'tall of stature, lean of body and face, with small crystalline eyes, of a pleasant and cheerful countenance, sober, mild, and courteous ;' yet did she so upbraid and goad her husband, that the little Ditcher, watching his opportunity, 'leaped (as Stow deposed) into his face, and that he feared he would have digged out his eyes, and was pulled off by the neighbours ; and also threw tileshreds and stones at Stow's apprentice, *till he was driven from off the stall at his work ;* and coming again to John's stall, the irate Ditcher vowed if he could catch that same apprentice, he would cart him, and swore he would accuse him to have killed the man at the Mile's End, in Whitsun week,' &c. &c. This quarrel, which is so petty and insignificant, that we could wager it originated all along with the women of the family—sprang from some jealousy touching the fineries of Stow's three daughters, who, having 'good services,' came jauntily home a' Sundays, and threw, by gay breast knots and smart hoods, the less smart finery of fiery Mistress Ditcher into contempt. This quarrel, we say, shows our historian's bland and gentle nature to great advantage. He was no brawler—did not return railing for railing, and would not have noticed all this evil talk, but for the preservation of the characters of his wife and daughters, which this family most falsely assailed ; and the breeze was but the forerunner of a storm of slander which followed the after career of the venerable man, who delighted so in his

were discarded in this room as early as the reign of Elizabeth, and "a large Persia carpet" purchased to cover it, and in 1601 so large a sum as £50 was spent on a new carpet, which was, in 1618, superseded by one of needlework. James I., Charles I. and his queen, and James II. were all accommodated here during their visits to the city, and the company spared no expense in entertaining them.'

city's celebrity. One other anecdote only we will relate, as picturing the power held and exercised by the great in those 'good old times ;' and we tell it the more readily, as it sets forth the generous nature and just mind of John Stow.

ALDGATE AND ITS NEIGHBOURHOOD.

Where now the hall of the drapers' company stands, stood formerly a palace, built on the site of a number of old and small tenements by Sir Thomas Cromwell, who was afterwards Lord Cromwell and Earl of Essex. One could almost fancy that a certain portion, and a very considerable one, of tyranny attached itself to that name, so omnipresent in England even to this day. 'Sir Thomas Cromwell's house being finished,' says honest John in his description of Bread Street ward, 'and having some reasonable plot of ground left for a garden, he (Cromwell) caused the palings of the adjoining gardens to the north part thereof on a sudden to be taken down, twenty-two foot to be measured forth, right into the north of every man's ground, a line there to be drawn, a trench to be cast, a foundation laid, and an high wall to be builded. My father had a garden there,' he continues, 'and there was a house standing close to his south pale ; this house they loosed from the ground, and bare upon rollers into my father's garden twenty-two foot, ere *my father heard of it.* No warning was given him, nor other answer, when he spake to the surveyors of that work, but that their master ; Sir Thomas, commanded them to do so! *No man durst go to argue the matter,* but *each man lost his land,* and *my father paid* his *whole* rent (six and eightpence a year) for that *half* which was left.' This is strange enough. The petted minister of Henry the Eighth had no dread of removing his neighbour's landmark. We wonder what would be said if modern ministers were to make such an attempt! Certainly, whatever we may think of old places,

ALDGATE.

the 'old times' were not always the best. It is also curious to know that the yearly value of a garden so situated in those days, was just the sum which you are now obliged to pay for an attorney's letter! Stow's parting observation upon this act of unjustifiable tyranny is quaint and pointed. He says, 'Thus much of mine own knowledge I have thought good to note, that the sudden rising of some men causeth them to forgot *themselves.*' This was a keen and cutting reproof to the son of the Putney blacksmith. And for all that, Sir Thomas Cromwell's injustice, gross as it was, did not force Stow to take a revenge which ordinary men would have taken—the revenge of silence as to his good deeds. Both are long since dust and ashes. The wounded feelings of the antiquary trouble him no more, and the overleaping ambition of Cromwell led to the scaffold ; yet Stow records his charity with right good will, and brings it forward when not called upon to do so, save by the right-minded justice of his honest nature. Mourning over the decay of public almsgiving, he says, 'I have oft seen, in that declining time of charity, at the Lord Cromwell's gate, at London, more than two hundred persons served twice every day with bread, meat and drink sufficient.

One of his bitter foes, we should imagine, was a fanatic curate of St. Catherine Cree, who has been known to leave his pulpit and preach from the boughs of a tree to the people. He is called 'Sir Stephen ;' and, when Stow lived over against Aldgate Pump,[33] excited the honest

---

[33] The portion of the old map of London engraved opposite, executed in the reign of Elizabeth, show's the district connected with Stow's life and residence. The church of St. Catherine Cree is seen to the spectators left in the street running toward Aldgate. At the point where Fenchurch Street joins with it stands Aldgate pump, which is probably repre-

citizens' bitter indignation, by causing to be hanged, by his false misrepresentation of simple words, the bailiff of Rumford—'a man well beloved.' He was executed upon the pavement by Stow's door, there being at the time much disturbance 'of the Commons' in 'Norfolk, Suffolk, Essex, and other shires.'

It was not until the year 1560 that, Stow addressed his 'cares and cogitations' to the compilation of his mighty chronicle, which was at first published in small volumes. It was then, to use his own words, that he consecrated himself 'to the search of our famous antiquities.' It was, indeed, a consecration to labour, and poverty, and evil report—the latter only for a time. There were literary pirates in those days, as well as in our own—miserable thieves, who pick brains when they dare not pick pockets. And such Stow found Grafton to be.[34] Our only astonishment is, that he treats him so mercifully, particularly when we consider the truthfulness of his own nature, and the extreme sensibility of his temper, which made him most painfully alive to things that might be considered nothings to other men. He was also subjected to the visits of government officers, who believed him to be an 'admirer of antiquity in religion as well as in history.' They sadly disturbed his books and shelves, making a rare dust, and yet, finding nought beyond some books and

---

sented in the map, by the small building standing by itself, opposite the point of the junction. These old city pumps and conduits were frequently very picturesque, and our initial letter represents one, the pump which formerly stood at the top of Bishopsgate Street, near the church of St. Mary Outwich. The house which Stow inhabited is certainly delineated amongst the rest in the view above, but it cannot now be identified. It will be seen that London was not at that time so closely built upon, and the houses had gardens attached to them. The city walls and bastions existed for its defence, and Aldgate (so called Stow says because it was one of the oldest of the city gates) his quite a fortified look ; and in the old time had seen sum sharp conflicts. The ditch beyond the walls which gives its name to Houndsditch will be observed, and the detached houses and gardens which bordered on London, and in which the citizens would disport themselves with buckler-play, foot-ball, and shooting at butts in the long summer evenings, when all were enjoined by law to 'draw a good bow and shoot a long shot.'

Aldgate as it appeared previous to its demolition in 1760 is given on the previous page.

[34] Richard Grafton had published a rival Chronicle of England, in which, as Stow says, 'he had set his mark on another man's vessel,' merely compiling from easily accessible materials, and had not like Stow searched in untrodden grounds. He indignantly styles his book, in allusion to his name, the 'noise of empty *tonnes* and unfruitful *graffes*.' To this Grafton replied by terming Stow's labours 'lyes foolishly *stowed* together.' The folly of literary squabbles is shown by posterity—Grafton is forgotten, but Stow is ever remembered.

tracts with odd names. But this investigation, out of which he came purer than ever, planted an arrow in his heart that rankled and festered therein until his death. 'The false servant,' as Strype calls him, who perjured his soul to destroy the antiquary, was his own brother! Sad, sad it is, that this should so have been : it is impossible to conceive the bitter anguish such a discovery must have produced on such a mind. He alludes to it frequently and painfully ; all other ills fade before it ; all other wrongs are forgotten in this great one ; it was as scarlet before his eyes until the day of his death. One of his marginal notes on this painful subject is singularly strong and expressive, and shows how bitterly he could feel upon a matter, which his own purity and simplicity of heart taught him to abhor : 'the ungrateful backbiter slayeth three at once— himself by his own malice, him that crediteth his false tales, and him that he backbiteth.'

He continued his labours despite every obstacle that malevolence and poverty threw in his way—studiously and fearlessly enduring and hoping all things. The charity he was so ready to defend ought not to have suffered him to want ; and yet he found none to do for him what he had recommended others to perform in their charities. He advised all, then, to make their hands their executors, and their eyes their overseers ; and yet the wealthy company of Merchant Tailors to which he belonged, and whom he once petitioned as to his distress, suffered the good old man to pine in comparative want,[35] when he was in the eightieth year of his age ; and they could not say they knew it not, for Stow memorialised also King James, and the king—base craven to all kingly greatness that he was!—gave—what?—a home,—a pension gilded with kind words? Not so ; he gave him a privilege!—he gave him permission—TO BEG!

---

[35] The company had done something for Stow, but not commensurate with his wants or his services. Herbert, in his 'History of the Twelve great Livery Companies of London,' notices an entry in the books of the Merchant Tailors Company, dated July 5, 1592, which supplies some hitherto unknown particulars of our antiquary. The first entry acquaints us with John Stow's having 'presented to this house his books entitled "Annals, &c., being a Brief Chronicle of English History ;"' and that the court in consequence settled on him an annuity of 4*l.* per annum. An after entry states this 4*l.* annuity to have been raised to 6*l.* and subsequently to 10*l.* on the motion of Mr, Dove, one of the assistants, and a worthy benefactor to the Merchant Tailors' Company. So that this valuable man's services to society were not altogether so ill rewarded as has been stated. Stow's 'Annals or General Chronicle' as afterwards enlarged by Hawes, was again presented to the company by the latter in 1614, who, it is not improbable from that circumstance, was also a member of the company. The Merchant Tailors' Company has the further honour of having restored John Stow's monument in St. Andrew Undershaft Church.

We saw this fact printed in the *Chronicle,* and deemed it a libel upon the memory of any that had worn our royal English crown. We would not believe it, and so posted off to the British Museum, hoping *not* to find what we sought—in the Harleian collection. Yet here is a true copy, from the original, there extracted :—

'James, by the Grace of God, King of England, Scotland, France, and Ireland, Defender of the Faith, &c. To all our well-beloved subjects greeting :

'Whereas our loving subject, John Stowe (a very aged and worthy member of our city of London), this five and forty yeeres hath to his great charge, and with neglect of his ordinary meanes of maintenance (for the generall good as well of posteritie, as of the present age) compiled and published diverse necessary bookes and chronicles ; therefore we in recompense of these his painfull labours, and for encouragement to the like, have in our royall inclination been pleased to grant our Letters Patents under our great Seale of England, dated Eighth of March, 1603, thereby authorising him, the sayd John Stowe, and his deputies, to collect amongst our loving subjects theyr voluntary contribution and kinde gratuities, as by the sayd Letters Patents more at large may appeare. Now seeing that our sayd Patents (being but one in themselves) cannot be showed forth in divers places or parishes at once (as the occasions of his speedy putting them in execution may require), we have therefore thought expedient, in this unusuall manner, to recommend his cause unto you, having already in our owne person, and of our speciall grace, begun the largesse,[36] for the example of others.

'Given at our palace at Westminster.'

How exceedingly touching, knowing this, are the brief words he speaks of the labours and hardships through which he had to make his way. 'It hath cost me,' he says, 'many a weary mile's travel, many a hard-earned penny and pound, and many a cold winter night's study.' How keenly will this be felt by all who seek by the labour of their fragile pen to earn a subsistence ; how little thanks they receive for the pleasure they bestow, or the knowledge they impart! The sympathies they enlist are for the sorrows of others, not their own ; and if they complain, or tremblingly put forth some claim to the aid and help of the wealthy and the great, they are either neglected or reproached with improvidence—as if they ever had more than they needed from year to year, or, it may be, day to day! Charles Knight supposes that Stow, 'who had long shown how secondary outward circumstances were, in his regard, and who felt

---

[36] There is no account of this 'largesse ;' it is more than probable than it was never given. The date of the letters patent cited in this document is March 8, 1603. Stow was then verging on eighty years of age.

that his poverty did him no dishonour, probably kept up his heart under the state of mendicancy to which he was reduced,' and also adds an anecdote for which he deserves thanks. Once, long before the poverty of Stow was anticipated, or the despicable meanness and shameful heartlessness of James established beyond dispute by his own sign manual, Ben Jensen told his friend Drummond of Hawthornden that he and Stow, walking together, met two lame beggars ; when Stow, as if with some half presentiment of how he was to end his days, gaily asked them 'What they would have to take him to their order?'

ENTRANCE TO THE EXCHANGE, CORNHILL.

With a weary heart must he have often trodden Cornhill and looked upon the wealthy merchant men who thronged Gresham's Exchange ; conscious of having done his work nobly as the historian their great city, yet unrewarded and unrecognised amid the throng, intent then, as now, on their own aggrandisement.[37]

---

[37] The curious view of Cornhill above engraved, forms the background to one of Hollar's large figures exhibiting female costume, dated 1643. It gives, with all the faithful minutiæ of this artist, the aspect of this principal London thoroughfare with its shops ; and it shows the entrance to Gresham's Exchange, with the square tower, which forms so conspicuous an object in old views of the interior. Opposite to this in the centre of the roadway stands the conduit known as 'the tun,' which was constructed in 1282 'by Henry Walles, mayor of London, to be a prison for night walkers and other suspicious persons, and was called the Tun upon Cornhill, because the same was built somewhat in fashion of

Those who would know farther particulars concerning this venerable man who hath drawn unto himself the highest honour the heart can give—must peruse his works, which contain the rare merit of being himself, and as such are better than any biography. It is a sad pity that his history of England has been lost ; and the greater content we have with

CHURCH OF ST. ANDREW UNDERSHAFT.

what he hath himself written, the greater regret we feel that we have not more. Our pilgrimage to his monument was quickly performed—and luckily ; for a very quiet patient sort of woman was cleaning the vestry ; she seemed much pleased by the admiration we expressed for the beauty and antiquity of the church, and assured us that many came to see the monuments, especially that of 'Master Stow.' She kept herself busied so as to have an eye to our movements, and yet was not in the least obtrusive. But first let us explain what Stow explained to us—that this church

a tun standing on one end.' So says honest John Stow, who adds, in 1401 it was made into a cistern 'for sweet water conveyed by pipes of lead from Tiborne, and was from thence called the Conduit upon Cornhill.' The well was planked over, and a strong cage for prisoners constructed upon it with stocks ; and on the top of the cage a pillory for bakers who gave short weight, scolds, and other offenders.

was called St. Andrew's *under-shaft*, because that, in old time, in every year, in May Day in the morning, a long shaft, or May-pole, was set up there in the midst of the street, before the south door of the church, which, when fixed in the ground, was higher than the steeple. Hence the name, St. Andrew *under*, below, the shaft. Chaucer[38] hath assisted to immortalise the said shaft—

   'As ye would beare
   The great SHAFT of Cornehill.'

We could tell you the history of its downfall, but our mind is with the monuments, and the church *within*, rather than the riots of 'Evil May Day,' and the destruction that followed *without*.[39] It is truly a beautiful church. There is a curious communion, or baptismal table, and railing, as you enter at first ; and a noble screen bordered with fine carving ; a window of painted glass, very beautiful in colour and execution. Stow speaks of the liberal donations and great charities of the inhabitants of this parish ; and for the first time for some years, in reply to our question concerning its present state, we were told that 'it had hardly any poor!'—of course in comparison with others. We were glad to hear this of the parish in which the remains of this good old pilgrim mouldered. There are a great many curious monuments and tablets in the church ; two, particularly, within the communion table ; that on the right must have been richly inlaid with brass, but has been shamefully defaced. The woman, wearied perhaps with our questions, and pleased a little with the interest we took in what she respected, opened a long chest that contains many old and valuable books, which, standing all the time close by our side, she permitted us to inspect. One we were greatly delighted to see—an old folio edition of the answer to Harding's reply to Bishop Jewel's Apology. It is bound and studded with steel entirely deprived of its brightness, and a long and strong chain is attached thereto, which the woman assured us 'was solid gold, used for marking the book!' There

---

[38] This passage is not to be found in Chaucer's published works, but was quoted by Stow from a MS. now lost.

[39] The riot of city apprentices on the 1st of May 1517, which ended in a general on-slaught against all foreigners, made stringent rules necessary for their turbulence, and May-games were for a time forbidden. From that time this famous maypole was hung upon hooks over the doors of the neighbouring houses, until a fanatical sermon was preached against it in the reign of Edward VI , which so inflamed the citizens, 'that after eating a hearty dinner to strengthen themselves, every owner of such house over which the shaft hung, with assistance of each ether, sawed off as much of it as hung over his prem-ises, each took his shire, and committed to the flames the tremendous idol.' *Pennant.*

are many other volumes of much value in that chest, and we wish they were carefully seen to, and repaired where age and insects have worn and eaten the leaves. They are with out doubt the remains of what Stow makes honourable mention of :—'At the lower end of the north aisle,' he says, 'is a wainscot press, full of good books, the works of many learned and reverend divines, offering at seasonable and convenient times the benefit of reading, to any that shall be as ready to embrace it, as they and their maintainers to impart it.'

STOW'S MONUMENT.

When we thought of this we pondered over the precious volumes the more ; and would have certainly seen all contained in the chest, had not our watchful friend observed that, though we had come to see Master Stow's monument, we had not yet looked at it, and she did not comprehend our feelings in the least when we told her, that if we had seen it first we should have seen nothing else. She also informed us how that some years ago, one of the churchwardens being a house-painter, painted the carved screen, and pulpit, and organ-loft, with 'oak paint ;' and Master Stow's monument with 'white paint,' and that the gentlemen ever since have had much work to got it off. If he had been a tinman, we suppose, he would have coated them all with tin! Oh, the wickedness of the world! We wonder he did not repaint the twelve apostles!

At last we approached the old pilgrim's tomb. We felt as if in the presence of a shrine, and prostrated our hearts before it.   There is something inexpressibly holy and happy in the figure of the venerable man : unlike all other monuments, not being marble, it has not a cold and chilling aspect. It was a long time reported to be made of terra cotta ; but as it was covered with paint, some of the warm tints of the stone beneath where the paint had been destroyed led to the mistake. It has the smooth, stained, shining (we had almost said *warm*)" look (if very old ivory, and no design could better express the character of the historian. He is seated at his table writing—there is an old swan-quill in his hand. Notwithstanding that the bridge of his nose has been carried away by some rude assault, the full-orbed brow, and the concentrated, yet benevolent mouth, are at once intellectual and amiable. We have seen no engraving that conveys this peculiar expression. There is a clasped book, of the same character as those we had just been inspecting, at either side of the little den in which he sits, and the inscription is simple and beautiful. It is in Latin, but may be translated—

'Sacred to the Memory.

'Here JOHN STOW, citizen of LONDON, awaits the resurrection in CHRIST. who, having exercised very accurate diligence in investigating ancient records, wrote, in a luminous manner, Annals of England, and a concise History of the City of London ; deserving well of his own, well of every future age. Continuing through life with piety, and gradually and happily retiring from it, he died in the 80th year of his age, on the 6th day of April, 1605. 'Elizabeth, his wife, as a perpetual testimony of her love, grieving.'

This quiet record of his old wife's love is not the less moving because of its simplicity. And there rests JOHN STOW ;—and there, of all other places would we have him rest ; for though there were thorns in his worldly career, HERE all is as he, if living, would desire—he is in the heart of his beloved city. If anything could be heard in his narrow resting-place, the peals of its thousand, bells would wake him before the day of final doom. The parish in which he sleeps is immortalised, by the charities he loved and preserved, from the pangs of starvation which have gnawed the very vitals of our enduring people. Strangely enough, beside his tomb are the shelves which, Sunday after Sunday, are piled with bread and money for the widow and the orphan ; nay, the very scales are there, to tell the justice of the weights. Right opposite the monument is the pure font he mentions, though its carved cover, one of the most exquisite both in elegant design and perfect execution we ever saw, is not noted in his 'Chronicle ;' but there it is—blessed to receive, and, in receiving, blessing, the younglings of Christ's flock. Surely he would rejoice to see those infant citizens received into the holy Church! There he lies among those he loved—the most honoured of those he delighted to honour—THE ONE JOHN STOW!

Let no one sneer at the toils of the antiquary : he has enjoyments peculiarly his own, but his labours are pregnant with instruction ; his enthusiasm may not be at all times intelligible but out of it proceeds enlightenment to thousands : he may work like the mole—often in darkness and underground—but that which he brings to the surface is fruitful and good. How many pleasures do we owe him : for how much of instruction are we his debtors, bringing together the present and the past,—illustrating history by proofs surer than hosts of witnesses. Rarely is the antiquary other than the advocate and ally of virtue ; it is the gentle and generous only who seek intercourse and intimacy with the dead and the forgotten.

The Tomb of John Kyrle.

'Rise, honest Muse, and sing the Man of Ross.'—Pope.

 N a rocky eminence overlooking the Wye, stands the town of Ross. Nothing can be more picturesque than its position : it is seen to most advantage from the Hereford road, from whence our view is taken. The church stands upon an elevated ridge of rock ; and the town occupies the rising ground ; while behind are wood-crowned hills, as grand in their character and as beautiful as many more celebrated Continental scenes. The view from the walks beside the church and from other parts of the town is singularly fine ; and the curve of the Wye, which flows at the base of the hills, is lovely in the extreme. It would be difficult to point out a more fascinating stream ; flowing as it does through a rich and well-wooded country, abounding in natural beauties, and over which the eye may rove untired for days,—the prospect is so rich and ever-changing, as it is sun-lit or shadowed by the passing cloud. It is a scene which Turner would have loved, and one that must be studied on the spot to be fully appreciated. The country is Arcadian ; the river rapid and clear, forms a curve of the most graceful form, wending its way among the Welsh hills ; the prospect has that most perfect union of grandeur and beauty, of pastoral simplicity and mountain sublimity, which, when combined, become the perfection of landscape scenery. But all these advantages, all these beauties, are to be found in various districts of our glorious country. Perhaps it is because the rich valley, the swelling hill, the fertilising river, the smiling village, are scattered so abundantly throughout England, that we only note them 'by their loss' when we visit other countries, where, however novel, all things must seem barren by comparison.

ROSS FROM THE HEREFORD ROAD.

Ross has been rendered remarkable : it has a reputation that will live as long as 'our land's language ;' a reputation created by the actual as well as the ideal ; an immortality founded by a good man, and celebrated by a man of genius, who honoured himself while honouring 'the right.' Yet it can boast of little historic interest ; but for *the Man* who has 'made it world-famous, it would have no other claim to celebrity than that which it derives from beauty of situation. The streets are all more or less upon acclivities, and are narrow and antique-looking, with many a gabled roof and bit of old carving ornamental plaster-work upon timeworn fronts. The market-house is a study worthy of the artist ; it is in a very decayed state, and is supported by columns of red sandstone, which have succumbed to the action of the weather so considerably that it looks as if it had been erected in the time of the Saxons rather than that of Charles II., in whose comparatively modern days it was constructed. Upon a market-day, when it is crowded with the peasantry from the neighbouring forest of Dean, that primitive and almost unvisited district, the scene is most picturesque and unsophisticated. No railways run near the town, and the heavily-laden coach, as it winds its slow way up the street beside the marketplace, does not jar with the old-world association of a scene which seems rather to belong to the last century than to our own.

The town of Ross is celebrated for the especial purity of its air and for the longevity of its inhabitants ; and the visitor who rambles in its churchyard[40] will meet with many inscriptions, recording the memory of those who had attained their eightieth, ninetieth, and even one hundredth year.

The entire aspect of Ross is that of a quiet mountain home. The shopkeepers seem to conduct their business in the simplest and plainest manner, without bustle, and with a due amount of attention. Carts jog quietly up and down the inclined planes called streets. People walk on the curb or in the road 'at their own sweet will,' and encounter none of the dangers of the tumultuous thoroughfares of London. There is a serenity about life in these country towns of which those 'in populous city pent' have no notion ; people do not rush along the path of life as if death were at their heels, and there was literally no time for thought or the enjoyment of existence. The clear well-opened eye, the ruddy cheek and fresh bright lips of rural health, tell of the absence of care and thought : if there is less evidence of intelligence and the knowledge of life which is seen in the haggard eye of the manufacturer, or the worn and anxious look of the pallid artisan, there is more of peace and contentment, and above all, of health, in those of the tiller of the soil.

---

[40] The church is a spacious and beautiful building, with a tower and elegant spire, for which it is indebted to 'the Man' whose body rests within its walls. Beside the pew which be used, trees have forced their way beneath the window in the wall, and grow with great luxuriance withinside the church, nearly covering the glass. They are two slight and elegant elms, which wave their branches over his pew, and which are regarded with much veneration. The local legend is, that some years ago a rector impiously cut down some of John Kyrle's favourite trees, with which he had adorned the churchyard, and which grew *outside* the window and immediately opposite to his pew, and that there-upon they threw out fresh shoots, which forced their way *withinside* the church, under the wall, and grew in the pew of him who planted them, where they have been suffered to remain and expand. Not a branch of these trees grows without the church, but they luxuriate within it ; reaching nearly to the ceiling, and closely clinging with their branches to the window-glass. They are carefully preserved and venerated ; and the singularity of their position and history is remarked by all. The other windows contain many fragments of old glass. There are several fine monuments in the church to the Rudhall family, who were the ancient proprietors of the Manor of Rudhall, in this neighbourhood. The recumbent figures of Judge Rudhall and his lady, of the time of Henry VII. and the martial effigy of Sir Richard Ruhall, who was knighted at Cadiz in the reign of Elizabeth, are fine specimens of the art of sculpture in those days.

We do not contend for the palm of intellect for our rural population : they are heavy, the men especially so, and hard to move, and their qualities and virtues are in the general way rather negative than active. But the sloth has always been transformed into the lion when a great occasion summoned the peasant from his cottage to protect his country and defend its liberty ; then other lights dance in his blue eyes ; a deeper colour mantles his ruddy cheek ; it is glorious to recall what English peasants effected when they rose against ship-money, and compelled justice to do her duty. Certainly there is a distressing contrast between the physical appearance of the 'Men' of Ross, and those of our close manufacturing districts : the anxious look and bloodshot eye that rests ever on machinery, and rarely sees a flower or a leaf ; the half-numbed ear, that hears no song of bird, save from within those rusty bars upon which even a defiled sunbeam seldom rests ; the sunken cheek, telling of hard labour and privation ; the narrow chest, never expanded by the fresh breeze of the hill ; the limbs, more than half deformed during an infancy spent in bending over the frames of some overgrown manufactory,—all tell the dismal story of eternal toil. The peasant has innumerable blessings which, however unconsciously he may enjoy them, contribute to that health of body and placidity of spirit, the latter of which tends to create a heavy indifference to passing events, which the keen and hungry-eyed manufacturer is driven by necessity, as well as by habit, to attend to. The peasant has fresh pure air ; he lives in constant communion with Nature ; by attention the small garden can be rendered a source of profit and enjoyment ; he has frequently the consciousness that those in better circumstances, placed as the world calls it, 'above him,' take an interest in his temporal and spiritual affairs. In all our agricultural districts schools have multiplied, and efforts are at last making by those who ought to have made them long ago, to rouse a spirit that will send labourers from the beautiful fields of our pastoral districts into the vineyards of our Lord. No one who has lived pent up in the close city, and is able to leave its feverish excitements,—its noise,—its atmosphere laden with pestilence—for the tranquillity of the country, but must feel renewed existence, at being permitted to breathe the air in which the lark sings, and which gives voice to the nightingale.

There are few things that so purify and uplift the spirit, as the consideration of that which mere WILL can achieve, even when unaided by what we consider wealth—wealth! which renders charity of such easy and happy performance, that the wonder is, how men so underrate the power it gives in creating happiness and conferring the enduring immortality of benevolence, as to abstain from its bestowal in the service of fellow-creatures ; yet nearly all our large Charities have been originated by persons of great minds, but small means. And the only regret we can have in contemplating the noble monuments to humanity which are up-springing around us, is, that in accordance—and an evil accordance it is,—with the taste of the times, there is too much money expended in decoration. Public charities should dwell within walls of severe simplicity, where show should be sacrificed to comfort. Pope, refined as was his taste, was of this opinion when he wrote his encomium on John Kyrle, "The Man of Ross."

KYRLE'S HOUSE.

Exactly opposite the market-place, and in the narrowest part of the town, still stands the house of John Kyrle, the world-famous 'Man of Ross,' it is a plain building, situated on the slope of the hill, and was a few years ago used as an inn, known by the sign of the King's Arms. While the house was an inn it was visited by Coleridge, and he commemorated his sojourn here in some beautiful and touching lines. It has since undergone alterations, and is now converted into a bookseller's shop. The adjoining house, now a chemist's, appears to have originally been a part of the building, and is ornamented with a plaster medallion representing in the centre 'the Man of Ross.'[41]   It is inscribed with Kyrle's name, and with the cognomen Pope has made more famous ; and on a band beneath is given the date of his decease—'Died November 7th, 1724, Aged 88.'

THE GALLERY OF KYRLE'S HOUSE.

The house bears traces of antiquity in the carved brackets and the massive woodwork which decorate the interior.   Our cut shows the gallery that runs along the first floor, and the reader will remark the solid beams upon which the ceiling rests.   The carved arch over the staircase, as well as some other 'bits' of the original work, would lead to the conjecture that it was constructed in the middle of the seventeenth century ; it is said to have been built by Kyrle.   The rooms retain much of their old appearance, being wainscotted in solid panels ; and in one of them appears a decorated compartment, believed to have been the work of Kyrle himself.   It exhibits his coat of arms, and the date 1689 executed in punctured or dotted outlines.

The house being in the centre of the town, has but a small garden in its rear.   It is a square plot of ground, reached by a sort of alley between the walls of the adjoining houses.   Here Kyrle erected the summer-house represented in our cut, but of which nothing now remains except the foundation.   It was here he read and ruminated ; but the advantages it possessed are few, as it is overlooked by houses on all sides, and is a town-garden at best.   The only pleasing feature is the church spire, which he aided in building, and which gracefully overtops the unpicturesque buildings around.

---

[41] He wears a flowing wig and long neckcloth, but *the likeness* appears to be but a very unsatisfactory one, inasmuch as it is a poor work of art.   In the 'Beauties of England and Wales,' mention is made of 'a tolerable portrait' preserved here when the house was an inn ; it is not here now, but the original is said to have been in the possession of Lord Muncaster.   All the portraits now sold here seem to lack *vraisemblance.*

THE SUMMER HOUSE.

The beneficence and goodness of John Kyrle owe their celebrity to Pope's noble lines. But for the Poet's acquaintance with his actions, and his record of them in never-dying verse, he might have been as little remembered as many other philanthropists whose mimes are only written in 'the Book of Life.' Pope made frequent visits to Holm Lacy, the seat of Viscount Scudamore, to whom he had been introduced by his relative Mr. Digby. He was near enough to Ross to hear of all John Kyrle's charities ; and he rendered due homage to them in his Moral Essays. The vivid colours of the Poet's description did not in this instance outdo the truth. Kyrle literally did all that Pope declared in his outline of the good man's works.

He was entered as a gentleman-commoner of Baliol College, Oxford, in 1654, and was intended for the bar ; but this intention he abandoned, and returning to his native county he devoted himself to agriculture and the improvement of his native town. He always lived with great simplicity, was an unmarried man, and had as housekeeper, an old maiden aunt. His was the olden hospitality ; beside his kitchen fire stood a large block of wood, which served as a bench for the poor and the passing traveller to sit upon and take the refreshment which was never refused them. His own table was served with much simplicity, and it is recorded that he never drank anything but malt liquors and cyder, and never had roast beef except on Christmas-day. He was exceedingly fond of cheerful society, and much enjoyed the weekly market dinners, when he would join the farmers and chat with them, being usually the last to leave the table.

He is described as tall and thin, but well shaped, and by his temperance insured so much good health, that his last illness was also his first ; he was fond not only of superintending the many public and private labours in which his mind was engaged, but of manually aiding in them ; and he would help the workmen at their labour, in road-making and planting. The latter occupation was his favourite one, and he delighted above all things in walking about with an enormous pot of water, and attending to the trees he planted. He was generally seen trudging from place to place with his spade on his shoulder.

His charities are so well told in Pope's lines, which are in the memory of all Englishmen, that we need scarcely do more than refer to them for the history of his actions. Every Sunday he cooked a large piece of boiled beef and made three pecks of flour into loaves, which was regularly distributed to the poor :

> 'Behold the market-place, with poor o'erspread,
> The Man of Ross divides the weekly bread ;
> He feeds yon alms-house, neat, but void of state,
> Where age and want sit smiling at the gate ;
> Him, portion'd maids, apprenticed orphans, bless'd,
> The young who labour, and the old who rest."

The universality of his benevolence and thorough honesty of his character, made him the referee in most disputes ; and his leisure and good-nature gave him means of settling many a case which might else have involved much wrangling and expense in law-courts. To the sick he was also a doctor and attendant :

> 'Despairing quacks with curses fled the place,
> And vile attornies, now a useless race.'

He set his heart on the improvement of Ross ; and its natural beauties and advantages were heightened by his taste and care. Previous to his time there was a want of trees about the town and in the plain below it. Kyrle felt this, and was a vigorous planter. It became ultimately his greatest enjoyment to plant and water and foster his sylvan children. The fine trees about the church and avenues in the Prospect-ground adjoining, were of his fostering. It was he 'who hung with woods yon mountain's sultry brew,

and who called into existence many conveniences and beauties which Ross has still to show. Kyrle died at the age of eighty-four, full of years and honour ; the real grief felt when a benefactor dies, was felt at Ross in 1724, when his remains wore carried to the last resting-place on the hilltop where he had often walked and prayed.   No stone marked his

grave for fifty-two years, but kind hearts cherished the spot and remembered it.   In 1776, the tomb shown in our cut was placed on the wall of the chancel close to the communion-rails.   Its history is told in this inscription which appears upon it :—'In virtue of a bequest under the will   of   Constantia, Viscountess Dupplin, great-granddaughter to Sir John Kyrle of Much Marcle in this county,   Bart.;   Lieut.-Col. James   Money   of   Much Marcle   aforesaid,   her executor and heir, erected this Monument in memory of his kinsman,   John   Kyrle, A.D. 1776.'   The tomb is a work of much elegance, it is of white and dove-coloured marbles edged with black.   A medallion in the upper part exhibits a bas-relief likeness of Kyrle, above which is hung a festoon.   Beneath is another medallion representing Charity and Benevolence supporting each other.[42]   The principal inscription, which occupies the centre, runs thus :—'This Monument was erected in memory of John Kyrle, commonly called the Man of Ross.'

Immediately adjoining the churchyard is *the Prospect-ground,* as it is termed, consisting of a public walk extending for nearly a mile to the

---

[42] It is engraved in our initial letter.

southward and which was formed by Kyrle. He planted it with trees, and evidently intended it for the ornament of the town as well as for the health of its inhabitants ; he constructed seats for the weary traveller, as described by Pope, and a summer-house at its termination. But his townsmen had not that thought for themselves which he in his benevolence had for them. They neglected his gifts, and the Prospect-ground became merely a field, instead of a cheerful garden or a parterre ; the seats were broken, the summer-house decayed, and many of the trees were cut down. Worse than all, the land became partially alienated from the people ; the walks have been declared 'not public ;' and Kyrle's townsmen, by their own neglect, have been deprived of the advantages his benevolence designed for them.

We cannot sympathise with those who had so little sympathy with the exertions made for their advantage by 'the Man of Ross ;' to us everything connected with his name is hallowed. We felt it a privilege to know how much could be done with small means towards, not ephemeral, but lasting good. We longed to show it to those who enrol a donation on a charity list and earn for themselves a great repute, by what is in fact, no sacrifice.

There is a fashion in all things, and the cant of religious charity is as degrading as any other. John Kyrle acted upon the great ennobling precepts left us by St. Paul, and all who love to see how—

'—the memory of the just
Smells sweet and blossoms in the dust,'

would be well rewarded by a pilgrimage to the resting-place of THE MAN OF ROSS.

The Grave of Sir Richard Lovelace.

F all the visitations of ill-fortune with which old London has been afflicted, the one most deplored by the historian and the antiquary is the great fire of 1666. The mementos of early ages, the momorials of great men, the localities on which the mind might dwell with pleasure, and conjure up the inhabitants who had made them famous, were all swept away, and with them many a written record, the want of which will be felt for ever ; many a work of ancient Art, with which the piety of our ancestors delighted to decorate the churches or the halls of the civic companies ; many a "flower of history" was withered and lost in that desolating flame.

In the pages of that noble old antiquary, John Stow, we have the best picture of ancient London. The patient and ill-rewarded chronicler has noted its ancient features with a minute truthfulness that will render his labours precious to all time. To understand the destruction which was spread amid the flame-girt city, we must know his pages well, and contrast them with the little that is left to us. Of the churches he describes, how few remain ; of the tombs he notes, how rare are they now to look upon ; the many memorials of great men which adorned St. Paul's are reduced to a few simple fragments. Little, indeed, did the fire leave but blackened and shapeless ruins. Such churches as were spared are therefore doubly dear to us ; and St. Helen's, Bishopsgate ; St. Andrew Undershaft ; St. Bartholomew's, Smithfield ; and a few others, hence assume an additionally sacred character.

How truly great are the names which connect themselves with the churches of London. Statesmen, churchmen, warriors, historians, legal and civic dignitaries, merchants, who made the city glorious and its trade world-renowned, are in the list, with the names of painter, poet, and dramatist, whose minds were engrossed by all that make mental life

ENTRANCE TO ST. BRIDE'S CHURCH.

captivating. But of many we know only the whereabouts of their last-resting place, 'no storied urn or monumental bust' remains to do them honour ; the last tribute of affectionate regard placed over their graves has fallen for ever amongst the ruins of burned London, and the pages of the older historians must be our guide merely to the spot.

It is thus with the tomb of Sir Richard Lovelace ; we know only that he was buried 'at the west end of St. Bride's Church,' in Fleet Street.[43] But the church was burned in the great fire, and no memorial of his resting-place remains ; nor do we know of any other view of the sanctuary where he re-

---

[43] The present church was built by Sir Christopher Wren, and completed in 1680. The steeple was originally thirty-two feet higher than the Monument, but having been struck by lightning in 1805, it was lowered to its present standard. Of the old church, we obtain glimpses in such views as that given above. 'The doorway into Mr. Holden's vault, erected April, anno 1657,' with his arms above, has been engraved as 'one of the few relics after the fire of 1666.' Pennant thus slightingly speaks of it : 'It was dedicated to St. Bridget ; whether she was Irish, or whether she was Scotch, whether she was maiden, or whether she was wife, I will not dare to determine.' The church was originally small, but by the piety of William Viner, warden of the Fleet, about the year 1480, it was enlarged with 'body and side aisles, and ornamented with grapes and vine leaves, in allusion to his name.'

posed after a toil-worn life, except that afforded by Hollar's view of London before the fire, where the steeple of St. Bride's is seen above Baynard's Castle.[44]

BAYNARD'S CASTLE.

We had spent our morning hunting through the books, the registers of St. Bride's church, for the entry of the burial of Sir Richard Lovelace, the very pink of cavalier-chivalry, differing, perhaps, from the ancient chivalry of England, in being *not* so deep seated and intense, but undoubtedly more glossy and brilliant—more of light burnished armour, the velvet, and plume, and broidered glove, than of casque and iron spear, heavy helmet, and weighty battle axe ; but the swords of both were of well-tempered steel, and, if the cavalier were perfumed in the

---

[44] Baynard's Castle was one of the two castles built on the west side of the city, with walls and ramparts, as mentioned by Fitz-Stephen. It was originally built by Baynard a nobleman, who, according to Stow, came in with the Conqueror. It was situated in Thames Street, and has been rendered immortal by Shakspeare, who makes it the scene of the Duke of Glo'ster's deceptive morality in his play of Richard III., when the citizens, with the mayor at their head, solicit him to be king. 'The Baynard's Castle of the time of Richard III.,' says Mr. Knight, was built by Humphrey, Duke of Glo'ster ; and it was subsequently granted by Henry VI. To Richard's father, the Duke of York.' It is frequently named by early writers as the place of embarkation for the mayor and nobility on solemn occasions. It was destroyed in the great fire ; but Stevens, in one of his notes to Shakspeare says, 'part of its strong foundations are still visible at low water.'

drawing-room, he was brave and faithful in the field. We had been hunting, we say, for this last sad entry, and afterwards, at home, when pondering over his chequered life, our cogitation's naturally ran upon a contrast of the past with the present. If our minds have been improved by the march of intellect, there certainly has been no improvement during these latter days in our manners ; on the contrary, no one who has

been much in the society of some of the young men of the present time, and can remember those of even the later period of George III.'s reign, but must confess that manner generally has imbibed a sort of roughshod 'egalité,' utterly at variance with right feeling and good taste. Impudence is too frequently confounded with ease—rudeness with frankness—the amalgamation of dress has caused an unfortunate amalgamation of persons, and, somehow or other, both persons and things have got misplaced. We have almost as much want of keeping in society as if we were a new country. The aristocracy of wealth has intruded its grossness upon the aristocracy of birth and talent, and we gaze upon it

INNER GATE OF THE CHARTER HOUSE.

as we would upon a Chinese joss placed amid Grecian statues, wondering at its rich but gaudy hues and uncouth form, and, above all, how it got where it is. We are opening our mouths in loud condemnation of American coarseness, while our middle class is getting into the same 'go-a-head' way, and loosing the refining belief that for the well-being of society good manners are only second to good morals ; we never were altogether a polished people, John Bull having some strange idea that his nature would be worn out if he attended too much to the courtesies of life ; and particularly of late he has, we imagine, begun to fancy that the graces, the small cares, the atten tions and etiquettes of society—the 'politeness' which Lord Shaftesbury defines to be *benevolence in trifles,'*—'interfere with his civil and religious liberty. He thinks himself more independent in a frock than in a dress coat, and will chuckle half the evening over his own cleverness, if he has succeeded in baffling the scrutiny of the doorkeepers, and getting into the pit of the opera in boots. He does not understand that he puts a slight upon the lady of the house if he enters the drawing-room in what *he* terms a 'friendly way,' but what she cannot fail to consider a palpable inattention to the duties—for they *are* duties—of the toilet, and duties which, if once rendered, as they ought to be, HABITUAL, would involve neither trouble nor expense. To contrast the manners of Old England with what we may almost term the manners of *New* England— the young, lounging, doing-as-they-like, cigar-smoking, indifferent, loose-coated men of the present with the courtly, polished, earnest, and well-dressed men of the past century is by no means agreeable.

The high-toned mind, the gallant bearing, the innate sense of chivalric honour, remain in the history and writings of the past. We know nothing of chivalry except from books—such books as those around us, the 'Poetic Chroniclers of England,' and above all those, Sir Richard Lovelace deserves especial note. A quaint collector of old songs, whose little volume is bound in roughest russet, says, that he can compare none to Colonel Lovelace, save Sir Philip Sidney, of which latter it is told by one in an epitaph made of him—

> 'Nor is it fit that more I should acquaint,
>   Lest men adore in one
> A scholar, souldier, lover, and a saint.'

The parallel between those two men naturally suggests itself to all who read their writings. They were both of noble parentage, Sir Philip's father being deputy of Wales, our colonel, of a viscount's name and family—both accomplished scholars ; the one celebrating his mistress under the name of 'Stella,' the other the lady regent of his affections under the banner of Lucasta ; both of them imbued with the spirit of true poetry, though its degree of strength was different, Lovelace being the feebler and less industrious of the two ; but both being of undoubted bravery, and overflowing with that true, unshaken loyalty, the unfailing offspring of nobler souls. It is impossible to think of Sir Richard Lovelace without admiration and sympathy. Woolwich has good reason to be proud of his birth, and the Charter House of his education.[45]

He graduated with due honour at Gloucester Hall, Oxford, in 1636.[46] On leaving college he 'retired,' as Wood phrases it, 'in great splendour to the court,' where he was well received ; and having attracted the attention of Lord Goring, he entered the army and became first an ensign, and afterwards a captain. On the pacification of Berwick he took possession of his estate, which was worth about 500*l.* per annum, and was deputed by the men of Kent to deliver their petition to the House of Commons, requesting the king to be restored and the government settled, which gave such offence that he was doomed to imprisonment in the old Westminster gatehouse, where so many were, from time to time, deprived of their liberty ; *there* he composed one of his favourite poems that well deserved the praise bestowed upon it by the old cavaliers :—

---

[45] The name of this noble foundation is a corruption of the French *Chartreuse,* and it obtained its name from the establishment of a monastery of Carthusians in the reign of Edward III. It became a rich place, and was among the first seized by Henry VIII.; but its inmates so inflexibly opposed his supremacy, that John Houghton, the prior, and many of the monks were executed at Tyburn, and their heads and quarters set on the gates of the city, the priors being reserved for exposure on the Charter House. After it had passed through the hands of many of Henry's rapacious courtiers, it was purchased by Thomas Howard, fourth Duke of Norfolk, who resided in it. It was purchased by Sutton in 1611 for the sum of 13,000*l.*, and converted into a hospital and school, making it one of the noblest foundations in England. Eighty pensioners and forty-two scholars are supported in the establishment. The former, according to Sutton's statutes, should be 'gentlemen by descent and in poverty ; soldiers that have borne arms by sea or land ; merchants decayed by piracy or shipwreck ; or servants in the household of the King and Queen's majesty.' But these regulations were soon enlarged for 'needy or impotent people' in general, who now have apartments, food, attendance, and 20*l.* yearly in money. There is no nobler or more liberal institution, and none which has been more instrumental in smoothing the last years of deserving unfortunates.

[46] Gloucester Hall, 'originally an ancient house of learning, built by the monks of St. Peter Gloster for the education of their novices in academical learning,' is now Worcester College. It changed its name early in the last century, when Sir Thomas Cooke, having by will, dated June 8, 1701, left 10,000*l.* for the increase of some house of learning, that sum remaining unapplied for some years, amounted to 15,000*l.*, it was given to Gloster Hall, which by letters patent, dated July 14, 1741, was called Worcester College. The old buildings gave way to a more befitting structure, and the features of Lovelace's place of education were obliterated so much as to destroy its connection with his name.

'Stone walls doe not a prison make,
    Nor iron bars a cage,
Mindes, innoceent and quiet, take
    That for an hermitage.
If I have freedom in my love,
    And in my soule am free,
Angels alone, that soar above,
    Enjoy such libertie.'

To us there has always been a most exquisite quaintness and simplicity in the lines

    'Mindes, innoceent and quiet, take
        That for an hermitage.'

But the whole is beautiful ; and, when his confinement produced a gem of such perfect workmanship as this, we are almost selfish enough to regret his liberation, which, however, did not take place until he had given secrurity, in a bail of 40,000*l.*, that he would not quit the country. Truly, his heart and hopes were too much with the kingly power to forsake it. According to old Wood, his biographer, he was accounted the 'most amiable and beautiful person that eye ever beheld ; a person, also, of innate modesty, virtue. and courtly deportment, which made him then, but especially afterwards when he 'retired' to the great city—much admired and loved by the female sex.' During the time of his confinement in London he lived beyond the income of his estate, either to keep up the credit and reputation of the king's cause, by furnishing men with horses and arms, or by relieving ingenious men in want, whether they were scholars, musicians, soldiers, friends, openly or secretly, of the royal cause—enjoying the freedom of generosity ; proving by his actions the poetry of his nature ; winging his thoughts upon such elastic verse, that the idea of his liberality and his genius became one and the same thing. His manners were of such gentle courtliness that he led those whom he obliged to the belief that they were obliging him. Lovelace is a just example of the poets of his time, when the making of verses was considered a chief excellence in a courtier—the most approved of all relaxations ; and when, to the good graces of women, more prone in those days to a love of poetry than a love of gold, it was a ready, if not a necessary, passport.

The lover then was invariably the laureate of his mistress, whose duty it was to record the most trifling incident that chanced to her, and to labour so that her smallest attraction might obtain immortality. Thus the compositions of Lovelace are chiefly the productions of happier hours, and tell of joys begotten by a smile, or easily-endured woes, the produce of a short-lived frown.   Unfortunately, the events they com-memorated were seldom such as have universal interest.   The wearing of a glove, the blemish of a pimple, or the infliction of a toothache, were considered topics more fitting to occupy a poet's thoughts and pen than the noble, enduring, and endearing ties which bind virtuous men to vir-tuous women.   Frequent instances of this straining after an undesirable effect is to be found amongst the old poets, mingled up with their chiv-alry, both of love and war.   This trifling was a species of courtly excres-cence, an excess of refinement less offensive in its weakness than the roughness of modern society ; the latter irritates, the former only creates a smile.

Lucy Sacheverell was the lady to whom Sir Richard addressed his love.   His beautiful lines to her, on his going to the wars, are worthy of any poet :—

'Tell me not, sweet, I am unkind,
    That from the nunnerie
Of thy chaste breast and quiet minde,
    To warre and arms I flie.

True, a new mistress now I chase,
    The first foe in the field ;
And with a stronger faith embrace
    A sword, a horse, a shield.

Yet this inconstancy is such
    As you, too, shall adore ;
I could not love thee, deare, so much,
    Lov'd *I not honour more.*'

In 1646 he formed a regiment for the service of the French king, became its colonel, and was wounded at Dunkirk.   In 1648 he returned to England with his brother ; but unhappily his mistress, hearing that her lover had died of his wounds at Dunkirk, had married another.   Thus disappointed in his love, and anguished past endurance by the death of his royal master, Charles I., the gallant and high-souled poet found him-self at liberty, after a second imprisonment,[47] without any residue of the fortune he had bestowed with too liberal a hand upon those who needed.

---

[47] In Peter House, London, to which he was committed soon after his return, and where he remained until after the king's death.

His monarch and his mistress, the continued and frequently-associated themes of his muse, both lost to him, he bowed his head to the dispensations of Providence, and prepared for death as for the friend

'who only could restore
The libertie he must enjoy on earth no more.'

No longer dressed as became his rank, the nodding feather fell away from the velvet hat, the satin dropped from the slashed sleeve, the threadbare hose became a world too large for the shrunk limb ; and so Sir Richard Lovelace pined and died, in the year 1658, in a miserable room in Gunpowder Alley, Shoe Lane, adding another to the list of unfortunate poets ; another to that of those who, endowed by nature with the richest and brightest of all earthly gifts, seem fated to an inheritance of misery! Wood says, that 'having consumed his estate, he grew very melancholy, which at length brought him into a consumption ; became very poor in body and purse ; was the object of charity ; went in ragged clothes (whereas when he was in his glory he wore clothes of gold and silver); and mostly lodged in obscure and dirty places, more befitting the worst of beggars and poorest of servants.' Were there none to alleviate the sorrows of his last hours? None to wipe the death-dews from his high and noble brow? None who, for the love of honour, for the sake of royalty—in memory of what be had been to all who needed—so unselfishly generous, so unsparingly liberal—was there not *one*, even of those who had chorussed his songs, and been warmed in the brightness of his glorious days, to sit by that lowly deathbed, and whisper the assurance that he was only passing through the dark valley to enter upon an immortality where sorrow and sighing should be no more, and where loyalty is perfected in homage to the Almighty? There might have been— there *must* have been—though of such there is no earthly record. But it would be en insult to human nature to suppose he died alone—alone in that room which echoed back the dreadful cough telling of the wasting disease that terminated the earthly career of as gallant and true a gentleman as ever wielded sword or pen.

And so he died, and was buried, according to all chronicles, in the beautiful church of Saint Bride's ; and thither we went to seek either for a tablet to his memory or for the record of his burial in the church books. Some charity-children were passing out as we entered the gate that may be called 'beautiful ;' and wandering along the aisles, attended by the intelligent and obliging sextoness, we found the spot where Richardson, the author of that everlasting 'Sir Charles Grandison,' is interred ; but we found nothing of Lovelace ; and then we passed into the vestry, and were much struck with an ancient *cofre,* the lid of which is one huge lock, and sundry curious relics, and then carefully examined the church books, some of which bore evidence, by their discoloured leaves, of having suffered in the great London fire, and found therein, about the date of his death, two buried of the name, but none by the Christian name of RICHARD.

The woman asked if he were of our kin. We told her no, not in the flesh ; but that we loved his memory well, and honoured him as one who, with a most worthy mixture of courtliness and benevolence, was of marvellous talent, unshaken loyalty, and bravery unsurpassed.

The Grave of Lady Rachel Russell

HE experience of every day confirms us more and more in the belief that women who make a great outcry about their *rights* have given but small attention to their duties. A woman's DUTIES are her RIGHTS ; and if we consider either her individual or her social position, the duties which belong to her as daughter, wife, or mother ; give her actual power, power of the highest and holiest kind,—power to form the minds and characters of men, and that without over-stepping the charmed circle within which Nature ordained her to move.

Women, blessed as was the LADY RACHEL RUSSELL, with a friend, a councillor, and a lover, in a husband,—women, so circumstanced, can, perhaps, form no idea of the perpetual misery a high-souled woman endures, upon whom the knowledge of a husband's unworthiness comes after all efforts have been made to have faith in him. To see, one by one, the feigned or imagined, virtues vanish ; to find that he who had wooed and wed for a purpose, at length, scorns even to assume the qualities he never cared to possess ; to obtain from experience the terrible knowledge that the companion for life, in whom the hopes of the future were treasured, the husband of her choice, the father of her children—is worthless in the sight of God and man,—is a grief so full of anguish, that no wonder the weak-minded either sink into helpless slavery, and in time become 'like what they loathe,' or, forgetting the solemn obligation of the vow, (uncondi-tional as it is) break into impotent rebellion and perish, the victims of opinions,—to alter which would be more fatal to the good order of soci-ety than their continuance, harsh as they are, and hardly as they bear upon the 'weaker vessel.'

But the right-minded, and above all the *Christian,* woman, should be most careful to avoid judging her own sex harshly. Silence towards an erring sister is more seemly than condemnation ; and one of the most

92

touching passages in the letters of the Lady Rachel Russell,—whose Life should be in the library of every daughter of England—is that in which she points to her *own unworthiness* ; never implicating those whose follies and vanity led her 'to like well the esteemed diversions of the town.' The woman who is so happy as to find a wise and worthy friend in her husband, one whom it is impossible not to reverence and love, whom she may delight to honour, and whose faults are but as dust in the heavy balance of his virtues, will do well to keep steadily in view the duty of the covenant made at God's altar, rendering thanks that she cannot choose but 'love, honour, and obey' what is so worthy of easy and pleasant service. But if she does well in this matter, she will do better to show by her actions what is the duty of a good and loving wife, than by heavily railing at women less blest than herself who, having none of her consolations, forget the duty they owe even to a bad husband, and with peevish discontent would invert God's order of things, and think they could more rightly perform man's duty than man himself. Such women ought to be especial objects of pity, for they are most unhappy. We never knew one of those who are for upsetting the Christian order of man's precedence, who was not a restless, discontented person, and even more to be pitied because more unhappy, than the meek and suffering woman, who, bearing her cross in humble imitation of HIM who, when 'reviled, reviled not again,' presses onward in her thorny path of duty, looking forward to the future, while enduring the present, and not unfrequently rewarded by winning back, even at the eleventh hour, the wandering heart. We owe much of the well-doing of society to those silent, patient, loving sisters,—wives and mothers,—who, with no pretensions to lofty intellect, but with a desire to do right and the rich treasure of a loving nature, are the guardian angels of many homes, which, but for them would run as wildly to ruin as their masters. How frequently a timid, shrinking woman, whose nerves have been shattered by the loud voice and midnight orgies of a brutal husband, 'keeps the house together,' one can hardly tell how ; by instinct rather than reason. And yet how can those whose homes are the temples of domestic peace, where happiness disposes its richest triumphs, judge of the temptations of her who hears no music in a husband's step, and whose every spar of hope has been shipwrecked by the reckless and cruel nature of him who swore to shield her from all sorrow?

It is interesting to know what were the preparations which sanctified the name of Lady Rachel Russel, and gave to her so high and prominent a place in English history. Let us, first pause a moment to say, that while it has been the custom to portray the virtues of the lower and middle class females of England, so as to excite sympathy and admiration, the female aristocracy of England have had no faithful portrait-painter, either with pen or pencil of late years, to do them justice. The so-called *'fashionable'* novels, have, with few exceptions, been written either by individuals of at least doubtful morality, acquainted only with the coarser features of rank, or by persons who knew nothing of its movements, except from public records ; and who have fallen into the error of confounding the so-called man or woman of *fashion*—mere 'fashion,'—the actually vulgar notoriety hunters—with the high-bred and high-born aristocracy, whose women are as remarkable for great beauty as they are for great talent and great virtue—describing the 'man about town' as the English gentleman, and the woman with the fag-end of an old, or the gaudy freshness of a new title, who exhibits her lolling sleepiness in 'the Ring' at Hyde Park, and scorns the name and duties of an English mother—as a type of those noble and high-bred ladies, who, rallying round the court of their Royal Mistress, devote, as she does, their thoughts, their time, and their talents, to the cultivation of those very domestic duties which we are so often told belong to a *class* and not to our country.

Surely it is high time for some one with genius and knowledge so to picture the female aristocracy of England, as they might be pictured with truth and honesty—as exemplary wives, devoted mothers, and zealous friends ; with hands open as day to melting charity, thoughtful of the dependants who surround their mansions ; foremost to establish schools and support dispensaries ; ever ready with the counsels that produce virtue. It is far too much the vice of our age to give notoriety to corruption in high places, and to forget the large balance of good that is to be found among the great.

Happily the example of the Lady Rachel Russell is by no means rare among the highborn women of England.

We have walked more than once up and down the north side of Bloomsbury Square, where Southampton House once stood, and where Lady Rachel and her husband resided, and felt half inclined to quarrel with this noble lady's grandson, Wriothesley, Duke of Bedford, for changing its name to Bedford House ; and still more grieved that Francis, Duke of Bedford, should have caused it to be taken down ; such buildings should be considered sacred ; they are monuments which no hands should touch to desecrate or to injure.

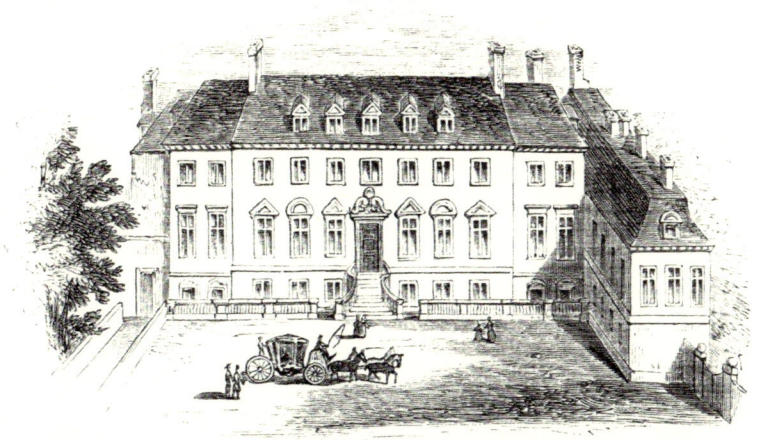

SOUTHAMPTON HOUSE, BLOOMSBURY.

We can now but contemplate the site of the dwelling, where Lord William Russell lived with one in all respects so worthy of him ;[48] yet it is some satisfaction to know that the Duke of York, his malignant foe, and the pusillanimous enemy of all civil and religious liberty, did not achieve his wicked will that this most injured nobleman should have been executed there—at his own threshold. But it is not upon 'houses built with hands' that the memory of Lord William and Lady Rachel Russell depends ; their names have imperishable renown in their country's history—watchwords they are of liberty, of truth, of uprightness, of dignity, of all and everything that can add lustre to human nature!

Lady Rachel Russell, who in every situation of life is so eminent an example of what a woman can be, and ought to be, was the child of an illustrious father—Thomas Wriothesley, *the* Lord Southampton, who, during the first dispute between Charles and his Parliament kept so honestly aloof from court, that he was considered as one of the Peers most attached to the people—yet was so struck by seeing the course of justice perverted on the trial of Lord Strafford (whom, be it remembered, he

---

[48] On Lady Russell's death, in 1723, it descended to her grandson, Wriothesley, Duke of Bedford, and received the name of Bedford house. It was pulled down by Francis, Duke of Bedford, in 1800. Our view is copied from an old print in the illustrated Pennant, now in the British Museum.

had never favoured), and noting how the current set against a monarchical government, that he felt himself impelled by his desire for the peace of England to attach himself to the Royalists. The violence of one party, and the mad obstinacy of the other, rendered his efforts at a reconciliation between the King and the Parliament abortive ; but when all was

RUINS OF TICHFIELD HOUSE.

over, he did not desert even the remains of his royal misguided master. *He* was one of the four faithful servants who asked and obtained permission to pay the last sad duty to his master's remains, divested of all ordinary ceremonial. Lord Southampton had married before these troubles a Huguenot lady, Rachel de Ruvigny, who soon died, leaving two infant daughters, of whom Lady Rachel was the youngest. There is to be found in Lady Rachel's character the exalted and enduring piety which so eminently belonged to the Huguenots of those days ; blended with the tolerant spirit of universal charity which distinguished her father. It seems also to us that though the crude imperfect style of her early letters, proves that her mere education, so called, was not strictly attended to, yet, during her father's retirement at Tichfield, in Hampshire,[49] her

---

[49] Tichfield House, Hampshire, was originally an old monastic foundation given by Henry VIII. to Lord Wriothesley, who built the mansion. At this house Charles I. was concealed after his flight from Hampton Court in 1647. It was then one of the seats of the Earls of Southampton, where his mother lived with her family : here Charles was met by Colonel Hammond, who was fetched by Sir John Berkley and Ashburnham, and from

mind and heart were both strengthened and refreshed. Nothing does this so effectually with women as early intercourse with high-minded and right-thinking men ; the piety and purity, the unflinching integrity of the father, were unconsciously imbibed by the child—healthful and invigorating to her soul as was the fresh country air to her constitution.

She was betrothed, according to the custom of the times, in childhood, to Lord Vaughan, whom she married, but soon became a widow ; and then, richly dowered, young and lovely, she chose wisely, in choosing from among her suitors, a younger brother of the right noble house of Russell. During their lives those two were seldom separated ; and when we first turned over all that is published of her few letters to her husband, we were sensibly struck by their *homeheartedness ;* their appreciation of happiness born of rational as well as passionate affection ; bearing the fruitage of cheerfulness and joy, yet prepared—as people seldom are—alike to bask in the sunshine, or meet the storms, of life. Lady Rachel's tender and almost prophetic exhortations both to her husband and herself, to merit the continuance of God's goodness, as much as we can be said to merit anything, assure us how perfectly she understood the great principle of the *balance of life*, which is exemplified as much in the peasant's cottage as in the prince's palace ; while his entire and absolute confidence in her character was only equalled by his affection and attachment to her society. Thus were they *united* in the holiest and highest sense of the word ; united in principle, in intellect, in views, and in all noble dispositions ; pursuing, according to the different means appropriate to their sex and situation, one common end—sustaining and strengthening each other ; no harshness, no tyranny, no depreciation on the one hand, no affectation, no small arts, no deceit or struggling for unwomanly power, on the other—each finding a candid and a brave judge in the understanding, and a warm and devoted advocate in the heart, of a dear companion.

It has been justly remarked, that there is as great a variety in the powers and compass of human hearts as of human intellects. Some are found hardly equal to the modified selfishness which produces attachment to their most immediate connections ; some have naturally strong feelings concentrated on a few objects, but which diffuse no warmth out of their own narrow focus ; while others again appear endowed with an

---

thence set out for the Isle of Wight. The view was taken in 1781, when great part of the mansion had decayed or been pulled down.

almost boundless capacity for every virtuous affection, which contracts undiminished to all the minute duties of social life, and expands unexhausted to all the great interests of humanity. Such was the heart, the large, full heart of Lady Rachel Russell, in which her husband, her three children, her family, especially her sister (whom she so exquisitely terms 'a *delicious* friend'), her friends, her country, and, above all, her religion, all found space.

THE RYE HOUSE.

How delightful it is to read the manner in which she requites the 'tender kindness' of her husband ; how her letters are filled with words of love and most delicate fondness! Yet with all a woman's care for the small domestic things, of a *right* woman's carefulness, are ever to be seen the brave energy and thoughtfulness of her nature—the indelible marks of an animated interest in her lord's pursuits, a mind open to all great public objects. Dear as was his society to her, there was no pitiful, vexatious whining after it, when his duties called him away, but every effort was used to strengthen him in his strength. Her account of the debate in the House of Commons on the king's message, in April, 1667, is clear and well given—a proof of the improvement of her style ; wherein are to be found passages intimating her minute acquaintance with political affairs, and with Lord Russell's participation in them. Above all others, she was impressed with the most perfect trust in the goodness of God, bringing her faith into daily exercise—her sweet faith ; for surely it sweetened all her cups of bitterness from first to last.

The one thing generally known and universally appreciated is Lady Rachel's conduct on her husband's trial, for a pretended connection with the Rye House Plot.[50] Of the events which preceded and followed this most disgusting mockery of justice, she herself has left no record. Her confidence in her husband's purity of intention and action, of course, could not be shaken ; and her mind, instead of being overwhelmed, expanded into more than human majesty. The dastardly policy of the court would have rejoiced if Lord Russell had fled ; it would have been a relief from the degradation of his death. They could have vilified his character with a show of reason, and this would have led to the more easily disposing of others, whose greater activity, as well as fewer scruples, made them, in fact, more dangerous enemies. It is on record that Lady Rachel was even sent to, to consult with Lord William's friends, whether or not he should 'withdraw himself.' But no : she loved his

---

[50] This conspiracy, which appears to have originated among some disaffected London tradesmen, was to have been carried out at the house of one of them, Rumbold a maltster, who was to lodge the conspirators in his house called "The Rye," near Hoddesden, in Hertfordshire. The Rye House is an old brick building situated in a picturesque spot on the river Lea, and has upon its exterior some ornamental features, which show it to have been once a building of some importance. All that now remains is but a fragment of the original building, and the interior has been so entirely altered to suit it to the exigencies of the parish workhouse, as to have no feature of interest remaining. It was afterwards an inn and fishing-house. The foundations are everywhere insecure, and the house is rapidly crumbling away. It cannot be expected to last many years longer. As a memento of one of the most interesting events in our history, it is well worthy of a visit before its fall. The names of Russell and Sidney forever make it famous, and their judicial murders give a thrilling solemnity to its name.

honour better than his life—loved that which *must* live, better than that which must die. No fears for the safety of her life of lives led this heroic woman to counsel what she did not consider would be consonant with her husband's innocence and honour. History, blushing at the perversion of justice, details what followed. During the fortnight—the bare fortnight which elapsed between Lord Russell's commitment to the Tower and this base mockery of jury-trial—Lady Rachel was unceasingly occupied in procuring information as to what was likely to be urged against him, and in adopting every means of precaution. She found it difficult to believe with her lord, that once within the poisoned coil of his enemies, his doom was fixed. A thrill of anguish ran through the court when, in reply to the Chief Justice's intimation that Lord William might employ any of his servants to assist in writing anything he pleased, he simply said, 'My wife is here to do it.' And she, pure, holy, and strengthened for such a task by the direct power and grace of God, that 'sweet saint' arose from her lord's side, and seated herself with most wonderful calmness and self-possession, to take notes of the proceedings that were to issue in his life or death. No heroism ever surpassed this. How many there present must have recalled her father's services, her husband's unsuspected patriotism, the excellence of their lives, their domestic happiness. It shook the hearts of their bitter persecutors, for even the 'atrocious judge' assumed a milder tone, and said, 'If my lady will give herself the trouble.' How she could have supported herself—how she could have controlled her feelings—during the feeble and most iniquitous mass of compounded nothings that were urged against her noble lord, especially by the pitiful Lord Howard, we know not. She had also to bear up against the news of the suicide in the Tower, of Lord Essex—her relation and friend. She heard this in the midst of the trial, tolling through the court like a death-knell, yet did she give no voice to the torture of her heart, nor distract her husband's attention by a single murmur. Day and night did she labour, after his condemnation, for a mitigation of his sentence ; but the unforgiving James gaped for blood ; the facile Charles laughed at mercy ; the venial Duchess of Portsmouth feared to risk her power over the king, even for the mighty bribe which Lord William's father, Lord Bedford offered her ; every plan was tried, save a desertion from those high principles which formed Lord William's sole crime in the eyes of his relentless enemy, the Duke of York. Now mark how she strengthened her husband's noble nature. While offering to accompany him into exile, never did she propose that he should purchase his life by a base compliance, or the abjuration of those glorious truths for which he endured persecution. How deeply he felt this, is proved by his mention of her in his last interviews with Burnet who tells us that Lord Russell expressed, even in his last hours, 'great joy' in her magnanimity. 'At eleven o'clock on Friday night' he says, 'they parted ; he kissed her four or five times, and *she kept her sorrow so within herself, that she gave him no disturbance at their parting.*' There was,' he said, 'a signal providence of God in giving him such a wife, where there was birth, fortune, great understanding, great religion, and a great kindness to him. *But her carriage in this extremity went beyond all ;* and it was a great comfort to him that he left his children in such hands.' And truly can we believe it. Well might he trust HER upon whom in this world he should look no more ; safely might be confide to *her* those dear pledges of unsurpassed love, who to the last moment, by a continuation of woman's sacrifice—a sacrifice of self-indulgence—a suppression of every selfish feeling—which nothing but the deepest tenderness could dictate to the most exalted mind— parted from his last embrace—looked her last look upon the honoured, the beloved, of her true heart, without permitting a single sob of anguish to disturb his serene composure. Away she went to the home which had known him for fourteen years, but should know him no more. Away— away—to count the fleeting minutes that were to elapse before his children were fatherless and his wife a widow.

Her beloved sister, that 'delicious friend,' was dead ; her infant children were incapable of thought or consolation—her half-sister, Lady Northumberland, was abroad—her cousin, Lady Shaftsbury, could only offer 'pity and prayers'—her father-in law?—they could but gaze upon each other. In those cruel moments she was left 'alone with God ;' this holy companionship enabled her to support her great agony, and feel, what many years after she avowed, that there was something so glorious in the object of her greatest sorrow, that in some degree prevented her from being overwhelmed.

She did not even for a moment, when all was over, sit down with sorrow, but roused by a knowledge of her duties to the dead, as well as the living, defended the memory of her husband, when his unsatiated enemies endeavoured to deny the authenticity of the paper he had delivered to the sheriffs on the scaffold—this, and the summoning of Tillotson and Burnet before the king and the Duke of York, who were taxed as the advisers of the declaration, drew forth Lady Rachel's memorable letter to Charles—a brave letter it was, the fearless expression of duty and innocence resolved to repel falsehood and assert truth. We may wonder how the Duke of York felt when it was read ; as for the vacillating Charles, he gave immediate permission that the mourning escutcheon for the murder he had been pleased to sanction should be placed over Lord Russell's house, and sent a kind word to Lady Russell, intimating that he did not mean to profit by the forfeiture of Lord William's personal property—poor fluttering shred of royal frippery! Is not *this* a great glory to woman? Is not *this* her genuine power, the power of superior virtue? Is not *this* her great, her mighty strength, the strength born of a purified nature? What woman's influence could have holier exercise? Just consider the power she (long since dust and ashes) holds at this moment over every well-regulated female mind. Her name is as a talisman—the watchword of truth, and virtue, and vigilance—of domestic love, and lofty heroism. In *her* the *moral power* is most perfectly exemplified. She was not beautiful, nor 'witty' (for *that* her husband blessed God), nor learned. Now-a-days she would hardly have been called *educated*. And yet surely, we behold a PERFECT WOMAN. Would any wish more love, more gentleness, more truth, more trust, more virtue, more heroism, more religion—and all without assumption or pretence. Does not this show that, however ornamented may be the structure, there can be no true glory for woman unless there be a righteous foundation? One of her friends laments her 'mighty grief ;' how it has wasted her body, though she struggle with it 'ever so hardly.' Bishop Burnet congratulates her on having resolved to employ so much of her time in the education of her children, *that they should need no other governess.* It irks us to hear the excuses mothers make to rid themselves of their maternal duties, leaving their children to hired teachers and low-bred menials, gadding abroad after new friends, new pleasures, and new whims—their children will not bless them in their graves. How different was this from Lady Rachel, training her two daughters, from whom she was never separated ; and strengthening her own mind, that she might strengthen that of her son. We remember one passage where she says—'I am very solicitous, I confess, to do my duty in such a manner to the children of one I owe as much as can be due to man, that if my son lives he may not justly say hereafter, that if he had a mother less ignorant or less negligent he had not then been to seek for what perhaps, he may then have a mind to have.

Her son's education was a matter of deep interest to her ; and the skill with which she parried Lord Bedford (his grandfather's) cares, lest she should put him to 'learn in earnest' at too early an age, is, as every thing else, a proof of how her judgment regulated her affections. Her eldest daughter's marriage with Lord Cavendish drew her at last from her retirement and her interest in all the world's doing, was kept painfully alive by the trial of the seven Bishops, and the stirring events of the times. Time passed on, she received the assurance of profound respect from the Prince and Princess of Orange, and at last when the Revolution settled into a new Monarchy, its first act was the reversal of Lord Russell's attainder ; his execution being termed a 'murder' by a vote of the House of Commons! She lived to see it! A less firm and comprehensive mind than her's might have been elated at the extraordinary respect paid to her, not only by the court, but by the intellect of the country. Dr. Fitzwilliam referred to her his conscientious resignation of preferment under the new government. Tillotson applied for her sanction to his acceptance of the dignity offered him by King William ; and even the stout sturdy, man-woman, Sarah, Duchess of Marlborough, would not dare an important step without consulting with 'the Lady Russell, of Southampton House.' Lady Rachel's energy and influence were constantly exercised for the good of others. She never suffered her repeated trials to interfere with her friendly duties, nor did her feelings become blunted either by age or sorrow. Immediately after the death of her halfsister, Lady Montagu, and her nephew, Lord Gainsborough, she makes this touching observation in one of her letters :—

'Every new stroke to a wearied and battered carcass makes me struggle the harder ; and though I lost with my best friend *all the delights of living,* yet I find *I did not lose a quick sense of new grief.'*

The honours we are justly proud of, the dress and ornaments of virtue, were showered upon the two noble houses she best loved ; Devonshire and Bedford were elevated to dukedoms, and most worthy mention was made of Lord William Russell in the royal letters patent. Lady Rachel's dread of blindness, with which she had struggled for years, had been removed ; 'she had seen the government which had oppressed, proscribed ; the power which she had found implacable, fallen in the dust ; the religion, whose political predominance she dreaded, in circumstances to require that toleration it had been unwilling to allow ; the man whose vindictive spirit had inflicted the greatest misfortune of her life, himself an exile, after having, with characteristic meanness, implored the assistance of him whom he had persecuted—the assistance of the father of the man he had murdered. She had seen the triumph of those principles for which her beloved Lord had suffered, the blessed effects produced by a steady adherence to them, and his name for ever coupled with the honour and freedom of his country.' Tried both by adversity and prosperity she remained unchanged. And so, she became old in years ; yet her heart was green within her, and she slumbered not, but actively and enduringly busied herself about her orphan grandchildren, enjoying in the depths of her chastened spirit the respect and honour due to the experience and the wisdom of length of days. No trace of the prejudices, peculiarities, or selfishness of age lingered around her. She scrutinised none so severely as herself ; and her personal inquisitions were directed not to the forms, but to the feeling, of Christian piety—to the Christianity which, to quote her own 'delicious' words, could not be distinguished by 'outward fashions, or by the professing a body of notions differing from others in the world, but by the renewing of our minds, by peaceableness, charity, and heavenly love.'

A halo of glory encircles her name : every spot where she resided is to us consecrated. We have filled a large space with poor words concerning one, of whom it seems to us we have said nothing. Lady Rachel Russell died on October the 5th, 1723, at Southampton House, her age being 86 years ; and she was buried at Chenies, in Buckinghamshire,[51] with her most dear lord.

---

[51] Iselhampstead, or Iselhampstead-Cheneys is on the borders of the county. 'It is now,' says Lysons, generally called Chenys, its original name is almost lost, having been exchanged for that, which was first given to distinguish it from the neighbouring village of Iselhampstead-Latimers, this place having been for many years the manor and seat of the ancient family of Cheyne.' It was, originally, a royal palace, and was given by Edward III. to Thomas Cheyne, the first of the family who settled in this county, and who was his shield bearer. It ultimately descended, by marriage, into the family of the Russells in 1560. Lord Russell upon coming into possession of the estate, rebuilt the greater part of the manor house, and made it his principal seat. 'The old house of Cheynes is so translated,' says Leland, 'by my Lord Russell, that hath his house in right of his wife, that little or nothing of it remayneth untranslated, and a great deal of the house is newly set up, and made of bricks and timber.' Queen Elizabeth was entertained here by Francis, Earl of Bedford, in 1570. When the Bedfords fixed their principal residence at Woburn they deserted this house, which was converted into a farmhouse.

In the parish church are some memorials of the Cheynes, and in the adjoining chapel, built by the heiress of the Sapcotes, by whom the estate was conveyed to the Bedford family,—Anne, Countess of Bedford,—is the monument for herself and her husband, John, first Earl of Bedford. There are also monuments of Francis, Earl of Bedford, who died in 1585, and his Countess ; Anne, Countess of Warwick, their daughter, and Lady Francis Bourchier, their grand-daughter ; Francis, Earl of Bedford, who died 1641, and of his Countess ; that of the first Duke of Bedford, and a medallion of William, Lord Russell,

Chenies, the once happy home and the last resting-place of Lady Rachael Russell and her martyred Lord, is situated in a secluded corner of Buckinghamshire ; the little village is environed by trees, and the quiet dells and waving corn-fields give a favourable picture of the fertile spots of our country. The old mansion is nearly deserted ; a greater part is used as a stable, and pigeons find a home in the upper stories. It is now inhabited by farmers, and used as the farmhouse. Yet externally it retains the features of its original beauties. To some of the gables are still appended the carved corbels, which speak of the elaboration and beauty of the old house in its palmy days. The ivy-covered turrets and gables, and the lofty firs, complete a picture of much interest—even apart from the glorious history with which it is associated.

CHENIES.

The church is immediately beside the house. It is a work of the sixteenth century, and the principal part is the large Mausoleum and carved Chapel, built by the first Countess for the Bedford family. Within the church is much to interest ; the roof is of open timber-work, and very ornamental ; there are a beautifully carved pulpit, and an early circular Norman font. In front of the communion-table are some interesting brasses of the Cheyne family, the original possessors of the estate.

who was buried here August 2nd, 1683, as well as some modern monuments to others of the family.

In the chapel adjoining are many magnificent tombs to the members of the Russell family. The principal one is shown in our engraving, and maybe considered as an historical memento of the principal members of the family. In the centre are full length figures of the first Duke and Duchess, leaning upon a column, supporting the ducal coronet, in attitudes of reflective sorrow. Above them is a medallion of Lord William Russell, the victim of Charles II.; at the sides are similar medallions of six other members, male and female, of the family, whose names are inscribed around each head ; above, cherubims are seen supporting the arms and crest of the house. This tomb is sumptuously executed in coloured marbles. Immediately in front is the grated entrance to the burial vault, where nearly sixty of the family lie. The Lady Rachel Russell has—strange and sad to say—no memento in this chapel ; her monument is the History of her country.

CHENIES CHURCH.

And behold what lustre the exercise of 'DUTIES' bestows upon a WOMAN! The celebrity of her character has been purchased by the *'sacrifice of no feminine virtue,* and *her principles, conduct, and sentiments, equally well adapted to every condition of her sex, will in all be found the surest guides to peace, honour, and happiness.'*

THE BEDFORD MAUSOLEUM.

The Monument of Wren.

ARE old London! It would be difficult for us to describe the affection we entertain for this noble city—venerable for its antiquity, and revered for its associations with our greatest men—although it combines so much that occasions us distress of mind with so much that is dear and honoured to our every feeling of existence. We should never have loved it so well if we had not become acquainted with the histories of some of its public buildings, its houses, its holy temples, one by one, almost stone by stone ; and yet how little we know of what we might know, and of what we hope yet to learn. We marvel more and more how we could ever have passed a peculiar-looking house without inquiring 'Who lived there?' Certainly, we move through life very listlessly ; we go along its highways and into its by-lanes without being stirred by the immortality around us ; we close our eyes against the evidences of change which are the accompaniments of life ; and we plod on, of the earth—earthy, with little more than a fluttering effort to raise our minds by the contemplation of the acts of those glorious spirits who elevated England to the rank she holds among nations.

We had been wandering through the human labyrinths of London—cogitating, rather than observing—musing, instead of rousing ourselves to enter into the feelings and occupations of those with whom we live, when suddenly we stood opposite the gate of the Church of St. Bride, Fleet Street. We never can pass any one of Sir Christopher Wren's churches without endeavouring to obtain a sight of the beautiful spire by which he loved to decorate his sacred buildings ; accordingly, we stepped down the paved court, and strained back the head to gratify desire. As we turned the corner to go on, St. Paul's, looming through the atmosphere of mingled smoke and fog, again recalled to mind the character of its mighty architect—that polished, high-minded, true-hearted, modest man, who loved his art with a depth and purity unknown in our times, and with the steady enthusiasm of his noble nature, not for the gold it brought, but because of its own high merits, and the power it gave him to elevate his country in the eyes of the whole world.

Born in 1632, Christopher Wren was nurtured in the highest principles of the Reformed Church ; his father, at whose rectory he drew breath, at East Knoyle, in Wiltshire, was also Dean of Windsor ; and his uncle, successively Bishop of Hereford, Norwich, and Ely, is celebrated in the Ecclesiastical history of England as having devoted himself to the royal cause, and remaining so firmly attached to the fortunes of the deposed King as to endure an imprisonment of nearly twenty years without being brought to trial. During a portion of this dismal time for all who held the true royalist faith, Mr. Christopher Wren, even then distinguished as a youth of equal modesty and talent, was a frequent visitor at Mrs. Claypole's, who was sure to distinguish and promote excellence. Here he occasionally met the stern Protector, who called to him one day, in his usually abrupt and determined manner ; to go immediately and 'tell his uncle that he might come out of the Tower if he liked.' The youth bowed his thanks. Knowing the equally determined nature of his uncle's spirit he proceeded with an anxious heart to the Tower. The shadows of the massive building lay heavily upon the waters, and, as the heavier gates groaned beneath the creaking chains and rusty bolts, he hoped that one he loved so well would come forth to the light and liberty so very, very dear to a young aspiring mind. So strongly did the value of this inestimable blessing seem to him, as he entered the dark and narrow room appropriated to his relative, that he could hardly forbear throwing himself upon his neck, and wishing him joy of the liberty he at first doubted whether he would or would not accept. The stern contempt which the prelate at once expressed towards the Protector's message— the air of offended dignity with which he regarded his nephew for being its bearer—the exalted nature that breathed in every word he uttered, proving his sincerity, and his determination to accept no favour from those he despised—were never forgotten by the future architect ; and unable to repress or direct the feelings he had roused, he listened with silent respect to his high-souled relative. 'Go back!' he exclaimed, 'to the man who holds the power of England within his blood-stained palm, and tell him that I will none of *his* permission to depart, but will tarry the LORD's leisure, and owe my deliverance to HIM alone!'

This noble disregard of things temporal, when contrasted with things eternal, was strongly characteristic of both the uncle and the nephew. Many of our paltry pilers of brick and mortar—builders of mere paper houses—creatures with not half as much architectural knowledge as the bee or the beaver—would think themselves insulted if required to superintend a square or a street in the suburbs of London at the remunerating rate that was paid the mighty architect of Saint Paul's. But long before he was distinguished as an architect, or thought of architecture, perhaps, but as a branch of the sciences to which his young mind rendered such ready homage, every man of knowledge in England considered the youth a prodigy. Like his remarkable contemporary, Pascal, his genius displayed itself at a very early age. At thirteen he dedicated the invention of an astronomical instrument to his father in a Latin ode ; and, though labouring under extreme delicacy of health, he was able to enter Wadham College, Oxford, at the age of fourteen ; here he secured the friendship of Bishop Wilkins, who introduced him to Prince Charles, the Elector Palatine, as a prodigy ; and Oughtred, in his preface to his 'Clavis Mathematica,' mentions his extraordinary promise as a youth of sixteen.

About this time, Doctor Willis, an eminent mathematician, collected together a knot of scientific men, chiefly from Gresham College, who gave the idea after the lapse of a few years of the formation of the Royal Society ; and Doctor Willis was another of his friends. Wren devoted much attention to the microscope, which caused both him and his cousin to be sneered at by the author of the 'Oceana,' as those 'who had an excellent faculty for magnifying an atom, and diminishing a commonwealth.' He then turned his attention to some astronomical theories, and many claim for him the invention of the barometer, though there exists little doubt that the discovery belonged to Torricelli. The exquisite Evelyn, so associated with all that is honourable to England, so dear to all who love the registers of old times, makes frequent mention of Wren, designating him as 'that rare and early prodigy of science,' 'that miracle of youth,' 'that prodigious young scholar.' Well, indeed, did he deserve this praise. At fifteen, Sir Charles Scarborough, an eminent physician of his time, employed him as a demonstrating assistant ; and it was the future architect of St. Paul's who first injected several liquids into the veins of living animals. But, turn where we will to the records of this great man's life, we find all illumined by his fame. Having abandoned his classic retirement he filled the chair of astronomy at Gresham College,[52] and the next year solved Pascal's celebrated

---

[52] Gresham College, as its name implies, is a foundation which owes its origin to the builder of the Royal Exchange ; and in his will he bequeathed all his interest in that build-

problem, that was issued in all magnificence as a challenge to the learned of England, and then posed the mathematicians of France by one that was never answered. So he continued his course, mingling the mild lustre of the morning and evening star with the splendour of the comet ; the perfection of human talent and human virtue ; alienating himself from the party quarrels of the day, yet feeding the sacred flame of loyalty within his heart.

COURT YARD OF GRESHAM COLLEGE.

After a period of much turmoil, during the most interesting epoch of England's history, Charles II. was received back into the bosoms of his loving subjects, and Wren was chosen to fill the highest chair (the Savilian) at Oxford. Then the Royal Society, aided by the learning of

---

ing, and also his dwelling-house, to the Corporation of London and the Mercers' Company, on condition that they provided seven professors to lecture publicly and gratuitously on the seven liberal sciences. At the death of his wife the professors entered on their duties, and had apartments assigned them in Sir Thomas's house, which was situated in Bishopsgate Street (upon the site of the present Excise Office), and which was in consequence now termed Gresham College. It numbered many eminent men among its professors, and flourished until the commencement of the civil wars, when it was occupied as a military garrison, and all the professors, save one, compelled to leave it. The restoration revived it, and the foundation connected itself with the newly-formed Royal Society. In the early part of the eighteenth century, dissensions arose between the professors and trustees, and the building was deserted and allowed to go to decay, until an act was obtained for its sale and the ground on which it stood. There is a curious bird's-eye view of the building in 1740, and that portion of it which shows the inner quadrangle has been delineated above.

England, was established firmly, Doctor Wren being one of its most efficient members, and yet we find him toying with all sciences — observing Saturn — mapping the Pleiades — calculating eclipses — writing on the longitude — most probably inventing mezzotinto engraving, and permitting the credit thereof (for which he never cared, except for truth's sake) to rest with his friend Prince Rupert. He also sacrificed, occasionally, to the Muses, but this most likely was in his love-making hours : *that* the wisest men must go through despite all other sciences.

But this human weakness was no stain upon his stainless career—as completely *sans reproche* as that of Bayard himself. At length, he went to Paris to study architecture and the mechanical inventions, and there saw the Louvre in progress.

OLD ST. PAUL'S CATHEDRAL.

Soon after the Restoration, our Charles, whose foreign sojourn had given him some taste in architecture, took it into his head to contemplate repairing St. Paul's, which was absolutely necessary from the dilapidations it had suffered during the Commonwealth, when Cromwell converted the Choir into a horse barracks. Wren was named in the royal commission to superintend the repairs, but it was decreed by a greater power that no one desecrated stone should remain above another. The mighty fire came in its terror upon the city, sweeping it away like chaff before the wind, and rendering old St. Paul's[53] a tottering ruin ; and there, amid the destruction, upon the burning cinders, fear less, amid the

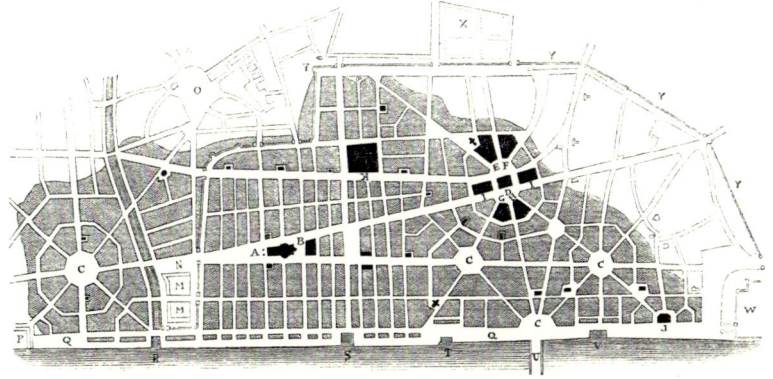

WREN'S PLAN FOR RE-BUILDING LONDON.

---

[53] Old St. Paul's was the idol of the Londoners. They seem to have looked upon it as the very perfection of its species, and were redolent of its praises. One of its great holds in popular affection consisted in the belief of its legendary history. It was supposed to stand on the site the Roman temple to Diana, and believed to be the spot where Christianity first found a home amongst us. All the older antiquaries fall in with this popular belief ; and the legends they tell may be comprehended by a reference to the pages of Camden. Its great antiquity and its constant connection with the historic and ecclesiastical history of our country, gave it however a strong interest. Its interior was enriched with the tombs of the great and the learned, some few relics of which are still preserved in the crypts of the present building. The long-drawn aisles were in the sixteenth century used as the meeting-place and lounge of the citizens. So began desecration, and the cathedral became a place for idlers and a noisy rendezvous not always respectable. In a short time dilapidation and decay began to appear, and during the reign of James I., strong measures were necessary to be adopted to preserve the building at all. Our cut shows its palmy state when the steeple was entire. It was destroyed by fire in 1561, some say by lightning, others by the neglect of plumbers, who left their fires burning in their absence. It was new roofed after this ; but was neglected until the reign of Charles I., who did that which had been urged during his father's reign unfruitfully, and set the example of restoration by building at his own expense a noble portico. Others followed the royal example and subscribed towards the work nobly, and in 1643 the renovation was completed at a cost of about one hundred thousand pounds. The Civil War came, and with it a desecration worse than any previous one to which the noble building had been subjected. Horses were stabled within its walls, and it received so much injury, that on the restoration of Charles, that of the cathedral became again necessary. It was slowly proceeded with when the Great Fire left it a mere mass of ruin's, to be succeeded by Wren's grander and more uniform conception.

embers that crumbled about him— calm, amid the desolation that surrounded him on every side-heedless of the smoke and *debris* of what
should be seen no more, was the fearless architect, concentrating a mind
of inconceivable strength, knowledge, solidity, purity, vastness, and
vigour, upon one point—the restoration of London! Up to this period he
had been one of whom no evil was ever whispered, but at once the un-
dercurrent of self-interest, that muddy, babbling, polluted stream, was
let loose upon him ; yet he stood between the glory of London and the
mean and paltry economy that would have neglected the clearance made
by the fire, and patched and cramped St. Paul's, emancipated from its
disjointed thraldom by what to individuals was a great calamity. If the
plans of this astonishing projector had been worked out altogether, as he
intended, we should have had a city as remarkable for the dignity of
uniformity as for extent.[54] He proposed a street ninety feet wide to pro-

---

[54] Wren's mode of operation is detailed by his son in his 'Parentalia.' He says, that
after his appointment as surveyor-general and principal architect for rebuilding the city, he
immediately 'took an exact survey of the whole area and confines of the burning, having
traced over with great trouble and hazard the great plain of the ashes and ruins ; and designed a plan or model of a new city, in which the deformity and inconveniences of the old
town were remedied, by the enlarging the streets and lanes, and carrying them as near
parallel to one another as might be ; avoiding if compatible with greater conveniences, all
acute angles ; by seating all the parochial churches conspicuous and insular ; by forming
the most public places into large piazzas, the centre of six or eight ways ; by uniting the
halls of the twelve chief companies into one regular square annexed to Guildhall, by making a quay on the whole bank of the river from Blackfriars to the Tower.' In his clear
sighted plans and useful improvements he designed 'the streets to be of three magnitudes ;
the three principal leading straight through the City and one or two cross streets to be at
least ninety feet wide ; others sixty feet ; and lanes about thirty feet, excluding all narrow
dark alleys without thoroughfares or courts.' An examination of his plan engraved opposite, will make these improvements apparent, and show how much London has lost by not
adopting Wren's views ; they were opposed by the 'vested interests of the citizens, which
then, as now, deprecated all changes even for evident advantages. They had insurmount-
able prejudices in favour of rebuilding in old localities and in old styles, and hence he lost
the opportunity of his wish to render London 'the most magnificent as well as commodious
city for health and trade of any upon earth. A glance at his plan will show how well he
had laid out main streets, and studied the proper position of public buildings, with an eye
as well to utility as to architectural effect. A shows the position of St. Paul's, which would
have been the first grand object that claimed attention when the western side of the city
was entered ; at B is Doctors' Commons, in close and proper proximity. The letters C
refer to the piazzas with which Wren intended to ornament London, where the principal
streets met. At D we have the principal buildings sacred to trade and commerce ; E is the
Post Office ; F, the Excise Office ; G, Insurance Office ; H, the Mint ; while at I are the
Goldsmiths shops. K shows the position of Guildhall ; L that of the Custom House. At M
are the public markets ; N, the Strand entrance to the City ; O, is Smithfield ; P, the Temple ; Q, a Quay along the entire bank of the Thames ; R, is the *debouchement* of the Fleet

ceed from St. Dunstan's Church to Tower Hill, there to terminate in a piazza ; this, besides its magnificence, would have ensured a world of air and health to the citizens ; he intended this to open into a circular piazza on its way, the centre of eight streets, leaving Ludgate prison on the left side, where, instead of the gate, he designed a triumphal arch to the renovator of London, Charles II. The street was then to divide into two other streets as large, and before they, spreading at acute angles, could have been clear, one of the other ; he intended them to form a triangular piazza, the basis of which would be filled by the Cathedral Church of St. Paul's. How glorious this picture! The magnificent structure would not have been cribbed up by those close-fitting gaudy shops ; and the proposed piazza would have given a majesty to the immediate neighbourhood in keeping with the cathedral ; though piazzas can never be generally adopted in England with advantage. If they shelter from rain they darken the houses ; and an Englishman connects some Italian idea with them ; something of 'lurking' and hiding, and 'secret stabbing ;' and indeed the more broad and wide and expanded streets are the better : still *there* they would have formed a noble base to the mighty pyramid. It was a fine idea of his also to make his highway to the Tower ; adorned with parochial churches ; setting before the people continually their Christian temples in the best situations, thus reminding them of their highest duties.

We can, without difficulty, imagine the magnificent appearance of our river, if he had been permitted to carry his quay along the whole bank of the Thames, from Blackfriars to the Tower, a canal being cut at Bridewell, with sluices at Holborn Bridge and at the mouth, and stores for coal at either side. What metropolitan magnificence would have arisen, had he erected twelve halls for the twelve chief companies, united into a regular square, annexed to Guildhall? He desired to banish trades that use great fires and create noisome smells, and all burying-grounds, out of the city. Our cemeteries are but the working out of one of his projects! Yet, necessary and useful as they are, we should be sorry to be buried in one of those dead high-ways ; we would rather

---

river at Bridewell ; S, Queen hithe ; T, Dowgate ; U, London Bridge ; and V, Billingsgate. W, shows the position of the Tower ; X, that of Moorfields ; and Y, the circuit of the City Walls. The small black blocks, which are isolated represent churches which he had intended to place in prominent positions in the main thoroughfares, but always free of the houses. It is only necessary further to remark, that that portion of our plan which is covered by lines of tint, represents that part of London, which was destroyed by the great fire.

repose quietly in a sheltered nook of an old churchyard, where the shadow of the trees we saw planted should fall upon our green-grass grave, while the voices of those we have loved, and who have loved us, echo above it.

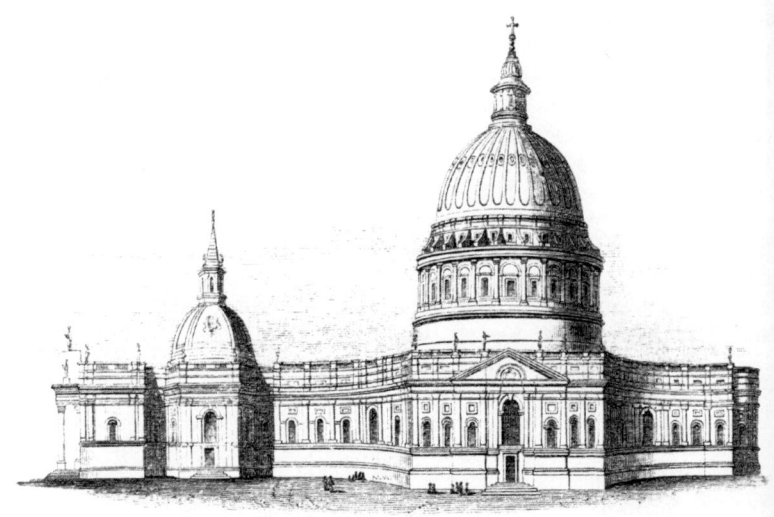

WREN'S ORIGINAL DESIGN FOR ST. PAUL'S.

It is evident to all who contemplate the plan of Sir Christopher Wren's renovation that St. Paul's was the sun of his system ; he would have ranged his planets and their satellites around it. His mind was as harmonious as the movements of the heavenly bodies ; and the more we thought upon, the more we felt the sublimity of his conceptions.[55] It is with a feeling of extreme diffidence that we object to his fondness for arcades, which except as a sort of amphitheatre for St. Paul's' church-yard, are, for the reasons we have mentioned, unsuited to our climate. But we cannot feel the objection which some have stated to his plan, on the ground of sameness and uniformity. Darmstadt, Carlsruhe, and Manheim, those uniform Continental cities, are dull enough, not from

---

[55] The dome of St. Paul's rises above his grave a noble monument ; but there ought to be another. There has been published a tribute to his memory —a pictured representation of the workings of his mind, beautifully grouped, by Mr. Cockerell. This fine representation of British architecture sets forth no less than sixty-two of Sir. Christopher's buildings the principal number being churches.

their uniformity, but from the absence of that moving world which is the variety of London.

Sir Richard Steele justly observed with reference both to Wren and the great fire, that 'That which produced so much individual misery afforded the greatest occasion that ever builder had to render his name immortal and his person venerable.' But though nothing could exceed the fortitude displayed by those who had seen their city swept, first by the plague, and then by fire ; and though 'the people' would have embraced his plans, yet the selfishness of some individuals, the conflicting interests of others, the intrigues of certain parties in both court and state, dispersed the architect's noble efforts as regarded the city ; and when he was, after innumerable vexatious and provocations from the prejudiced and the ignorant, really permitted to set about his great work of St. Paul's, he did so with superhuman patience and perseverance.

Nurtured in the purest Protestantism, his first plan of the cathedral did not include the length of the aisle necessary for the processions and pageantry of the Roman Catholic worship, but unnecessary in our Reformed cathedral service.[56] The Duke of York, afterwards the tyrannical and bigoted James, insisted on the lengthened aisles and the addition of side oratories, thus preparing the cathedral for a religion, the subsequent attempt to re-establish which cost him his crown. This infringement on Wren's plans and principles caused him to shed bitter tears ; but his Royal Highness, who would have hardly ventured to interfere with the design of a sculptor, altered the plan of the architect ; and Wren began his work of immortality—laying the first stone of London's landmark on the 21st of June, 1675. And in the year 1710 the good old man, having attained the seventy-eighth year of his ago, having spent thirty-five years

---

[56] The unfortunate circumstance of the Duke of York's tendency to the Roman Catholic faith deprived England of possessing the only Protestant cathedral in the world. Wren's notions of church building for the reformed faith were well expressed in his report to the King, where he declares that our own ritual and its form should guide the architect solely in his designs for the buildings sacredly devoted to such service. 'The Romanists,' he says, 'indeed, may build larger churches ; it is enough if they hear the murmur of the mass, and see the elevation of the host ; but ours are to be fitted for auditories.' Impressed with this view, he omitted the long aisles and side chapels necessary to the Romish ritual and its processions, and made the body of the building a compact centre as a grand substructure to the dome, and forming an enormous receptacle for a large auditory. But the Duke, who had, no doubt, long cherished the idea of restoring Popery, insisted on the long aisles and side chapels being inserted. Wren was therefore obliged to alter his design entirely to one less original and beautiful, to gratify the wish of one who sat upon our throne but two short years and was banished for ever.

of his life in the actual and daily labour of this erection, having seen the
terminations of three reigns, having experienced a revolution which
drove the Stuarts from the throne, and witnessed the going out of the
Orange dynasty and the coming in of the Hanoverian, saw his son lay
the highest stone of the lantern on the cupola. The toils, and taunts, and
vexatious he had endured were forgotten at this triumphant moment.
The shouts of a grateful people rent the air ; he was surrounded still by
long-tried friends, and his character was as stainless as when he took his
first lesson in the dignity of a fixed purpose from his uncle within the
Tower walls.

And what now, gentle friends, suppose you was the sum allotted to
Sir Christopher Wren for building *your* St. Paul's—*our* St. Paul's?—
what to remunerate him for the learning, the labour, the untiring
attention he brought to his work of love? *Two hundred pounds a year!*
And the commissioners had the pettiness to stop a portion of this until
the work was completed ; nor could he obtain his money without an
application to Parliament.   Well might that splendid vixen Sarah,
Duchess of Marlborough, remonstrate with her architect, when, as she
said herself, 'It is well known that Sir Christopher Wren was content to
be dragged up in a basket three or four times a-week to the top of St.
Paul's, and at a great hazard, for 200*l.* a year.'   Poor Sarah! she took
little into consideration his mind or talent, but thought mightily of his
swinging in a basket for such a paltry sum! His payment, as architect of
the City churches, was hardly better ; being no more than 100*l.* a year ;
though the parish of St. Stephen, Walbrook, voted his lady a present of
twenty pounds! on the completion of that admirable building.

He was not suffered to continue uninterruptedly at his St. Paul's.
Papers of the Privy Council speak of his being hurried to Knightsbridge
to decide if the site of a projected brew-house was far enough from
town ; then to report concerning buildings to be made in the rear of St.
Giles's Church.   Nobody but the hard-worked and ill-paid Sir Christopher could be found to make arrangements for the accommodation of the
Lord Mayor and Aldermen and their officers, and also the livery of the
twelve companies, in Bow Church!   He was appointed jointly with
Evelyn to conduct the sale of Chelsea College to Government ; upon him
devolved the task of detecting and abating all nuisances, irregular buildings, defects in drainage that might prove prejudicial to public health or
the beauty of the Court end of the town.   These and all other tasks con-

cerning the laying out of roads imposed upon him too much personal exertion and extensive and intricate calculations.

He laboured diligently ; the Monument, Temple Bar ; Chelsea Hospital, many of the halls of the great companies, seventeen churches of the largest parishes in London, and thirty-four out of the remaining parishes on a large scale, were rebuilt *under the direction and from the designs of Wren, during the time that he was engaged upon St. Paul's.* And when Queen Anne passed an act of Parliament for the erection of fifty additional churches in London and Westminster ; the omnipotent Wren was appointed one of the commissioners.

What other man has left such records of a life behind him? Michael Angelo, so gloriously associated with St. Peter's, had as strong a struggle against prejudice and meanness as our 'Hero Architect,' and their characters were cast in the same mould, alike high-souled—alike poor in this world's riches—loving Art for its own sake—sacrificing their time, their knowledge, and themselves for their city's glory ; but Angelo's hot southern nature lacked the fine tempering of Wren's, for he earnestly, at the expiration of seventeen years, implored Cardinal Carpi 'to liberate him from his vexatious employment.' Wren completed his task in thirty-five years, but St. Peter's occupied a space of 145 years, during the pontificate of nineteen Popes.

BOYER HOUSE.

His name has filled our imagination with images of his works. They rise before us, distracting our mind with their magnitude and number. Recollections of his life, too, crowd upon us, and we see him in a hundred situations of his varied career. With an effort we banish these visions, for we have a Pilgrimage to make.

At Camberwell there is a quaint old house called Boyer House or Manor House ; and Evelyn records a visit to Sir Edmund Boyer at his 'melancholic house at Camerwell. He has,' he says, 'a pretty grove of oakes, and hedges of yew in his garden, and a tall row of elms before the door.' This house is still standing in the London Road ; and in that house, not 'melancholie' to our thinking, Sir Christopher Wren resided during a great portion of the time occupied in building St. Paul's. Most likely Wren rented the house from Sir Edmund. And, as Evelyn is believed to have introduced cedars into England, who knows but Sir Christopher obtained the very tree which we regret to see looking so really 'melancholie,' from the sweet author of the Sylva?' The house, as you may see, has a very different appearance from any other in this particular neighbourhood ; and the wide-spreading branches of the cedar ; now the wreck of what it was, invite attention. Tradition calls it 'Queen Elizabeth's tree ;' but there is a certainty that her Majesty never saw it. The house has a sufficient claim to our attention without this distinction—Evelyn entered the gateway, Sir Christopher Wren resided within those walls!

There are no people in the world more misunderstood than the English. Our 'shyness' is termed 'coldness ;' our 'timidity and reserve heartlessness ;' no one ever knocked at the proper door of an English heart without having it opened. Here were we personal strangers to the lady who resides in this venerable mansion ; and yet a mere expression of a desire to see Wren's house, sufficed not only to secure us admission, but such kind attention as we can never forget. The steps ascended, the hall is entered by a glass door ; and you immediately find yourself where taste and judgment have presided, and where care is still taken of the work of their hands. From the gloomy aspect without you are astonished at the cheerfulness within, for the hall is spacious and lightsome ; and, though it has been deprived of many of its ancient honours, still the plainness of its panelling is in keeping with the character of the building, and though it has lost much—for its present occupant informed us that when she took it the owner of the mansion removed the 'carved imageries of fruit and flowers,' and various other beauties, that decorated an exquisitely perfumed room, still called the 'cedar parlour'—though much has unhappily been removed from this house of noble memories, nothing has been introduced in violation of the pure taste that presided over its adornment. The 'cedar parlour' is of a mellow and yet delicate colour ; panelled with that expensive wood from the floor to the lofty ceiling. The adjoining room is finely proportioned ; but the room on the opposite side of the building is the one that particularly attracted the attention of our artist friend. The chimney-piece still boasts some undisturbed carving, and there is a door remarkable for its simplicity.

This probably was the architect's study ; his own proper room. We would give much to know whose bust originally occupied the position which its present possessor has assigned to Sir Walter Scott. Per-

DOOR AT BOYER HOUSE.

haps Inigo Jones or Michael Angelo. And the window, which now only looks forth towards a chapel, then opened upon a trim parterre, guarded from all harsh winds by the 'hedges of yew,' and enjoying a sight of the 'pretty grove of oakes' that commanded even Evelyn's commendation, despite the 'melancholie' of 'Camerwell.' Here the most wonderful of men reposed from his fatigues, and, relying with the high faith of a Christian spirit upon the God who works all things together for good to them that trust in Him, was never bowed down, never shaken, never turned from his loyalty to his maker ; to his ruler ; to his art. Well might Steele aver that 'his personal modesty overthrew all his public actions ; the modest man built the city, and the modest man's skill was unknown!'

Here, perhaps, originated the meeting which Herder asserts was the origin of the Freemasonry of St. John. Here, with a few friends, to save his journey home to dinner ; he arranged to dine somewhere in the neighbourhood of St. Paul's ; and a club was thus formed, which by degrees introduced a formula of initiation and rules for the conduct of the members expressed by symbolic language, derived from the masonic profession. Knight thinks it rather corroborative of Herder's assertion, that, while the biographers of Wren mention the attendance of the lodge of Freemasons, of which he was the master, at the ceremony of placing the highest stone of the lantern, no mention is made of their attendance at laying the foundation stone ; and every lodge in Great Britain is an offshoot from the lodge of antiquity of which Sir Christopher was master! We can fancy these walls covered with his plans, and, as the twilight gathered round us, might almost hear the music of his clear ; sweet, demonstrative voice replying kindly to those who questioned upon all points, by short but satisfactory answers.   Perhaps when at breakfast in this very room, when told that the frightful hurricane of the previous night had damaged all the steeples in London, he observed, with his quiet, faithful smile, 'Not St. Dunstan's, I am sure.'[57]

The admirable order of his mind gave him time for all things.   He never abandoned his scientific pursuits ; and here were written many of his interesting letters to the Royal Society.   One in particular partakes so much of the simplicity of the man and dignity of the philosopher, that it occurred to us while gazing on the beautiful proportions of the door.   'It is,' he said, 'upon billiard and tennis balls, upon the *purling* of sticks and tops, upon a vial of water, a wedge of glass, that the great Des-Cartes has built the most refined and accurate theories that human wit ever reached to ; and certainly nature, in the best of her works, is apparent enough in obvious things, *were they but curiously observed ;* and the key that opens treasures is often plain and rusty.'   'But,' he adds, with the pen of experience and prophecy, *'unless it be gilt, it makes no show at court.'*

As we walked round what is but a remnant of the garden that belonged to the house, and learned that it is now occupied as a school for the education of young ladies, we could not but think of the fine associations (those creators of noble thoughts) the young could not fail to imbibe in such a residence.   We are sure the lady, who felt so thoroughly the purity, even more than the vastness, of Wren's character, will not fail to impress upon their minds the great lesson taught by his life ; how much can be done by the right employment and division of

---

[57] The St Dunstans alluded to is the Church in Tower Street, London, known as St Dunstans in *the east*.   There is a tradition that the plan of this elegant tower and spire was furnished to Wren by his daughter, Jane Wren, who had seen and admired the famous one of St. Nicholas, at Newcastle.   She died in 1702, aged twenty-six, and was buried under the choir of St. Paul's Cathedral.   The storm which occasioned Wren's remark, raged in London through the night of the 26th of November, 1703, and some of the steeples and pinnacles in the City suffered serious injury.

time, and how surely a noble object, when persevered in, will be, *must* be, accomplished.   When we entered, we did envy her that house, but when we left it, we thought it could not, in the present day, be more worthily occupied.

We have deferred as long as we could the last public act of England towards Sir Christopher Wren, because we are ashamed to record it. His talents, his uprightness, his exertions, his deeds, were forgotten ; and almost beneath the very shadow of London's chief glory, when his head was crowned with those snows of age which kings might envy, in the eighty-sixth year of his earthly pilgrimage—when he had been half a century architect to the crown, George I., whose mind was just sufficiently large to contain corruption and intrigue, dismissed him!   For once Horace Walpole forgot that the dismisser was a king, and the dismissed a subject.   He speaks of Wren as 'having enriched the reign of several princes, and *disgraced the last of them.*'   God bless his honesty! We say this heartily, for he seldom affords us so great a luxury.

The retirement of this great man was as glorious as his career—the sunset of a long summer-day of untiring, untired life, which he laid down, not as a burden, but a duty.   We may surely accept his character as a man of science upon the testimony of Newton, who in his 'Principia' joins his name with those of Wallis and Huygens, whom he styles *hujus ætatis geometrarum facile principes.*

Retiring from the immediate neighbourhood of London to Hampton Court, he spent the remaining five years of his life chiefly in the study of the Scriptures.   Time, which had enfeebled his limbs, left his faculties unclouded nearly to the last day of his existence.   His chief delight up to the very close of life was to be carried once a year to visit his great work ; and we once met a lady who had heard her grandfather describe having seen him assisted by two friends up the steps of the cathedral. He was a little child then, but he never forgot following the architect into the holy building, and wondered, when he heard the people, who uncovered as he passed, say, that that old man, whose every smile was a blessing, had built the great St. Paul's.   After one of those visits, he rested at his lodging in St. James's Street, after his dinner ; on the 25th of February, 1723.   His servant, thinking he dosed longer than usual in his chair, found, to use the emphatic words of Scripture, 'that he had fallen asleep.'

TOMB OF WREN.

Of course, he had a splendid funeral. His remains were deposited in the crypt under the south side of the choir of THE cathedral.[58]

---

[58] Wren's tomb, a simple ponderous slab, bears the following inscription : — 'Here lieth Christopher Wren, Knt., who dyed, in the year of our Lord, M.DCC.XXIII., and of his Age XCI.' At the head of the tomb, on the wall above, is a more ambitious Latin epitaph, enclosed in an ornamental border after the fashion of a Roman tablet. It runs thus : 'Subtus conditur hujus Ecclesiæ et urbis conditor Christophorus Wren, qui vixit Annos ultra nonaginta non sibi sed bono publico : Lector si monumentum requiris circumspice. Obiit XXV. Feb. Ætatis XCI. Anno MDCCXXIII.' On the opposite wall, at the foot of the tomb, is the monument of Dean Holder, who married Wren's sister ; and on one of the massive pillars is that of Jane Wren, his daughter, who officiated as organist in the Cathedral, and is here represented playing on her favourite instrument to listening angels.

The Grave of William Penn.

DISTINGUISHED American observed to us, not long ago, that 'of all lawgivers there are none whose names shine so brightly on the page of history as do those of GEORGE WASHINGTON and WILLIAM PENN,' both of whom he claimed for his country. The former was, indeed, truly a great man ; perhaps of all Patriots who over lived he is the one most 'without spot or blemish'—pure, faithful, unselfish, devoted : yet, all things considered, it may be that William Penn is entitled to even higher admiration : the one nurtured in liberty became its high priest ; the other cradled in luxury, lived to endure a long and fierce struggle with oppression ; and yet, amid sore temptations and seductive flatteries, he passed, with the innate consciousness of genius, and a human desire of approbation, conquering not only others but himself, and finally doing justice among the 'Red-men' of a new country whom all his predecessors had sought to pillage and destroy. The sense of RIGHT must indeed have been of surpassing strength in the nature of William Penn. In an age fertile of slander against every act of virtue, and of calumny as regarded all good men, the marvel is how his reputation has descended to us so unscathed ; living, as he did, with those who make us blush for England, and often in contact with the low-minded and the false who were ever on the watch to do him wrong, still the evil imputed to him is little, if it be any, more than tradition ; while his goodness is to this day as a beacon, casting its clear light over the waves of the Atlantic, and his name a watchword of honour and a synonyme for probity and philanthropy.

It is a joy and a comfort to turn over the pages of this great man's life ; to view him as a statesman, acting upon Christian principles in direct opposition to the ordinary policy of the world ; and it was to us a source of high enjoyment, to reflect upon his eventful career ; while spending, during the past summer ; some sunny days wandering amid scenes in Buckinghamshire,—in places which bear his honoured name.

125

In Penn Wood there are trees yet in all the vigour of a green old age, beneath the shadow of which the peaceful lawgiver of Pennsylvania might have pondered on the true and rational liberty he would have gladly died to establish.[59]

There is one spot—the most hallowed of them all—of which we shall write presently : a simple, quiet, resting-place, for those who have gone to sleep in peace ; but, ere we pause at this Shrine, we must recall the lawgiver, amid the billows of life, buffeting the waves which in the end floated him into a haven of rest.

The family of William Penn were of Buckinghamshire, and from them sprang the Penns of Penn's Lodge, on the edge of Bradon Forest ; from the Penns of Penn's Lodge *our* William Penn came in direct descent. His father was, by profession, far other than a man of peace. He was one of England's rough bulwarks, braving

'The battle and the breeze ;'

obtained professional distinction while almost a boy ; commanded (in 1665) the fleet which Cromwell sent against Hispaniola ; and, after the Restoration, behaved so gallantly in a sea-fight against the Dutch, that be was knighted, and was 'received,' runs the chronicle, 'with all the marks of private friendship at court.'

Charles II.'s 'private' friendship could have been of small value to Admiral Penn ; indeed, be seemed to have cared little which was in the ascendant—King or Commonwealth ; but his sailor-nature *did* care for the glory of England, and he improved her navy in several important departments. Admiral Sir William Penn married Margaret, the daughter of John Jasper, of Rotterdam, and in due time the fair Dutch-woman's son became the 'PROPRIETOR' of Pennsylvania.[60] William was born in the parish of St. Catherine's, Tower Hill, on the 14th day of October ; 1644;[61] doubtless his mother left her home at Wanstead in Essex to be

---

[59] Further traces of this family are to be found in Penlands, Penn Street, Penhouse, al in the same county. The name given in after years to the American colony—Pennsylvania—is but a remembrance of the locality.

[60] This phrase is copied from the tomb of one of his grandsons, in the Church of the Village of Penn.

[61] This district has entirely changed its aspect ; twenty years ago it was densely and not very reputably populated. The Collegiate Church and Alms Houses stood in the midst of dirty streets, down which few strangers ventured : the Hospital of St. Catherine was removed to the Regent's Park ; and the pariah cleared away to an enormous extent to form on its site the Docks which bear the same name.

confined in London, although the neighbourhood of the Tower could not have been a very quiet retreat. The beat of the drum and the blast of the trumpet must have often disturbed the couch of the young mother. The fashionable world of those days knew nothing of the 'west end,' except from the salubrity of its fields and mulberry gardens, and the locality of Tower Hill was well adapted to suit the taste and calling of the Admiral, who had there chosen his 'town house.'

WANSTEAD IN ESSEX.

In due time the mother and child returned to Wanstead ; and the Archbishop of York having a little time previously founded a grammar school at Chigwell,[62] the embryo lawgiver was sent there at a very early age, where he was sufficiently near the family residence to give his mother the opportunity of frequently seeing her beloved son.

The localities thus connected with the early life of Penn are on the borders of Epping Forest, and although but a few miles from London, lie in a district but little visited. Wanstead is a picturesque spot, and the village green with its thickly planted over-arching trees, and large red-

---

[62] The free schools at Chigwell were founded in the year 1629, by Archbishop Harsnet ; one for teaching children reading, writing, and arithmetic, the other for their instruction in the Greek and Latin tongues. There is a fine brass to the founder in the church here ; he commenced life as master of the grammar school in his native town of Colchester, and became successively bishop of Chicester and Norwich, and ultimately Archbishop of York. He died in 1631.

brick houses, give it still an air of old-fashioned dignity. We were pleased with the aspect of the place, and left it with regret to journey on to Chigwell. The latter is an old and silent village ; the church, with its row of arching yews ; the large inn opposite, with its deep gables and bowed windows, and the entire character of the village carried the mind insensibly back. The school is an ivy-covered building ; and the room in which the after governor of Pennsylvania was educated bears traces of considerable antiquity.

EXTERIOR OF CHIGWELL SCHOOL.

The temperament of William Penn was sensitive and enthusiastic ; and must have caused his parents much anxiety. It is certain, that while at Chigwell, his mind became seriously impressed on the great subject of religion. The Admiral, we may suppose, if he knew of this impression, would not have regarded it favourably ; and if it were known to him, it made him hasten his son's departure from Chigwell, for the following year we find him at school near his birthplace on Tower Hill, and most likely at a *day* school, for his father to augment his scholarship kept a private tutor for him at his own home. Sir William had high hopes for this darling child. His talents were of a lofty order ; his accomplishments were many, and he won all hearts by his captivating manners. When fifteen, he entered Christ Church, Oxford, as a gentleman commoner. There, without neglecting his studies, he took great delight in manly sports and in the society of his companions, numbering among his friends Robert Spencer and John Locke ; but though the seed may remain long in the earth and give no sign of life if the soil be but favourable, it will spring up as surely as it has been sown—to "bring forth fruit in due season.

INTERIOR OF CHIGWELL SCHOOL.

About this time a certain Thomas Loe was drawn into what his college considered the heresy of Quakerism, and, like all sincere men who believe they have discovered truth, he sought to win others over to his new faith, or rather to a purifying of the old. Accordingly, the meetings and devotional exercises of him and his friends gave offence to the heads of the college, who fined all of them for nonconformity. This opposition strengthened their determination to persevere ; and those who had been simply devotional, rushed into fanaticism. While these youths were fusing in the fire of increased zeal, a command from Charles II., to Oxford, directed that the surplice should be worn according to the custom of ancient times. His Majesty loved to see religion in full dress— outward pomp seemed to him a good excuse for absence of the vital principle—but William Penn, his friend Robert Spencer ; and others who believed that the robe would impair the spirituality, fell upon the students who appeared *en robe* and tore the dresses to pieces—for which they were all expelled. There was much more of the father's spirit than of the mother's gentleness, in this outbreak ; but his father was not moved to approbation thereby ; on the contrary, he was sorely grieved ; the Admiral was terror-stricken at his son's becoming 'religious ;' he knew that Quakers were men who professed to hold all worldly distinctions in contempt—whose political principles were hardly defined, but who refused to remain uncovered in the presence even of Royalty—whose plain speech, and uncompromising faith, left no loop-holes for 'excuses' or 'expedients'—whose nay was nay—whose yea was yea—without *compromise ;*' and, above all, who were men of peace. It was not to be expected that a hero such as Admiral Penn, could have endured the idea of his son—endowed with all the accomplishments that charm society, and the high qualities which engrave their possessor's name on the page of history—subsiding into Quakerism in the days of his youth ; hiding his fortunes beneath a broad-brimmed hat ; and abandoning for ever the graces of society—the established learning of the schools ; and what was far more dear to the Admiral the sword—then the badge and birthright of the English gentleman.

Even in this more tolerant age, when no sorrow or misfortune visits our country without testing and proving the social value of the Quakers, as most faithful labourers in the cause of charity and most loyal and peaceful subjects—even we can fancy the rage of some old Admiral—the very Hotspur of the ocean—if his son were found guilty of going over to sectarianism ; deserting his church being in his eyes almost as criminal, as deserting his gun. Admiral Penn was so annoyed at William's conduct that he turned him out of doors, well-be loved as he was. There is no record of William Penn's conduct at this time ; probably he had not been sufficiently schooled into forbearance to endure patiently ; and yet when his father's wrath subsided, his mother's tears and entreaties prevailed : overcome by his own affectionate nature on the one hand, and her expostulations on the other ; the father forgave the son, who was again sheltered beneath his roof ; but not long destined to remain there.

The unenviable distinction which France enjoys of being the country where no serious thought can arrive at maturity, tempted Sir William to send his son to Paris. Foreign travel was then considered indispensable to the gentleman, and he, doubtless, thought that the gaieties of Paris would do more towards emancipating young Penn from the thraldom of sectarianism than the reproof of the college, or his repented-of severity. It is believed that for a time his father's wishes were gratified ; but only one anecdote is preserved of his conduct there, and that tells greatly to his honour. He was attacked one night by a person who drew his sword upon him in consequence of a supposed affront. A conflict ensued, proving that the youth had not in all things conformed to the habit of those whose influence was so dreaded by his father. William disarmed his antagonist, but spared his life, when, according to the record of all those who relate the fact, he could have taken it ; thus exhibiting, says Gerard Crosse, a testimony not only of his courage but of his forbearance.

But if touched by the dissipations of Paris, he was not tainted by them.[63] In 1662 and 1663, we find him residing with a Protestant minister of Calvinistic faith, the very learned M. Amyrault of Saumur ; whose character and works recommended him to the notice of Cardinal Richelieu, who imparted to him his design of uniting the two churches.

The privilege of receiving instruction from such a man was appreciated as it deserved by William Penn ; the teaching of the schools is widely different from the knowledge communicated by the wise and true to a docile and eager pupil, in the comparative silence and solitude of a private family. At Saumur ; Penn pondered over 'the Fathers,' became more deeply interested in theology, and laboured diligently to acquire a perfect knowledge of the French language ; from thence he proceeded to Turin, where he received a letter from his father informing him of his taking sea against the Dutch, and commanding his immediate return to England. The Admiral was perhaps too busied to enquire much as to the state of his son's mind ;—satisfied, as many are, with the ease and grace to which foreign travel seldom fails to mould the young, he commended his improvement and Lincoln's Inn had the honour of receiving William Penn as a student for a year ; when the 'great plague' set him free from the dry, but—as regarded his future—useful, study of the law.

---

[63] It has been said indeed, that at this period of his life he dallied with the enervating pleasures of the time ; we have not only no evidence of this, but the supposition is inconsistent with his indignant exclamation, when before the Lieutenant of the Tower, Sir John Robinson, who charged him with having 'been as bad as other folks,' 'abroad, and at home too,' which elicited from William Penn the following : —'I make this bold challenge to all men, women and children, upon earth, justly to accuse me with ever having seen me *drunk*, heard me *swear*, utter a *curse*, or speak one *obscene word* (much less that I ever made it my practice); I speak this to GOD'S GLORY, that has ever preserved me from the power of these pollutions, and that from a child, begot an hatred in me towards them ;' concluding his outbreak thus —'Thy words shall be thy burden, and I trample thy *slander* as *dirt* under my feet.'

The sacred fire kindled in his bosom, though it smouldered for a time, was never extinguished. The awful visitation that had driven him from Lincoln's Inn was well calculated to revive his more serious thoughts and lead them from the present to the future. The fatal pestilence had not subdued the restless spirit of religious controversy ; men cried more loudly than ever 'I am of Paul,' 'and I of Apollos.' But, for a time, he spoke less and pondered more ; he had completed his twenty-first year ; and with his manly robe, assumed a grave and manly bearing. His father returned from the expedition flushed with glory and triumph ; but his proud pulses beat less quickly when he noted the gravity of his son, and his evident leaning towards serious matters. Again he determined to change the scene, and draughted him to the viceregal court of Ireland, then glowing with the brightness and animation of the accomplished Duke of Ormond. The means were too violent for the end : the young man grew disgusted with the court and courtly doings. The Admiral, fertile in expedients, then turned over to him the management of his Irish estates in the county of Cork.[64]

The task was after his son's own heart, and he performed it to admiration ; this occupation most likely sowed the seed of his wisdom in territorial management and, as there were no gaieties to annoy or perplex him, he might have continued long to delight his father in this capacity, but for the accident of his hearing WILLIAM LOE, the layman of Oxford, preach at a Quaker's meeting in Cork from the text,—'There is a faith which overcomes the world, and there is a faith which is overcome by the world.' This convinced him of the necessity for religious vitality ; and at length he was, according to the custom of those 'rare old times,' apprehended at a Quakers' meeting in Cork, and thereupon committed to prison ; but thanks to Lord Orrery, his term in 'the dark prison-house' was not long. His nature was strengthened in his new faith, as all noble natures are, by the invigorating power of persecution ; for

> '—who would force the soul, tilts with a straw
> Against a champion cased in adamant.'

From this time all wavering and indecision passed away, and he was considered a confirmed Quaker. Sir William, refusing to believe

---

[64] 'He had large estates in Ireland, one of which, comprehending Shannigarry Castle, lay in the barony of Imokelly, and the others in the baronies of Ibaune and Barryroe, all of them in the county of Cork.'—*Clarkson*.

that every means he had taken to dispel, had but established, his son's faith, commanded his return ; it would seem that at first William Penn desired to meet his father's wishes, were it possible to do so. His adherence to what was called the ceremony of the 'hat,' and his communion only with those of the same faith, convinced the Admiral that he embraced the 'heresy' more fondly than ever. The stormy and sorely-tried father used every means in his power to get his son even to appear to the world what he was not. The great point of dispute, the wearing or not wearing the *hat* in the presence of Royalty, may seem to us a light matter ; but it was not so to 'the Friends,' and is not so to this day.[65] And so the father again turned the son from beneath the shelter of his roof, a houseless and moneyless wanderer ; his situation would have been most pitiable, but for his mother's watchful tenderness and affection.

The young Quaker now put forth his faith in printed books, and was not slow in disputation ; evincing, occasionally, rather more of the fiery zeal of Peter than the discretion of Paul ; combating the attacks of certain Presbyterians with marvellous intrepidity, and attacking in his turn, which attacks ended in his being committed to the Tower. His imprisonment was rigid, but he wrote continuously ; and in one tract, 'Innocency with her open Face,' explained away the anti-Christian charges made against his faith. After seven months' incarceration he was liberated ; it is believed, by the intercession of the Duke of York, to whom, from this or some other cause, he was personally attached. Certainly, in nothing did his purpose waver ; for he left the gloom of the prison to attend the death-bed of Thomas Loe, his friend and guide. And then the heart of his father yearned towards him ; the Admiral could not but respect his son's earnestness and consistency of purpose ; the chords of both were the same, but they were tuned in different keys, and for different ends. He relented gradually, giving permission to the

---

[65] Clarkson has very clearly summed up the reasons of the early Quakers for discarding *Hat-worship* as they termed it. Taking it for granted that the ceremonious removal of the hat was intended to be indicative of honour, respect, submission, or some similar feeling of the mind, they contended, that, used as it then was, it was no more a criterion of these than mourning garments were criterions of sorrow ; hence, they argued, the falsity of the custom. If used as indicative of respect, they contended, that it was more generally applied to the purposes of flattery, and equally objectionable. But the strongest reason of the three, was that which declared, that the removal of the hat in the worship of God precluded the possibility of giving any of his creatures an equal amount of honour.

mother again to receive her son, and sanctioning his resuming the management of his Irish property.

OLD NEWGATE PRISON.

He performed to admiration the duties with which he was entrusted ; and on his return to England was received with open arms by a father no longer stern or unforgiving ; his mother had the joy of seeing them once more united. Nor does it appear that his son's after disputatious, or preachings, or imprisonments, caused any new breach between them, though we find the young 'friend' preaching in Gracechurch Street, and expressing his opinions so freely upon various matters—especially the famous Conventicle Act passed in 1670, prohibiting dissenters from worshipping God in their own way—that he was, with another of the society, one William Mead, seized upon by constables, conveyed

THE MONUMENT TO ADMIRAL PENN.

at once to Newgate,[66] where they were left until the following session, and then had the good fortune to be tried by one of the most steadfast and honest juries ever impanelled even in England.[67] The indignities endured both by prisoners and jury can hardly be credited ; but ultimately the Quakers were liberated upon the payment of a fine, which was privately discharged by Sir William Penn.

When William Penn was freed from the Tower ; it may be remembered that he passed from its walls to the deathbed of his spiritual father ; William Loe, and he hastened from the loathsome cells of Newgate to the deathbed of his earthly father ; whose career was terminating at an age when men calculate on length of days to enjoy the repose

[66] Newgate had been a prison since 1218, and was used for persons of distinction even before the Tower. It was a most miserable dungeon, originally termed Chamberlain's Gate ; and when re-constructed by Whittington was called New Gate, it being then one of the gates of the City. It was destroyed in the Great Fire.

[67] The trial of Penn is an extraordinary picture of the legal tyranny of the times. It took place at the Old Bailey in September, 1670. The indictment was for preaching in Gracechurch Street ; Penn's conduct was most heroic. He argued manfully and well against the persecution to which he and others were subjected, and appealed to the jury so powerfully, exhorting them to preserve their integrity of action uninfluenced by the lawyers, that they would only bring in their verdict 'Guilty of speaking in Gracechurch Street.' And, although sent back to re-consider this verdict frequently, 'until,' as the Recorder told them, 'they brought such a one as the court would accept' they continued firm for two days and nights. The court indulged in brutal language toward them, and the infamous Recorder lamented the want of the Inquisition in England, declaring England 'would never be well' till something equal in 'policy and prudence' to it was established. When finally pressed to deliver a verdict, —guilty, or not guilty,—they, to a man, returned an answer in the negative ; for which they were each fined forty marks and sent to Newgate, as also were Penn and Mead for refusing to pay the fines.

which is so needful as the evening of life approaches. At the age of forty-nine, his warring but chastened spirit passed to the God who gave both peace and Christian wisdom to his latter days.[68] It throws, however, a good deal of light on the 'king-loving' habit which was made a cruel reproach to William Penn's after course, by those who could not separate the *man* from the monarch—to remember ; that in his last illness, indeed, towards its termination, Admiral Penn, foreseeing that while the existing laws of the country remained, his son would have many trials and much suffering to undergo, sent one of his friends to the Duke of York to entreat him, as a deathbed request, that he would endeavour to protect his son as far as he consistently could, and to ask the king to do the same in case of future persecution. The answer was such as the Admiral deserved, and for once the *Stuart*-promise was faithfully kept ; be it also remembered, the Duke of York had previously befriended the young Quaker ; who was personally attached to him ; and all know that every member of the house of Stuart possessed an extraordinary power of attaching to them those they desired to bring under their influence.

Now that he was his own master, with a fortune of fifteen hundred pounds a-year, it would be impossible, within our limits, to trace his career abroad and at home, remarkable as it was for spiritual zeal, activity of body and mind, close penmanship in his closet, and so many perils and imprisonments, that he might compete with holy Paul in the eloquent list of perils and trials. At one time he publishes 'The People's Ancient and Just Liberties Asserted ;' then he disputes with Jeremy Ives touching Baptist matters, at Wycomb ; then he lets fly a barbed arrow against Popery : is again taken up and sent first to the Tower ; and then to Newgate, for preaching ; yet imprisonment no way damped his zeal, but seemed only to give him time for letters, essays, pamphlets, addresses.[69] He was never more fluent—never more industrious than when in bonds ; his spirit of endurance, his hope, his enterprise, were astonishing. He no sooner quitted Newgate than he travelled into Germany

---

[68] The father of Penn was buried in Redcliffe Church, Bristol, and a monument was erected there to his memory by his wife, which, narrating his early promotions in the Navy until the time when "he withdrew and made for his end ; and with a gentle and even gale, in much peace arrived and anchored in his last and best port, at Wanstead in the County of Essex, the 16th of September, 1670; being then but forty-nine years and four months old."

[69] In a catalogue of 'Friends' Books' (J. Soule, 1708) we find a list of his written productions from 1668 to 1700, in number no fewer than *one hundred and nine*.

and Holland, seeking and making converts. Returning, when in the twenty-eighth year of his age, he sought and found a loving and lovely wife, Gulielma Maria Springett, daughter of Sir William Springett, of Darling, in Sussex. For a brief time he enjoyed the quiet of domestic happiness at Rickmansworth, in Hertfordshire, but he would not, perhaps, could not, give up for domestic tranquillity, the life of excitement, wherein he had cast his lot ; and in those days there was always something fresh to stir up the spirit of an independent mind. Charles II. had issued a declaration of indulgence to tender consciences in matters of religion, in consequence of which five hundred Quakers were released from prison ; but William Penn again went forth on a self-imposed mis-

SWARTHMOOR HALL.

sion, accompanied by his lovely wife, and behold, amid the rant and turmoil of Bristol fair ; they encountered George Fox, the great fountain of Quakerism, who had just then landed in Bristol, after a sojourn in America. Though subsequently much engaged in very stormy controversy, there can be little doubt that this meeting determined William Penn to investigate human nature in the New World. We may diverge a little from our subject to introduce two engravings, interesting as associated with this period of the history of William Penn. With Fox he travelled much ; and in the Journal of that celebrated man he is frequently referred to. They visited each other's houses ; and while we know that Fox resided at Worminghurst, we have the traditional certainty of his visiting Fox, at his house, Swarthmoor Hall, on the borders of Lancashire. This mansion was his by marriage with the widow of Judge Fell ; and in the memoirs of Margaret Fox, she records his first visit there in her husband's lifetime, in 1652, who, from being opposed to Quakerism, became a convert on hearing Fox, and she says—'He let us have a meeting in his house the next first day after ; which was the first public meeting that was at Swarthmoor, our meetings being kept at Swarthmoor about thirty-eight years, until a new Meeting-house was built by George Fox's order and cost, near Swarthmoor Hall.'

In 1676 Penn became 'manager of Property concerns' in New Jersey ; invited settlers, sent them out in three vessels, and occupied himself in the formation of a constitution, consisting of terms of agreement and concession. Perfect religious liberty was of course established, and William Penn left on record that 'he hoped he had laid the foundation for those in after ages of their liberty both as men and Christians, and by an adherence to which they could never be brought into bondage but by their own consent.'

SWARTHMOOR MEETING HOUSE.

How evident it is that such-like exercises qualified him for his after-charge of 'his property' of Pennsylvania! In these days it is little more than a pleasure trip, to those who like, or do not absolutely dislike, the sea, to cross the Atlantic ; but in the time of William Penn it was a serious undertaking ; yet nothing obstructed his progress ; when once he fixed within his mind, that it was *right* to act, the act was 'a-foot.' It would be the PILGRIMAGE of a life to follow his steps ; we have taken but a condensed view of his movements, yet what space it has occupied ; and still his journeyings are only commenced! What meetings and preachings in Holland and Germany—what disputatious abroad and in England—what petitions on behalf of the peaceful, but most persecuted Quakers—what answers to libels, and what loving epistles to God's people! Stimulated by the hot blood of his father, which at times boiled within his veins, he for a time forgot his consistency and made common cause with Algernon Sidney in his contested election at Gildford ; but his 'plainness' did not move the people 'more than eloquence,' for Sidney lost his election, and Penn was forced from the hustings. And all this time his mighty head was projecting, and his mighty heart beating with plans for the good of New Jersey : mingling the divine and secular in a way which cannot be comprehended by those who have not known what it is to contend with the restlessness and suggestions of an enterprising and fervent spirit. His heart was rent asunder by the persecutions endured by his people—especially in the 'rough' city of Bristol—and anxious as he then was for the grants, which he in aftertime obtained, the fear of 'great ones' never prevented his raising hand and voice against tyranny.

At length one of his great objects was attained ; the Charter, granting him the tract of land which he himself had marked out, bears date the 4th of March, 1681. Let none suppose this was a free gift from the Majesty of England to the Quaker,—not at all ;—he had petitioned for land in 'the far West,' where brethren might dwell together in unity, in love, and in security, chiefly as the liquidation of a debt which the government owed his father.[70] And when his petition was granted, then commenced the career by which his name is chiefly known and honoured ; his sayings and doings, his writings, his wearyings and journeyings, are only parts of the political and religious contention which disjointed England in those days, and show forth the restless and truth-seeking spirit of one whose aim was to keep alive the purer and simpler forms of religion, while contending manfully for its liberty. Happily, the spirit of persecution—at least of legalised persecution—has been

---

[70] 'His father had advanced large sums of money from time to time for the good of the Naval service, and his pay had also been in arrears. For these two claims, including the interest upon the money due, government were in debt to him no less a sum than 16,000*l.*'—*Clarkson*.

extinguished in our age ; and now, instead of sitting in terror under our own 'vine and fig tree'—

> 'We rather think, with grateful mind sedate,
> How Providence educeth, from the spring
> Of lawless will, unlooked for streams of good,
> Which neither force shall check, nor time abate.'

But the grand feature, the climax—the crowning of the capital—is PENN at PENNSYLVANIA ; the just man, rising above all temptations. Let quibbles be raised, and old rumours revived,—the facts of Penn's legislation prove the greatness of his mind and the purity of his intentions. He had the strong feelings, passions, and thoughts inseparable from a large brain ; and the wonder of all who look upon him dispassionately, must be, not that some evil has been asserted of one who accomplished what he desired, and commanded the respect of the voluptuous, as well as the affection of the good, but that so little has been found or written to his discredit.

Gathering 'a favoured people' together from wherever he had preached 'the word,' we find that, at a very early period, he freighted two ships with Irish Quakers.

Mercurial as the Irish are, there is no country where Quakers are more beloved and trusted to this day, than in Ireland ; and well they may be so! At all times the Quakers stand forth between 'the people' and destruction ; no matter whether the peasantry are assailed by pestilence or by famine, the firm, calm, unpresuming, but steadfast Quaker ;[71] comes forward with his store of wealth, and energy, and industry, and charity (pure charity in its most comprehensive sense), and *mind,* ready to save, and employ, and instruct ; we have met with some who remember having heard from their parents, that their grandsires remembered the wailing of the poor when the 'great law-maker ;' William Penn, induced so many of the 'neighbours' to go to the New World. The 'conditions,' as it pleased him to call his code of laws,—laws made as much for the advantage of a people given carelessly into his hand by a power which evidently thought little of the 'Peltries,' or 'hunting-ground,' of the Red-men—as for the good of those who sought a home in an un-

---

[71] It is worthy of record, that during the rebellion of 1798, there was but one instance of a Quaker being put to death by the rebels ; and that act was perpetrated in ignorance of the calling of the victim.

known land, in full reliance upon their leader ;—the 'conditions' are all stated in Clarkson's life of Penn.[72]

The closeness and simplicity and wisdom of his legislation are admirable commentaries on the multitude and mystery of involvments which sepulchre our laws. It is evident that in all he did he sought not only that his own people should be well treated, but that they should treat others well. He put far away all attempts at religious persecution ; and strove rather to make men upright and just in their old faith, than to tempt them into a new one.

The embarkation of this Quaker colony must, if we recall it by help of imagination, have formed a strange contrast to the going out of an 'emigrant ship' in our own day. The well-clad, well-organised, steadfast, earnest, subdued, yet hopeful people, taking leave of those whom they loved, yet left, subduing, as is their custom, all outward indications of anguish, and seeming ashamed of the emotion which sent tears to their eyes and tremors to their lips! Two of the good ships—well ordered, well appointed, well provisioned—sailed from London ; another from Bristol. How different from those wretched hulks which are now sent staggering across the seas, to convey a diseased, half-naked, and enfeebled multitude to the promised land!

Penn's letter to the Indians, transmitted by one of the earlier ships, is a masterpiece of what worldlings call policy, but which is simply, justice and right feeling. This letter preceded his visit, and was well calculated to excite the confidence and curiosity of the Red-men, who must have felt deeply anxious to see the 'Pale-face' who addressed them, and was disposed to treat them, as brethren.

The death of his mother at this time spread a gloom over his loving spirit, and delayed his departure ; but the interests of the New World summoned him from the Old. His letter to his wife and children, written on their separation, is such a record of pure love and true wisdom, that we should like to see it published as a tract, to find place among the treasures of every young married woman, and be unto her and her chil-

---

[72] Philadelphia, the name which Penn gave to his new city, is a compound from the Greek, signifying brotherly love. The 'conditions' were also published in French, German, and Dutch, in 1682, and were extensively circulated over the Continent, inviting adventurers of all nations, creeds, and tongues, to join him in his enterprise at the city of 'Brotherly Love.'

dren a guide through life.   He dates this letter from Worminghurst, where his family resided some considerable time.

He at length sailed for the new colony, in the ship 'Welcome,' and was there greeted by his future subjects, consisting of English, Irish, Dutch, and Swedes, then in number about 3000. He had people of many creeds and many lands to deal with, as well as an unseen and almost unknown nation, but he commenced with so noble an act of justice, in

PENN'S TREATY GROUND.

paying the Indians for the lands already *given* him in *payment* by the king of England, that 'Pale-faces' and 'Red-skins' were alike convinced of his certain honesty of purpose.   There are few persons whose pulsations are so numbed that they will not beat the quicker when they hear of a generous action ; the soul is revived, even in a worldly bosom, by the throbs of immortality which tell us there are great and righteous deeds prompted by God himself.   With what an upright gait and open brow must William Penn have met the tribes at COAQUANNOC—the Indian name for the place where Philadelphia now stands—foremost of a handful of Quakers, without weapon, undefended, except by that sure protector which the Almighty has stamped on every honest brow.

Here the peace-loving law-maker awaited the pouring out of the dusky tribes.

Amid the woods, as far as eye could reach, dark masses of wild uncouth creatures, some with paint and feathers, and rude, but deadly weapons, advanced slowly and in good order ; grave, stern chiefs, and strong-armed 'braves' gathering to meet a few unarmed strangers, their future FRIENDS, not MASTERS! There was neither spear nor pistol, sword nor rifle, scourge nor fetter ; open or concealed, among these white men ; the trysting-place was an elm-tree of prodigious growth at Shackamaxon, the present Kensington of Philadelphia.[73] Towards this tree the leaders of both tribes drew near, approaching each other under its widely spreading branches ; front to front, eye to eye, neither having a dishonest or dishonourable thought towards his fellow-man—comprehending each other by means of that great interpreter—Truth! How vexatious, that history should be so mute as to this most glorious meeting, and that there is little but tradition,—that faintest echo of the mighty past,—to tell of the speeches made by the Indians, and replied to by William Penn after his first address had been delivered. The Quaker used no subterfuge, employed no stratagem to draw them into confidence ; imposed not upon their senses by a display of crown, sceptre, mace, sword, halbert, or any of the visible signs of stately dominion or warlike power ; to which, like all wild men, they were inclined to render homage ;—and this is a thing to look at with pride and thankfulness, when man in a righteous purpose, and with simplicity, and steadfast intent, becomes so completely one of Heaven's delegates, that he is looked up to, and respected by his fellow mortals, who are not so richly en-

---

[73] Penn, in his letter to the Earl of Sunderland, thus describes the great event which gives this spot celebrity : he says—'In selling me this land they thus ordered themselves : the old in a half-moon, upon the ground ; the middle-aged in a like figure at a little distance behind them ; and the young fry in the same manner behind them.' 'We have thus,' says Watson, in his Annals of Philadelphia, 'a graphic picture of Penn's treaty, as painted by himself ; and to my mind the sloping green bank presented a ready amphitheatre for the display of the successive semi-circles of Indians.' The large elm under which Penn concluded his treaty is seen to the right in the foreground of the above cut ; it was blown down on the 3rd of March, 1810. In its form it was remarkably wide-spread, but not lofty : its main-branch inclining towards the river measured 150 feet in length ; its girth around the trunk was twenty-four feet ; and its age, as it was counted by the inspection of its circles of annual growth, was 283 years ; it stood on the edge of the bank, which sloped to the river. The avenue of trees seen in the view, and Fairman Maurian opposite, was constructed in 1702. Penn greatly desired to purchase it as a country residence for himself, but failed to do so.

dowed by GOD. It must have been a sight of exceeding glory when
Penn, whose only personal distinction was a netted sash of sky-blue silk,
cast his eyes over the mighty and strange multitude, who observed him
with an undefined interest, while his followers displayed to the tribes
various articles of merchandise, and he advanced, steadily, towards the
great *Sachem,* chief of them all, who, as Penn drew near ; placed a
horned chaplet on his head, which gave his people intimation that the
sacredness of peace was over all. With one consent the tribes threw
down their bows and arrows, crouched around their chiefs, forming a
huge half-moon on the ground, while their great chief told William
Penn, by his interpreter, that the 'nations were ready to hear him.'[74]

This scene has never been either recorded or painted as it might be.
The great fact that he there spoke fearlessly and honestly, what they
heard and believed—pledging themselves, when he had concluded, according to their country's manner, to live in love with William Penn and
his children as long as the sun and moon should endure—is more suggestive than any record in modern history.

After arranging all matters as to the future city, well might William
Penn write home—'In fine, here is what Abraham, Isaac, and Jacob
would be well contented with, and service enough for God, for the fields
are here white with harvest. Oh, how sweet is the quiet of these parts!
freed from the anxious and troublesome solicitations, hurries, and per-
plexities of woeful Europe!

---

[74] Watson, in his *Annals of Philadelphia,* tells us—'After the death of the great law
giver of Pennsylvania, his family appear to have much degenerated. One member became
remarkable for dissolute and ungovernable habits, and ultimately the property passed into
other hands. The settlers, however, still retained a sense of respect for the descendants
and upon a visit of one of them in the early part of the eighteenth century, who had been
shopkeeper ; they received him with so much general rejoicing and public honours, that th
poor man, totally unused to it, was frightened out of all propriety.

SLATE-ROOF HOUSE PHILADELPHIA.

But much as the lawgiver[75] eulogised the 'quiet' of his new colony, he was not content to remain there. His mind was anxious ; his affections were divided between the two hemispheres ; his ardent, restless nature longed to act wherever action was needed. If the English government had hoped to get rid of him when they sold him the land for an inheritance, they were mistaken ; several of those he loved were in sorrow and imprisonment ; the Stuarts gave liberty of conscience one day and withdrew it the next ; he therefore returned to England. Charles II. was trembling on the verge of the grave, which soon closed over him, leaving nothing for immortality but the fame of weakness even in vice. William Penn records James telling him, soon after his accession, that now he meant to 'go to mass above board :' upon which the Quaker replied quaintly and promptly, 'that he hoped his Majesty would grant to others the liberty he so loved himself, and let all go where they pleased.' His renewed intimacy with James strengthened the old reproach of 'time-serving,' and 'trimming,' and William Penn was frequently called

---

[75] Slate-roof House, the city residence of William Penn and family while in Philadelphia, on his second visit in 1700, is remarkable as the birthplace of the only one of the race of Penn born in the country. Here John Penn, "the American," was born one month after the arrival of the family. After Penn's decease, the house was retained as the governor's residence ; and John Adams, and other members of the Congress had their lodgings in the Slate house.

Jesuitical. Those who so reproached him had forgotten the long friend-ship which had subsisted between the King and himself, and the fact that never had his influence in high places been used except for right and righteous purposes. Whatever was said against him either then or now lacks proof, and is no more history than the bubble on the surface of the stream is the stream itself. He resided then in a house at Charing Cross, most probably one ready furnished, as it has not been pointed at as a residence. His journeyings to and fro were resumed, and as he was known to be affectionately attached to James, (who certainly showed him great favour), when William came to the throne he was persecuted nearly as much as in the old times. Pennsylvania, too, became dis-turbed, not by the discontent of the Red-men, but by discontent with another governor. The wife of his bosom died in her fiftieth year ; and soon after his son, in the prime of youth and hope, was taken from him. He married, however ; again, feeling it hard to superintend a household without the overlooking care of a steadfast woman. From those of his own people who could not comprehend his liberal views he experienced great opposition and reproof, some of them thinking he entered too much into the world of politics.

'Time and the hour run through the longest day ;

Penn outlived evil report and persecution. After a lapse of seven-teen years he again sailed with his family to Pennsylvania ; again was received by 'white and red' as their father and their friend ; dispelled many differences, healed many sores, saw the city he had planned, ris-ing rapidly on every side. These seventeen years seemed to have done the work of seventy, and the prosperity of Pennsylvania was secured. He had shown the possibility of a nation maintaining its own internal policy amid a mixture of different nations and opposite civil and relig-ions opinions, and of maintaining its foreign relations also, without the aid of a soldier or a man-at-arms. The CONSTABLE'S STAFF was the only symbol of authority in Pennsylvania for the greater part of a century!

He had still abundant vexations to endure. His circumstances had become embarrassed. He returned with his family to England an aged man, though more aged by the unceasing anxiety and activity of his life, than by years.

RUSHCOMBE.

There are traditions of his dwelling at Kensington and Knights-bridge ; but it is known that he possessed himself of a handsome mansion at Rushcombe, near Twyford, in Berkshire ;[76] here a stroke of apoplexy numbed his active brain, and rendered him unfit for business ; that such 'strokes' were repeated, until he finally sank beneath them, is also certain ; but those who visited him between the periods of their infliction, bore testimony to his faith, and hope, and trust in the Lord, and of his unfailing loving-kindness and gentleness to those around him. Thus, through much faintness and weakness, he had but little actual suffering, though there was a gradual pacing towards eternity, during six years, and on the 30th day of July, 1718, in the seventy-fourth year of his age, he put off the mortal coil which he had worn, even to the wearing out, and joined in Heaven those he had loved on earth. There was an immediate and mighty gathering of his friends and admirers, who attended his remains to the burying-ground of Jordans. It must have been a thrilling

---

[76] Rushcombe is a quiet little village on the borders of Berkshire ; it lies in a valley, and the gently-rising hills afar off add to the placid beauty of the scene. Some very old cottages and farms constitute the homes of its inhabitants, which remain much as they must have been when Penn was here resident. The house in which he died was destroyed nearly twenty years ago ; and an old countryman, who noticed our scrutiny of the village and entered freely into the interest of our visit, described it as a large and quaint old mansion, which stood opposite the church, and commanded the view exhibited in our woodcut ; a view entirely unaltered by modernisation, and upon which the eye of Penn must often have rested.

sight ; the silent and solemn people wending their way through the embowered lanes leading from Rushcombe into Buckinghamshire, that hallowed land of Hampden, consecrated by so many memories, of which
Penn, if not chiefest, is now among the chief! The dense unweeping
sorrow of a Quaker funeral once witnessed can never be forgotten.[77]

The sun had begun to make long shadows on the grass, and the
bright stems of the birch threw up, as it were, the foliage of heavier
trees, before we came in sight of the quaint solitary place of silence and
of graves. The narrow road leading to the Quakers' Meeting-house was
not often disturbed by the echo of carriage-wheels, and before we
alighted an aged woman had looked out with a perplexed yet kindly
countenance, and then gone back and sent forth her little grand-daughter
who met us with a self-possessed and quiet air ; which showed that if not
'a friend,' she had dwelt among friends. The Meeting-house is, of
course, perfectly unadorned—plain benches, and a plain table, such as
you sometimes see in 'furniture-prints' of Queen Anne's time. This
table the little maid placed outside, to enable Mr. Fairholt to sketch the
grave-yard, and that we might write our names in a book, where a few
English and a number of Americans had written before us,—it would be
defamation to call it 'an album,'—it contained simply, as it ought, the
names of those, who, like ourselves, wished to be instructed and elevated by a sight of the grave of William Penn.

The burying-ground might be termed a little meadow, for the long
green grass waved over ; while it in a great degree concealed, the several undulations which showed where many sleep ; but when observed
more closely, chequered though it was by increasing shadows, the very
undulations gave an appearance of green waves to the verdure as it
swept above the slightly raised mounds ; there was something to us sa-

---

[77] In Thomas Story's Journal, he narrates the circumstances of Penn's death and fu
neral with touching simplicity :—'On the 31st of fifth month, 1718, I received a letter from
Hannah Penn, of the decease of her husband, our ancient and honourable friend, William
Penn, who departed this life on the 30th, between two and three in the morning, of a shor
sickness.' He then notes his visit on the 1st of the succeeding month to Rushcombe, where
'I staid till the 5th (of August), and that day accompanied the corpse to the grave, at Jor
dans meeting-place, in the County of Bucks, where we had a large Meeting of Friends an
others from many places ; and as the Lord had made choice of him in the days of his yout
for great and good services, and had been with him in many dangers and difficulties o
various kinds, so he did not leave him in his last moments, but honoured the occasion with
his blessed presence, and gave a happy season of his goodness to the general satisfaction o
all, the Meeting being well spoken of by strangers afterwards.'

cred beyond all telling in this green place of nameless graves, as if having done with the world, the world had nothing more to do with those whose stations were filled up, whose names were forgotten! it was more solemn, told more truly of actual death, than the monuments beneath the fretted roofs of Westminster or St. Paul's, labouring, often unworthily, 'to point a moral or adorn a tale,' to keep a memory green, which else had mouldered!

The young girl knew the 'law-giver's' grave amongst the many, as well as if it had been crushed by a tower of monumental marble.

She pointed it out, between the graves of his two wives ; some pilgrim to the shrine had planted a little branch, a mere twig, which had sprouted and sent forth leaves, just at the head of the mound of earth, — an effort at distinction that seemed somewhat to displease the old woman, who had come forth looking well satisfied at what she called the 'quiet place' being so noticed. 'All who came,' she said, 'knew the grave of William Penn ; there was no need of any distinction ; *there it was*, every one knew it ; yes, many came, —especially Americans. Ladies now and then plucked a little root of the grass, and took it away as a treasure ; and no wonder, every one said he was a man of peace, —a GOOD MAN!'

THE GRAVE OF WILLIAM PENN.

We walked along the road that leads to the upland, and leaning against a stile, saw the shadows of the tall trees grow longer and longer ; as if drawing themselves closer to the hallowed earth. The Meeting-house had a solemn aspect ; so lonely, so embowered, so closed up,—as if it would rather keep within itself, and to itself, than be a part of the busy world of busy men.

How still and beautiful a scene! How grand in its simplicity ; how unostentatiously religious,—those green mounds, upon which the setting sun was now casting its good-night in golden benisons, seemed to us more spirit-moving than all the vaunted monuments of antiquity we had ever seen. How we wished that all law-givers had been like him, who rested within the sanctuary of that green grass grave. We thought how he had the success of a conqueror in establishing and defending his col-ony ; without ever ; as was said of him, drawing a sword ; the goodness of the most benevolent ruler in treating his subjects like his own chil-dren ; the tenderness of an universal Father ; who opened his arms, without distinction of sect or party, to the worthy of all mankind ;—the man who really wishes to establish a mission of peace, and love, and justice to the ends of the earth, should first pray beside the grave of William Penn.

Shrines in Buckinghamshire.

E have made frequent Pilgrimages to Shrines that enrich Buckinghamshire. It is one of the most interesting—if not the most interesting—of our English counties ; and once, thanks to the kindness of the late Sir John ; and Lady Frankland, Russell, we spent a day at Chequers Court,[78] interested not only by the tell-tale dwelling—its long galleries, its Cromwellian portraits,[79] its stores of gems, its varied trophies of the past and beauties of the present time—but by the memory of those sorrows which enshrine the name of Lady Mary Grey, whose sufferings excite sympathy, and who would have slept for ever in a forgotten grave, but for the cruelty practised towards her by Elizabeth. Her room, at Chequers Court, is a small dark chamber, looking over the roofs and walls of a house that was her prison. We shall presently make some notes concerning the melancholy course of her young life.

The mansion—successively the residence of the Hawtreys and Russells—is situated in a little valley, surrounded by irregular eminences, clothed to their summits with beech trees, interspersed with box, larch, and holly, in a very picturesque manner. The house is said to have been

---

[78] Chequers takes its name from the King's Exchequer, he having palaces here and at Hawtree.

[79] On the death of Sir F. Russell, in 1664, who had been governor of Ely and Lichfield, and one of the Parliamentary Assessors in the time of the Civil Wars, as also one of Oliver Cromwell's lords, Sir John Russell, of Chippenham, having succeeded to the title, married Frances, youngest daughter of the Lord Protector Cromwell, relict of Robert Rich, son of Lord Rich, and grandson of Robert, Earl of Warwick, by which means so many relics of the Cromwells came into the possession of the family. Among the portraits are those of Cromwell when a child, and at mature age ; his mother ; his wife ; his son Richard, after-wards Protector ; and Henry, Lord Deputy of Ireland ; his eldest daughter, Bridget ; Elizabeth, wife of Mr. Claypole ; his third daughter, Mary, wife of Thomas Falconberg ; his youngest daughter, Frances, above named, who became possessed of Chequers. There are other mementos of the period preserved within these walls, in portraits of Thurloe, Lambert, Cornet Joyce, &c., as well as Cromwell's swords and slippers.

151

originally built about 1326, re-erected about 1566, and modernised, with great taste, by the late Sir Robert Greenhill Russell, Bart., and still more recently improved by its last possessor, Sir Robert Frankland Russell, Bart. It stands on a small but very elegant parterre, ornamented with beds of shrubs and flowers, and enclosed by a light iron fence.

CHEQUERS COURT.

The grounds are full of valuable records—associations with the past—near the south-west angle of the building are the remains of an elm known for centuries as King Stephen's tree, and said to have been one of sufficient magnitude even in his day to have supplied the monarch shade and shelter. It is banded with iron, and conjectured to have been at least

KING STEPHEN'S TREE.

coeval with the foundation of the house. It is only to he regretted that it could not have been the old Haw-tree of primeval celebrity, from which the family, who during many years inhabited the mansion, might be conjectured to have derived their name.

Yes, many happy, thoughtful, and, at least to ourselves, profitable, days, have we spent in that birth-county of liberty—Buckinghamshire ; but that of last autumn—when our visit was to the grave of William

Penn—was especially delightful, not only because of the places we examined, but because of the companionship of those who accompanied us on our way.

The country was reposing in all the self-satisfied luxury of an abundant harvest. The tangled hedges, rich in their winter store of 'blaes' and berries, were of every variety of tint ; the partridge whirred over the stubble ; and but few birds chaunted the vespers of summertime.

The foliage of the trees was hardly changed, and as we drove towards Beaconsfield, we passed some timber that might be called unrivalled. The tomb of EDMUND BURKE, who is buried in the village church, and who died in the house not far off, is worthy of a pilgrimage ; and to this Shrine—honourable alike to Ireland and to England—our earliest visit must be made ; but the neglected churchyard of Beaconsfield—where the dock and the nettle triumph over the graves, and pigs are permitted to go and come without hindrance—is sadly at war with the reverential feeling which the memory of an eloquent and able statesman—one upon whose words the senate hung, and whose eloquence told as much in the closet as in the crowded hall where his country's laws were made and defended—naturally summoned up. It was well to have looked upon his monument, and entered the pew where he had worshipped in earnestness and truth, and prayed for consolation during his time of trial. Our own memories and musings were, perhaps, a thought too much tinged with pride, because that he was a native of our own island—never more beloved than when most miserable ; and the galaxy of glorious names which have illuminated the whole world by their radiance, will always serve to show what its people might have been, but for the neglect and misconception of one party, and the unwise agitation of the other.

In this churchyard is the grave of another great man—that of Edmund Waller ; but the name of the poet is far less truly famous than that of the orator and statesman.

Hall Barn, the ancient mansion of the Wallers, was a large quadrangular edifice, now destroyed ; Gregories, another portion of the estate, was situated close to Beaconsfield Church, and here the poet resided in 1686, and his widow, after his death. Waller's tomb is one of the most conspicuous in the churchyard, and is of quaint and peculiar design, as will be seen from our faithful delineation of its aspect ; the

pyramid which surmounts the tomb is supported by skulls, to which
bat's wings are appended, a ghastly memento of the last end of man.

THE TOMB OF EDMUND WALLER.

Edmund Waller, the son of Robert Waller, Esq., of Agmonde-
sham, Bucks, and the descendant of an ancient and honourable family,
was born at Coleshill, Herts, on the 3rd of March, 1605. His mother, to
whom he was indebted for the early direction of his mind, was the sister
of the patriot John Hampden. He was twice married ; between the death
of the first, and his union with the second wife, the more valuable productions of his muse were given to the world. He had become the suitor
of the Lady Dorothea Sidney, daughter of the Earl of Leicester, whom
he immortalised as Saccharissa, a name 'formed, as he used to say,
pleasantly,' from *saccherum*, sugar. Yet he describes her as haughty
and scornful, and places the passion with which she inspired him in

contrast with his love for the more gentle Amoret. Although unsuccessful with both, his fate sat lightly on him.[80]

As a politician, he was unworthy his mother's blood ; fickle and unsteady—shifting like a weathercock—from the Commonwealth to the King, from the King to the Commonwealth, and then to the King again. Meanly securing his own safety, by appearing as a witness against his associates, in a conspiracy to overthrow the Commons when arrayed against the Crown, and whining out a pitiful moan for pardon at the Bar of the House, in which he had previously held the language and maintained the bearing of a man, he succeeded in purchasing his life at the expense of honour, and was for many years an exile in France. Through his various changes of fortune he was followed by his yielding and convenient muse. The most vigorous of all his poems is a 'Panegyrick to my Lord Protector,' whom he praises in the extreme of poetic extravagance ; but—the Second Charles ascends the throne, and the zealous royalist is ready with his greeting to the monarch 'upon his happy return.' The political poet, however, seems to have been estimated at his full value, and was left with no other recompense than his laurels.

He died in London, in the autumn of 1688, disappointed in his wish to have relinquished life on the spot that gave him birth, 'to die like the stag where he was rous'd.' He is described as possessing rare personal advantages, exceedingly eloquent, and as one of the most gallant and witty men of his time ; so much so, that, according to Clarendon, 'his company was acceptable where his spirit was odious.'

Waller obtained a reputation greater than his deserts. He has been absurdly styled the father of English verse—lauded as 'finding English poetry like the ore in the mine, some sparkling bits here and there, and leaving it refined and polished ;' and, 'as understanding our tongue the best of any man in England.' Even Dryden says, 'The excellence and dignity of rhyme were never fully known till Mr. Waller taught ;' and one of his biographers, after quoting the panegyrics of some of his contemporaries, adds, with stranger simplicity, 'we must confess there is something more great and noble in Milton.' As a lyrical poet, however, his claims upon our admiration are by no means inconsiderable. 'Waller's smoothness' was the theme of Pope ; but this is his chief merit. To

---

[80] Saccharissa and her lover met long after the spring of life had passed, and on her asking him 'when he would write such fine verses upon her again,' the poet somewhat ungallantly replied, 'O, madam when you are as young again!'

compare him with Shakspeare and Ben Jonson, his predecessors, or with Milton and Cowley, his contemporaries, even in smoothness, that second-rate quality of the poet, is absurd.

His mind was undoubtedly a narrow one. In his conceptions there was nothing grand nor lofty ; in all he produced there is not the slightest token that any topic of his muse had ever touched his heart. He was a flatterer—and a servile one. His devotion to women was mere gallantry—a fashion of the age in which he lived. Of tenderness, pathos, or that true love which breathes from the soul as well as the lips, he knew nothing.

How opposite in all things great and good was he to that far greater Poet whose home we visited next.

As the day advanced, we found ourselves in the primitive village of Chalfont, where Milton resided when, terror-stricken, he fled from the great plague of London, sheltering within a ragged vine-covered cottage, not far from that of his Friend Elwood the Quaker ; this house, at the extremity of the village, is supposed to have been built by some of the Fleetwood family, whose arms are over the door. Elwood's acquaintance with the poet resulted from Jeremy Pennington, son of the Mayor of London who was executed as a regicide in the days of Charles II., and 'he had an intimate acquaintance with Dr. Paget, a physician of note in London, and he with John Milton, a gentleman of great note for learning throughout the learned world, for the accurate pieces he had written on various subjects and occasions ; this person having filled a public station in the former times, lived now a private and retired life in London, and having wholly lost his sight, kept always a man to read to him, which usually was the son of some gentleman of his acquaintance whom in kindness he took to improve his learning.' For the advantage of thus reading with Milton Elwood took a lodging in Jewin Street. When the plague came, Milton desired him to take a house in the neighbourhood where he resided. He says, 'I took a pretty box for him in St. Giles's Chalfont, a mile from me, of which I gave him notice.' Elwood was imprisoned, but on his release he made a visit of welcome to him, and proposed 'Paradise Found' as a theme for the poet, and a pendant to his greater work. Milton made no answer ; but on his return to London wrote 'Paradise Regained,' and in a pleasant tone said to me, 'This is owing to you, for you put it into my head by the question you put to me at Chalfont, which before I had not thought of.'[81]

MILTON'S HOUSE AT CHALFONT.

We stood beneath the over-hanging beams, where a tall man could not more than stand erect. We noted the thick walls, the deep embrasure of the quaint windows, the ochrey hue of the cracked tiles, the ambitious roses, blushing beneath the broad vine-leaves, and vying in beauty with the purpling grapes ; the housewife's pride, sweet rosemary, which only flourishes where woman loves to labour ; the antique lavender knotted and knarled to the root but sending forth such spikes of fragrance, that the very earth was grey from its sweet blossoms ; the sheds around, such as an artist loves, their patched, worm-eaten roofs, mosaic'd by all hues and growths of mosses : the shining path-stones that marked the way from the low unprotecting gate to the house-door might have been hallowed by the poet's tread, and the huge trees on the other side of the road, screened him from the hot sun during his hours of meditation, or while listening for the horses' tramp, that told of news from the plague-stricken city. What a day of interest and emotions—of mysterious combinations between the present and the past—did we spend amid these scenes! how all the movement of our own actual times seemed low, and speculative, and void of high ambition. But *that* feeling did not often jar upon our senses ; there was so much to see beyond the beauty of the full, rich, ripe, glowing scenery of the hills and valleys, so much that

---

[81] Life of Elwood, by Himself.

made the heart beat and the eyelids moist, so much to make us proud
that England reared such men ; for we had recognised the outline of
those well-known hills—the Chilterns—where HAMPDEN drank in the
pure air of liberty ; and we had sheltered beneath the roof that sheltered
MILTON, and we had knelt beside the tomb of BURKE, and then forward!
to seek the grave of PENN, in the lonely burying-ground of Jordans!

But we have lost sight of the sad story of the Lady Mary Grey, and
its associations with the ancient and venerable Mansion of Chequers
Court ; we must therefore intreat the reader to accompany us thither
once again.

While we think over the sad destinies of many noble houses, some
claim more than others the sympathy it is impossible not to bestow, in
different degrees, upon all.   More of this has been given to the lovely
Queen of Scotland than perhaps to any other woman, and to the end of
time her history will suggest themes for poetry and painting ; but the
unoffending daughters of the house of Grey command, in addition to our
sympathy, feelings of reverence and respect winch cannot be yielded to
Mary Stuart.   The deplorable destiny of Lady Jane Grey, eldest born of
Henry, Duke of Suffolk, by the imperious daughter of Henry VII., is
recorded in one of the darkest pages of English history.   The fate of
Jane's sister Catherine was almost as unhappy,—in punishment for con-
tracting a marriage with the Earl of Hartford without previously obtaining the Queen's consent, she was doomed to the Tower ; where she
passed the remainder of her days, and was only liberated by God's
mercy, in 1567, from the vile prison-house of earthly bondage, in which
her youth and loveliness withered like a sickly plant deprived of light
and air.   One of the Harleian MSS. contains a most affecting paper entitled 'The manner of her departing,' which no eye can linger over without being dimmed by tears.   But there was yet another sister—from what
can be gathered, not over wise, or witty, or even blessed with comeli-
ness—appointed, in the spirit of concentrated cruelty, by the Queen, as
one of her Maids of Honour ; described by Cecil as the most diminutive
lady at Court, and by Sandford as slightly deformed.   It has been argued, that with the example of the fate of her two sisters before her, this
little creature should never have thought of matrimony!   Those who so
said, knew little of the deep-seated yearning in every woman's heart for
affection ; yet, in bestowing her affections upon the giant-like Serjeant
Porter—Mr. Thomas Keys—she doubtless considered he was far too
humble to be suspected of any 'treason,' and fancied that with her lowly

choice she might have been permitted to pass into the disgrace and ob-scurity, which would have been elysium compared to her position about the Royal person. But no. All the ruffs at court stood upright at the outrage perpetrated against propriety by the Lady Mary Grey. Sir Wil-liam Cecil noted it in a letter to Sir Thomas Smith, saying, 'The Ser-jeant-Porter, being the biggest gentillman in all this Court, hath marryed secretly the Lady Mary Grey, the *lest* (*i.e.,* smallest) in all the Court. They are committed to several prisons ;' and again, *'the offence is very great.'*

It was evident that her Royal Mistress lay in wait for an opportu-nity to destroy the last of these ill-starred sisters. The insignificance of the 'great giant Porter ;' the witlessness and simplicity of his lady-wife ; their utter incapacity to injure or even offend, might have protected them against any tyrant in the world—even in those days—except Elizabeth Tudor ; but the indignation of the sycophant court rose in arms against the sister of Lady Jane Grey! And in the State-Paper Office are some documents, a portion in the handwriting of Sir William Cecil, entitled 'Articles for the Examination of the Lady Mary Grey.' The marriage was performed, it appears, by a somewhat unsightly priest—'old, fat, and of low stature'—in the 'Serjeant Porter's Chamber ; by the Water Gate, at Westminster ;' and the questions asked at that examination were no less frivolous than impertinent ; the little gifts she confesses to—the 'love-tokens'—are touching from their simplicity. The 'giant-lover' had given her first 'two little' rings'; next 'a ring with four rubies and a diamond ;' 'a chain,' and 'a little hanging bottle of mother-of-pearl.' The honeymoon was certainly passed in separate prisons ; two days after the marriage was known to the Queen ; the husband was committed to the Fleet ; and a letter was dispatched to the keeper, stating that 'her Majesty had taken his *offence much to heart.'* The words in italics are underlined in the original.

The poor lady's immediate fate is more obscure ; but at last it was determined by the PRIVY COUNCIL that she should be sent to the country, and given in charge to a certain Mr. Hawtrey, of 'Chequers,' in Buck-inghamshire ; there to remain *'without conference with any, suffering* only one waiting-woman to attend upon her, without liberty of going abrode, for whose charges the Queen's Majesty will see him the said Mr. Hawtrey, *in reason,* satisfied ;' subsequently, however, the Lady Mary was allowed a groom as well as a gentlewoman, and the clause concerning her 'going abroad' was in a degree modified.

Any one not sleeping under the nightmare of Elisabeth, and whose dreams were not disturbed by memories of the absent, must have enjoyed Chequers Court, even as a prison! It is a place to linger in and love, a delicious vision of beauty and romance, one of the 'places'—see one ever so many—that can never be forgotten.

Whether the poor prisoner was permitted to wander over 'velvet lawn,' or visit the 'silver spring,' or enjoy the refreshment of the 'happy valley,' we cannot now ascertain ; the persecutor and the persecuted have long since gone to 'their account ;' and the dark waters of oblivion have passed over the sufferings of the young bride. Perhaps she never lost herself or her sorrows in the labyrinths of the hill, she could not oven see from the window of her attic. We must not look upon those abundant beauties, and conjure her fairy-like form as adding to their interest.

It seems that Lady Mary was removed from Chequers Court after an imprisonment of two years, and delivered to the care of her maternal step-mother, the Dowager Duchess of Suffolk, who lived—in the Minories! but the Mineries *then* and *now* were very different. Still the change must have been great from Chequers, to a neighbourhood so unhealthy. Her step-mother had small 'plenishing' to store her rooms, and even entreats the Queen to lend her 'some old silver pots to fetch her drink in.' 'A basin and an ewer,' she adds in a housewifely letter extant, 'I fear were too much ; but what it shall please her Majesty to apoint for her (*i.e.*, the Lady Mary), shall be always redy to be delyvered againe whensoever it shal please her Majestie to call for it.'

The Queen seems to have had pleasure in moving her victim from place to place, for we next find her under the roof of Sir Thomas Gresham, who sorely felt the heavy weight of the charge ; frequently, during a period of three years, praying she should be removed from him. Toward the latter end of this time poor Keys died, most likely in prison. Sir Thomas writes that she (Lady Mary) hath grievously taken his death, and that she desires the Queen's leave *to keep and bring up his children.* The entire kindness and lovingness of her nature is greatly shown in this simple and beautiful request ; moreover, during his lifetime, though she had always signed herself 'Mary Grey,' doubtless to pleasure Elizabeth, after his death her womanly sense of right conquered every other feeling, and in her heart's first grief she signed herself 'Mary Keys.'

In process of time her liberty was restored, and it may be she was restored also to what the world would call 'favour ;' for on the first of January, 1577-8, she presented the Queen at Hampton Court with 'two pair of swete gloves, with foure dozen buttons of golde, in every one a side perle, and received in return a cup with a cover weighing eighteen ounces.

Soon after this she died—on the 20th of April, 1578—in the parish of St, Botolph Without Aldersgate.

Truly the memory of this simple-minded and most unfortunate lady, was more with us at Chequers Court than was perhaps consistent with more striking and important associations. The sombre air of several of the rooms, the stillness and loneliness of the scene, the deep shadows that came and went, seemed to belong especially to this youngest of three most unfortunate sisters. And yet, but for the persecution and persevering cruelty of Queen Elizabeth, we should not have given a sigh to the memory of that sister of 'Lady Jane Grey,' who could so far forget herself as to marry the Serjeant-Porter of the palace which some might have held to be her birthright? Such will be the invariable result of persecution.

The Garden of Sir Thomas More.

HILE living in the neighbourhood of Chelsea, we determined to look upon the few broken walls that once enclosed the residence of Sir Thomas More—a man, who, despite the bitterness inseparable from a persecuting age, was of most wonderful goodness as well as intellectual power. We first read over the memories of him preserved by Erasmus, Hoddesdon, Roper, Aubrey, his own namesake, and others. It is pleasant to muse over the past, —pleasant to know that much of malice and bigotry has departed, to return no more, —that the prevalence of a spirit which could render even Sir Thomas More unjust, and, to seeming, cruel, is passing away. Though we do implicitly believe there would be no lack of great hearts, and brave hearts, at the present day, if it were necessary to bring them to the test— still, there have been few men like unto him. It is a pleasant, and a profitable task, so to sift through past ages, as to separate the wheat from the chaff—to see, when the feelings of party and prejudice sink to their proper insignificance, how the morally great stands forth in its own dignity, bright, glorious, and everlasting. St. Evremond sets forth the firmness and constancy of Petronius Arbiter in his last moments, and imagines he discovers in them a softer nobility of mind and resolution, than in the deaths of Seneca, Cato, or Socrates himself ; but Addison says, and we cannot but think truly, 'that if he was so well pleased with gaiety of humour in a dying man, he might have found a much more noble instance of it in Sir Thomas More, who died upon a point of religion, and is respected as a martyr by that side for which he suffered.' What was pious philosophy in this extraordinary man, might seem phrensy in any one who does not resemble him as well in the cheerfulness of his temper as in the sanctity of his life and manners.

Oh, that some such man as he were to sit upon our woolsack now ; what would the world think, if when the mighty oracle commanded the next cause to come on, the reply should be, *'Please your good lordship, there is no other!'* Well might the smart epigrammatist write :—

> When MORE some time had Chancellor been,
> No MORE suits did remain ;
> The same shall never MORE be seen,
> Till MORE be there again!

We mused over the history of his time until we slept—and dreamed : and first in our dream we saw a fair meadow, and it was sprinkled over with white daisies, and a bull was feeding therein ; and as we looked upon him he grew fatter and fatter, and roared in the wantonness of power and strength, so that the earth trembled ; and he plucked the branches off the trees, and trampled on the ancient enclosures of the meadow, and as he stormed, and bellowed and destroyed, the daisies became human heads, and the creature flung them about and warmed his hoofs in the hot blood that flowed from them ; and we grew sick and sorry at heart, and thought, is there no one to slay the destroyer? And when we looked again, the Eighth Harry was alone in the meadow ; and, while many heads were lying upon the grass, some kept perpetually bowing before him, while others sung his praises as wise, just, and merciful. Then we heard a trumpet ringing its scarlet music through the air, and we stood in the old tilt-yard at Whitehall, and the pompous Wolsey, the bloated King, the still living Holbein, the picturesque Surrey, the Aragonian Catharine, the gentle Jane, the butterfly Anne Bullen, the coarse-seeming but wise-thinking Ann of Cleves, the precise Catherine Howard, and the stout-hearted Catherine Parr, passed us so closely by, that we could have touched their garments—then a bowing troop of Court gallants came on—others whose names and actions you may read of in history—and then the hero of our thoughts, Sir Thomas More— well dressed, for it was a time of pageants—was talking somewhat apart to his pale-faced friend Erasmus, while 'Son Roper,' as the Chancellor loved to call his son in law, stood watchfully and respectfully a little on one aide. Even if we had never seen the pictures Holbein painted of his first patron, we should have known him by the bright benevolence of his aspect, the singular purity of his complexion, his penetrating yet gentle eyes, and the incomparable grandeur with which virtue and independence dignified even an indifferent figure. His smile was so catching that the most broken hearted were won by it to forgot their sorrows ; and his voice, low and sweet though it was, was so distinct that we heard it above all the coarse jests, loud music, and trumpet calls of the vain and idle crowd. And while we listened, we awoke ; resolved next day to make our Pilgrimage, perfectly satisfied at the outset, that though no fewer than four houses in Chelsea contend for the honour of his residence, Doctor King's arguments in favour of the site being the same as that of Beaufort House—upon the greater part of which now stands Beaufort-row-are the most conclusive ; those who are curious in the matter can go and see his manuscripts in the British Museum. Passing Beaufort-row, we proceeded straight on to the turn leading to the Chelsea *Clock-house.*

CLOCK HOUSE.

It is an old, patched-up, rickety dwelling, containing perhaps but few of the original stones, yet interesting as being the lodge-entrance to the offices of Beaufort House ; remarkable, also, as the dwelling of a family of the name of Howard, who have occupied it for more than a hundred years, the first possessor being gardener to Sir Hans Sloane, into whose possession, after a lapse of years, and many changes, a portion of Sir Thomas More's property had passed. This Howard had skill in the distilling of herbs and perfumes, which his descendant carries on to this day. We lifted the heavy brass knocker, and were admitted into the 'old clock-house.' The interior shows evident marks of extreme age, the flooring being ridgy and seamed, bearing their marks with a discontented creaking—like the secret murmurs of a faded beauty against her wrinkles! On the counter stood a few frost-bitten geraniums ; and drawers, containing various roots and seeds, were ranged round the walls, while above them were placed good stout quart and pint bottles of distilled waters. The man would have it that the 'clock-house' was the 'real original' lodge-entrance to 'Beaufort House ;' and so we agreed it might have been, but not, *perhaps,* built during Sir Thomas More's lifetime. To this insinuation he turned a deaf ear, assuring us that his family, having lived there so long, must know all about it, and that the brother of Sir Hans Sloane's gardener had made the great clock in old Chelsea Church, as the church books could prove. 'You can, if you please,' he said, 'go under the archway at the side of this house, leading into the Moravian chapel and burying-ground, where the notice, that "within are the Park-chapel Schools," is put up.' And that is quite true ; the Moravians now only use the chapel which was erected in their burying-ground to perform an occasional funeral service in, and so they 'let it' to the infant school. The burying-ground is very pretty in the summer time. Its space occupies only a small portion of the Chancellor's garden ; part of the walls are very old, and the south one certainly belonged to Beaufort House. There have been some who trace out a Tudor arch and one or two Gothic windows as having been filled up with more modern mason-work ; but that may be fancy. There seems no doubt that the Moravian chapel stands on the site of the old stables.

'Then,' we said, 'the clock-house could only have been at the entrance to the offices.' The man looked for a moment a little hurt at this observation, as derogatory to the dignity of his dwelling ; but he smiled, and said 'Perhaps so ;' and very good-naturedly showed us the cemetery of this interesting people. Indeed, their original settlement in Chelsea is quite a romance. The chapel stands to the left of the burying-ground, which is entered by a primitive wicket-gate ; it forms a square of thick grass, crossed by broad gravel walks, kept with the greatest neatness. The tomb-stones are all flat, and the graves not raised above the level of the sward. They are of two sizes only : the larger for grown persons, the smaller for children. The inscriptions on the grave-stones, in general, seldom record more than the names and ages of the persons interred. The men are buried in one division, the women in another. We read one or two of the names, and they were quaint and strange : 'Anne Rypheria Hurloch ;' 'Anna Benigna La Trobe ;' and one was especially interesting, James Gillray, forty years sexton to this simple cemetery, and father of Gillray, the H.B. of the past century. One thing pleased us mightily—the extreme old age to which all the dwellers in this house seemed to have attained.

A line of ancient trees runs along the back of the narrow gardens of
Millman's-row, —which is parallel with, but farther from town than,
Beaufort-row, — and affords a grateful shade in the summer time. We
resolved to walk quietly round, and then enter the chapel. How strange
the changes of the world! The graves of a simple peace-loving, unambi-
tious people were lying around us, and yet it was the place which Erasmus describes as 'Sir Thomas More's estate, purchased at Chelsey,' and
where 'he built him a house, neither mean nor subject to envy, yet magnificent and commodious enough.' How dearly he loved this place, and
how much care he bestowed upon it, can be gathered from the various
documents still extant.[82] The bravery with which, soon after he was
elected a burgess to Parliament, he opposed a subsidy demanded by
Henry the Seventh, with so much power that he won the Parliament to
his opinion, and incensed the King so greatly, that out of revenge he
committed the young barrister's father to the Tower, and fined him in
the fine of a hundred pounds! That bravery remained with him to the
last and with it was mingled the simplicity which so frequently and so
beautifully blends with the intellectuality that seems to belong to a higher
world than this. When he 'took to marrying,' he fancied the second
daughter of a Mr. Colt, a gentleman of Essex ; yet when he considered
the pain it must give the eldest to see her sister preferred before her, he
gave up his first love, and framed his fancy to the elder. This lady died,

---

[82] After the death of More this favourite home of his, where he had so frequently gathered 'a choice company of men distinguished by their genius and learning,' passed into the
rapacious hands of his bad Sovereign, and by him was presented to Sir William Pawlet
ultimately Lord High Treasurer and Marquis of Winchester ; from his hands it passed into
Lord Dacre's, to whom succeeded Lord Burghley ; then followed his son, the Earl o
Salisbury, as its master ; from him it passed successively to the Earl of Lincoln, Sir Arthur
Gorges, the Earl of Middlesex, Villiers, Duke of Buckingham, Sir Bulstrode Whitelock
the second Duke of Buckingham, the Earl of Bristol, the Duke of Beaufort, and ultimately
to Sir Hans Sloane, who obtained it in 1738, and after keeping it but two years razed it to
the ground ; an unhappy want of reverence on the part of the great naturalist for the home
of so many great men. There is a print of it by J. Knyff, in 1699, which is copied over
leaf ; it shows some old features, but it had then been enlarged and altered. Erasmus ha
well described it as it was in More's lifetime. It had 'a chapel, a library, and a gallery
called the New Buildings, a good distance from his main-house, wherein his custom was to
busy himself in prayer and meditation, whensoever he was at leisure.' Heywood, in his *I
Moro* (Florence, 1556), describes 'the garden as wonderfully charming, both from the
advantages of its site, for from one part almost the whole of the noble city of London was
visible ; and from the other, the beautiful Thames, with green meadows by woody emi
nences all around ; and also for its own beauty, for it was crowned with an almost perpet
ual verdure.' At one side was a small green eminence to command the prospect.

after having brought him four children ; but his second choice, Dame Alice, has always seemed to us a punishment and a sore trial.   And yet how beautifully does Erasmus describe his mode of living in this very place :—'He converseth with his wife, his son, his daughter-in-law, his three daughters and their husbands, with eleven grandchildren.   There is not a man living so affectionate to his children as he.   He loveth his old wife as if she were a young maid ; he persuadeth her to play on the lute, and so with the like gentleness he ordereth his family.   Such is the excellence of his temper, that whatsoever happenoth that could not be helped, he loveth, as if nothing could have happened more happily.   You would say there was in that place Plato's academy ; but I do his house an injury in comparing it to Plato's academy, where there were only disputatious of numbers and geometrical figures, and sometimes of moral virtues.   I should rather call his house a school, or university of Christian religion ; for though there is none therein but readeth and studyoth the liberal sciences, their special care is piety and virtue.'[83]

The King was used to visit his 'beloved Chancellor' here for days together to admire his terrace overhanging the Thames, to row in his state barge, to ask opinions upon divers matters, and it is said that the royal answer to Luther was composed under the Chancellor's revising eye.   Still, the penetrating vision of Sir Thomas was in no degree obscured by this glitter.   One day, the King came unexpectedly to Chelsea,

---

[83] The conduct of this great man's house was a model to all, and as near an approach to his own Utopia as might well be.   Erasmus says, 'I should rather call his house a school or university of Christian religion, for though there is none therein but readeth and stedyeth the liberal sciences ; their special care is piety and virtue ; there is no quarrelling or intemperate words heard ; none seen idle ; which household discipline that worthy gentleman doth not govern, but with all kind and courteous benevolence.'   The servant-men abode on one side of the house, the women on another, and met at prayer-time, or on church festivals, when More would read and expound to them.   He suffered no cards or dice, but gave each one his garden-plot for relaxation, or set them to sing, or play music.'   He had an affection for all who truly served him, and his daughters' nurse is as affectionately remembered in his letters when from home as are they themselves.   'Thomas More sendeth greeting to his most dear daughters Margaret, Elizabeth, and Cecily ; and to Margaret Giggs, as dear to him as if she were his own,' are his words in one letter ; and his valued and trustworthy domestics appear in the family pictures of the family by Holbein. They requited his attachment by truest fidelity and love ; and his daughter, Margaret, in her last passionate interview with her father on his way to the Tower, was succeeded by Margaret Giggs and a maid-servant, who embraced and kissed their condemned master, 'of whom he said after, it was homely but very lovingly done.'   Of these and other of his servants, Erasmus remarks, 'after Sir Thomas More's death, none ever was touched with the least suspicion of any evil fame.'

and, having dined, walked with Sir Thomas for the space of an hour in the garden, having his arm about his neck. We pleased ourselves with the notion that they walked where then we stood! Well might such condescension cause his son Roper—for whom he entertained so warm an affection—to congratulate his father upon such condescension, and to remind him that he had never seen his Majesty approach such familiarity with any one, save once, when he was seen to walk arm in arm with Cardinal Wolsey. 'I thank our Lord,' answered Sir Thomas, 'I find his Grace my very good Lord, indeed ; and I do believe, he doth as singularly love me as any subject within the realm ; however, son Roper, I may tell thee I have no cause to be proud thereof, for if my head should win him a castle in France, it should not fail to go off.'

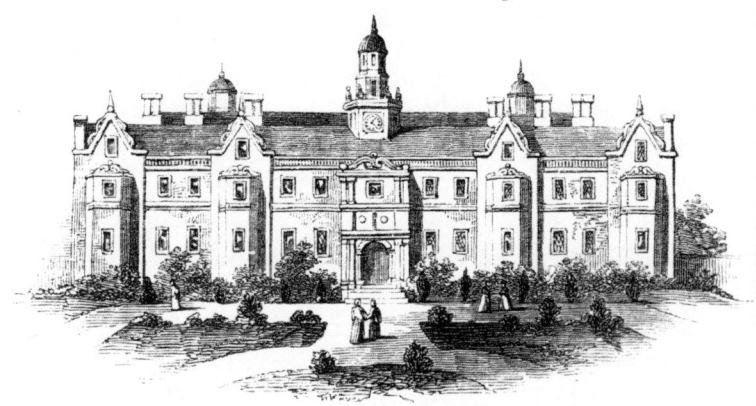

MORE'S HOUSE.

With the exception of his own family (and his wife formed an exception here), there are few indeed of his cotemporaries, notwithstanding the eulogiums they are prone to heap upon him, who understood the elevated and unworldly character of this extraordinary man.

The Duke of Norfolk, coming one day to dine with him, found him in Chelsea Church, singing in the choir, with his surplice on. 'What! what!' exclaimed the Duke, 'What, what my Lord Chancellor a parish clerk!—a parish clerk! you dishonour the King and his office.' And how exquisite his reply, 'Nay, you may not think your master and mine will be offended with me for serving God his master, or thereby count his office dishonoured.' Another reply to the same abject noble, is well graven on our memory. He expostulated with him, like many of his other friends, for braving the King's displeasure. 'By the mass, Master More,' he said, 'it is perilous striving with princes ; therefore I wish you somewhat to incline to the King's pleasure, for *"indignatio Principis mors est."'* 'And is that all, my lord?' replied this man, so much above all paltry considerations ; 'then in good faith the difference between your Grace and me is but this—that I may die to-day, and you tomorrow.'

CHELSEA CHURCH.

He took great delight in beautifying Chelsea Church, although he had a private chapel of his own ; and when last there they told us the painted window had been his gift. It must have been a rare sight to see the Chancellor of England sitting with the quire ; and yet there was a fair share of pomp in the manner of his servitor bowing at his lady's pew, when the service of the mass was ended, and saying, 'My lord is gone *before*.' But the day after he resigned the great seal of England (of which his wife knew nothing) Sir Thomas presented himself at the pew-door, and, after the fashion of his servitor, quaintly said, 'Madam, my lord is *gone*.' The vain woman could not comprehend his meaning, which, when, during their short walk home, he fully explained, she was greatly pained thereby, lamenting it with exceeding bitterness of spirit.

We fancied we could trace a gothic door or window in the wall ; but our great desire would have been to discover the water-gate from which he took his departure the morning he was summoned to Lambeth to take the oath of supremacy. True to what he believed right, he of-

fered up his prayers and confessions in Chelsea Church, and then returning to his own house, took an affectionate farewell of his wife and
children, forbidding them to accompany him to the Watergate, as was
their custom, fearing, doubtless, that his mighty heart could not sustain a
prolonged interview. Who could paint the silent parting between him
and all he loved so well—the boat waiting at the foot of the stairs—the
rowers in their rich liveries, while their hearts, heavy with apprehension
for the fate of him they served, still trusted that nothing could be found
to harm so good a master—the pale and earnest countenance of 'son
Roper,' wondering at the calmness, at such a time, which more than all
other things bespeaks the master mind. For a moment his hand lingered
on the gate, and in fastening the simple latch his fingers trembled, and
then he took his seat by his son's side ; and in another moment the boat
was flying through the waters. For some time he spoke no word, but
communed with and strengthened his great heart by holy thoughts ; then
looking straight into his son Roper's eyes, while his own brightened with
a glorious triumph, he exclaimed in the fulness of his rich-toned voice,
'I thank our Lord, the field is won.' It was no wonder that overwhelmed with apprehension, his son-in-law could not apprehend his
meaning then, but afterwards bethought him that he signified how he had
conquered the world.

The Abbot of Westminster took him that same day into custody, on
his refusal to 'take the King as head of his Church ;' and upon his repeating this refusal four days afterwards, he was committed to the
Tower. Then, indeed, these heretofore bowers of bliss echoed to the
weak and wavering complaints of his proud wife, who disturbed him
also in his prison by her desires, so vain and so worldly, when compared
with the elevated feelings of his dear daughter Margaret.

How did the fond foolish woman seek to shake his purpose? 'Seeing,' she said, 'you have a house at Chelsea, a right fair house, your
library, your gallery, your garden, your orchard, and all other necessaries so handsome about you, where you might in company with me
your wife, your children, and household, be merry, I marvel that you,
who have been always taken for so wise a man, can be content thus to be
shut up among mice and rats, and, too, when you might be abroad at
your liberty, and with the favour and good will both of the King and his
council, if you would but do as all the bishops and best learned men of
the realm have done.'

And then not even angered by her folly, seeing how little was given her to understand, he asked her if the house in Chelsea was any nearer Heaven than the gloomy one he then occupied? ending his pleasant yet wise parleying with a simple question :—

'Tell me,' he said, 'good Mistress Alice, how long do you think might we live and enjoy that same house?'

She answered, 'Some twenty years.'

'Truly,' he replied, 'if you had said some thousand years, it might have been somewhat ; and yet he were a very bad merchant who would put himself in danger to lose eternity for a thousand years. How much the rather if we are not sure to enjoy it one day to an end?'

It is for the glory of women, that his daughter Margaret, while she loved and honoured him past all telling, strengthened his noble nature ; for, writing him during his fifteen months' imprisonment in the Tower, she asks, in words not to be forgotten, 'What do you think, most dear father, doth comfort us at Chelsey in this your absence? Surely the re-membrance of your manner of life passed amotigst us—your holy con-versation—your wholesome counsels—your examples of virtue, of which there is hope that they do not only persevere with you, but that they are by God's grace much more increased.'

After the endurance of fifteen months' imprisonment, he was ar-raigned, tried, and found guilty of denying the King's supremacy.

Alack! is there no painter of English history bold enough to im-mortalise himself by painting this trial? Sir Thomas More was beheaded on Tower Hill, in the bright sunshine of the month of July, on its fifth day, 1535, the King remitting the disgusting quartering of the quivering flesh, because of his 'high office.' When told of the King's 'mercy,' 'Now, God forbid,' he said, 'the King should use any more such to any of my friends ; and God bless all my posterity from such pardons.'

One man of all the crowd who wept at his death, reproached him with a decision he had given in Chancery. More, nothing discomposed, replied, that if it were still to do, he would give the same decision. This happened twelve months before. And, while the last scene was enacting on Tower Hill, the King, who had walked in this very garden with his arm round the neck which by his command the axe had severed, was playing at Tables in Whitehall, Queen Anne Bullen looking on ; and when told that Sir Thomas More was dead, casting his eyes upon the

pretty fool that had glittered in his pageants, he said, 'Thou art the cause
of this man's death.'—The COWARD! to seek to turn upon a thing so
weak as that, the heavy sin which clung to his own soul!

Some say the body lies in Chelsea Church, beneath the tomb we
have sketched—the epitaph having been written by himself before he
anticipated the manner of his death.[84] It is too long to insert ; but the
lines at the conclusion are very like the man. The epitaph and poetry are
in Latin : we give the translation :—

> "For Alice and for Thomas More's remains
> Prepared, this tomb Johanna's form contains.
> One, married young ; with mutual ardour blest,
> A boy and three fair girls our joy confest.
> The other (no small praise), of these appear'd
> As fond as if by her own pangs endeared.
> One lived with me, one lives, in such sweet strife,
> Slight preference could I give to either wife.
> Oh! had it met Heaven's sanction and decree,
> One hallow'd bond might have united three ;
> Yet still be ours one grave, one lot on high!
> Thus death, what life denied us, shall supply."

Others tell that his remains were interred in the Tower,[85] and some
record that the head was sought and preserved by that same daughter
Margaret, who caused it to be buried in the family vault of the Ropers,
in St. Dunstan's Church, Canterbury ;[86] and they add a pretty legend

---

[84] Wood and Weever both affirm that the body of More was first deposited in the
Tower Chapel, but was subsequently obtained by his devoted and accomplished daughte
Margaret Roper, and re-interred in Chelsea Church, in the tomb he had finished in 1532
the year in which he had surrendered the Chancellorship, and resolved to abide the issue o
his conscientious opposition to the King's wishes, as if he felt that the tomb should then be
prepared.

[85] Faulkner, in his history of Chelsea, adheres to this opinion, and says that the tomb
in that church is but 'an empty cenotaph.' His grandson, in his Life, says, 'his body was
buried in the Chapel of St. Peter, in the Tower, in the belfry, or, as some say, as one
entereth into the vestry ;' and he does not notice the story of his daughter's re-interment of
it elsewhere.

[86] The Ropers lived at Canterbury, in St. Dunstan's Street. The house is destroyed
and a brewery occupies its site ; but the picturesque old gateway, of red brick, still re
mains, and is engraved above. Margaret Roper, the noble-hearted, learned, and favourite
daughter of More, resided here with her husband until her death, in 1544, nine years afte
the execution of her father, when she was buried in the family vault at St. Dunstan's
where she had reverently placed the head of her father. The story of her piety is thus told

how that, when his head was upon London-bridge, Margaret would be rowed beneath it, and, nothing horrified at the sight, say aloud, 'That head has layde many a time in my lappe ; would to God, would to God,

it would fall into my lappe as I passe under now,' and the head did so fall, and she carried it in her 'lappe until she placed it in her husband's, 'son Roper's' vault, at Canterbury.

The King took possession of these fair grounds at Chelsea, and all the Chancellor's other property, namely, Dunkington, Trenkford, and Benley Park, in Oxfordshire, allowing the widow be had made, twenty pounds per year for her life, and indulging his petty tyranny still more by imprisoning Sir Thomas's daughter Margaret, 'both because she kept her father's head for a relic, and that she meant to set her

TOMB.

by Cresacre More, in his life of his grandfather, Sir Thomas : —'His head having remained about a month upon London Bridge, and being to be cast into the Thames, because room should be made for divers others, who in plentiful sort suffered martyrdom for the same supremacy, shortly after, it was bought by his daughter Margaret, lest, as she stoutly affirmed before the council, being called before them after for the matter, it should be food for fishes ; which she buried, where she thought fittest.' Anthony-a-Wood says that she preserved it in a leaden box, and placed it in her tomb 'with great devotion ;' and in 1715 Dr. Rawlinson told Hearne, the antiquary, that he had seen it there 'enclosed in an iron-grate.' This was fully confirmed in 1835, when the chancel of the church being repaired, the Roper vault was opened, and several persons descended into it, and saw the skull in a leaden box, something like a bee-hive ; open in the front, and which was placed in a square recess in the wall, with an iron-grating before it. A drawing was made, which was engraved in the *Gentleman's Magazine* of May, 1837, which we have copied in our initial letter ; Summerly, in his Handbook to Canterbury, says—'in the print there, however, the opening in the leaden box enclosing the head is made oval, whereas it should be in the form of a triangle.' We have therefore so corrected our copy.

father's works in print.'

We were calling to mind more minute particulars of the charities and good deeds of this great man, when, standing at the moment opposite a grave where some loving hand had planted two standard rose-trees, we suddenly heard a chant of children's voices, the infant scholars singing their little hymn—the tune, too, was a well-known and popular melody, and very sweet yet sad of sound—it was just such music as, for its simplicity, would have been welcome to the mighty dead ; and, as we entered among the little songsters, the past faded away, and we found ourselves speculating on the hopeful present.

ROPER'S HOUSE.

The Grave of Edmund Burke.

 T has been said that we are inclined to overvalue great men when their graves have been long green, or their monuments grey above them, we believe it is only then we estimate them as they deserve. Prejudice and falsehood have no enduring vitality, and posterity is generally anxious to render justice to the mighty dead ; we dwell upon their actions,— we quote their sentiments and opinions,—we class them amongst our household gods—and keep their memories green within the sanctuary of our HOMES ; we read to our children and friends the written treasures bequeathed to us by the genius and independence of the great statesmen and orators—the men of literature and science—who *'have been.'* We adorn our minds with the poetry of the past, and value it, as well we may, as far superior to that of the present : we sometimes, by the aid of imagination,—one of the highest of God's gifts—bring great men before us : we hear the deep-toned voices and see the flashing eyes of some, who it may be, taught kings their duty, or quelled the tumults of a factious people : we listen to the lay of the minstrel, or the orator's addresses to the assembly, and our pulses throb and our eyes moisten as the eloquence flows—first, as a gentle river, until gaining strength in its progress, it sweeps onwards like a torrent, overcoming all that sought to impede its progress. What a happy power this is!—what a glorious triumph ever time!—recalling or creating at will!—peopling our small chamber with the demigods of history ; viewing them enshrined in their perfections, untainted by the world ; hearing their exalted sentiments ; knowing them as we know a noble statue or a beautiful picture, without the taint of age or feebleness, or the mildew of decay.

If these sweet waking dreams were more frequent, we should be happier ; yes, and better than we are ; we should be shamed out of much baseness—for nothing so purifies and exalts the soul as the actual or imaginary companionship of the pure and the exalted ; no man who purposed to create a noble picture would choose an imperfect model ; no

175

one who seeks virtue and cherishes honour and honour-able things, will endure the degradation of ignoble persons or ignoble thoughts ; no one ever achieved a great purpose who did not plant his standard on high ground.

A little before the commencement of the present century, England was rich in orators, and poets, and men of letters ; the times were favourable to such—events called them forth—and there was still a lingering chivalric feeling in our island which the utilitarian principles or tastes of the present period would now treat with neglect, if not contempt.

The progress of the French Revolution agitated Europe ; and men wondered if the young Corsican would ever dare to wield the sceptre wrenched from the grasp of a murdered king ; people were continually on the watch for fresh events ; great stakes were played for all over Europe, and those who desired change were full of hope. It was an age to create great men.

Let us then indulge in visions of those, who, in mere recent times that we have yet touched upon,—save in one or two PILGRIMAGES,—illumed the later days of the last century ; and, brightest and purest of the galaxy was the orator, EDMUND BURKE. Ireland, which gave him birth, may well be proud of the high-souled and high-gifted man, who united in himself all the great qualities which command attention in the senate and the world, and all the domestic virtues that sanctify home ; grasping a knowledge of all things, and yet having that sweet sympathy with the small things of life, which at once bestows and secures happiness, and, in the end, popularity.

EDMUND BURKE was born on Arran Quay, Dublin, January the 1st, 1730; his father was an attorney : the name, we believe, was originally spelt Bourke. The great grandfather of Edmund inherited some property in that county which has produced so many man of talent—the county of Cork ; the family resided in the neighbourhood of Castletown Roche, four or five miles from Doneraile, five or six miles from Mallow—now a railroad station—and nearly the same distance from the ruins of Kilcolman Castle, whose every mouldering stone is hallowed by the memory of the poet Spenser and his dear friend, "the Shepherd of the Ocean," Sir Walter Raleigh. There can be little doubt that Edmund—a portion of whose young life was passed in this beautiful locality—imbibed much thought, as well as much poetry, from the sacred memories which here accompanied him during his wanderings.

Nothing so thoroughly awakens the sympathy of the young as the imaginary presence of the good and great amid the scenes where their most glorious works were accomplished ; the associations connected with Kilcolman are so mingled, that their contemplation produces a variety of emotions—admiration for the poem which was created within its walls—contemplation of the "glorious two" who there spent so much time together in harmony and sweet companionship despite the storms which ravaged the country ; then the awful catastrophe, the burning of the castle, and the loss of Spenser's child in the flames, still talked of in the neighbourhood, were certain to make a deep impression on the imagination of a boy whose delicate health prevented his rushing into the amusements and society of children of his own age. There are plenty of crones in every village, and one at least in every gentleman's house to watch 'the master's children' and pour legendary lore into their willing ears, accompanied by snatches of song and fairy tale. All these were certain to seize upon such an imagination as that of Burke, and lay the foundation of much of that high-souled mental poetry—one of his great characteristics ; indeed, the circumstances of his youth were highly favourable to his peculiar temperament—his delicate constitution rendered him naturally susceptible of the beautiful ; and the locality of the Blackwater, and the time-honoured ruins of Kilcolman, with its history and traditions, nursed, as they wore, by the holy quiet of a country life, had ample time to sink into his soul and germinate the fruitage which, in after years, attained such rich perfection.

An old schoolmaster, of the name of O'Halloran, was his first teacher ; he "played at learning" at the school, long since in ruins ; and the Dominie used to boast that 'no matter how great Master Edmund (God bless him) was, HE was the first who ever put a latin grammar into his hands.'

Edmund was one of a numerous family ; his mother, who had been a Miss Nagle,[87] having had fourteen or fifteen children, all of whom died young, except four,—one sister ; and three brothers : the sister, Mrs. French, was brought up in the faith of her mother, who was a rigid Roman Catholic, while the sons were trained in their father's belief,

---

[87] Sylvanus Spenser, the eldest son of the Poet Spenser, married Ellen Nagle, elder daughter of David Nagle, Esq., ancestor of the lady, who was mother to Edmund Burke.

this, happily, created no unkindness between them, for not only were they an affectionate and a united family, but perfectly charitable in their opinions, each of the other's creed. As the future statesman grew older, it was considered wise to remove him to Dublin for better instruction, and he was placed at a school in Smithfield kept by a Mr. James Fitzgerald ; but, fortunately for his strength of body and mind, the reputation of an academy in the lovely valley of Ballitore, founded in the midst of a colony of Quakers, by a member of that most benevolent and intelligent society—the well-known Abraham Shackleton—was spreading far and wide ; and there the three young Burkes were sent in 1741, Edmund being then twelve year's old.

He was considered not so much brilliant, as of steady application. Here, too, he was remarkable for quick comprehension, and great strength of memory ; indications which drew forth at first the commendation, and as his powers unfolded, the warm regard of his master ; under whose paternal care, the improvement of his health kept pace with that of his intellect, and the grateful pupil never forgot his obligations : a truly noble mind is prone to exaggerate kindnesses received, and never detracts from their value ; it is only the low and the narrow-minded who underrate the benefits they have been blessed with at any period of their lives.

In 1743 he entered Trinity College, Dublin, as a pensioner. He gained fair honours during his residence there, but, like Johnson, Swift, Goldsmith, and other eminent men, he did not distinguish himself so as to lead to any speculation as to his after greatness, although his elders said he was more anxious to acquire knowledge than to display it ;—a valuable testimony. His domestic life was so pure, his friendships were so firm, his habits so completely those of a well-bred, well-born IRISH GENTLEMAN—mingling, as only Irish gentlemen can do, the suavity of the French with the dignity of English manners—that there is little to write about, or speculate upon, beyond his public words and deeds.

Like most young men of his time, his first oratory was exorcised at a club, and his first efforts as a politician were made in 1749, previous to his quitting the Dublin University, in some letters against Mr. Henry Brooke, the author of 'Gustavus Vasa.' His determination was the bar, and his entry at the Middle Temple bears date April 23, 1747. His youthful impressions of England and its capital are recorded in graceful language in his letters to those friends whom he never lost, but by death ; one passage is as applicable to the present as to the past. 'I don't find that genius, the "rath primrose which forsaken dies," is patronised by any of the nobility, so that writers of the first talents are left to the capricious patronage of the public.'

It was the taste of his time to desire, if not solicit patronage. In our opinion literature is degraded by *patronage,* while it is honoured by the friendship of the good and great. Nothing is so loathsome in the history of letters as the debased dedications which men of mind some years ago laid at the feet of the so-styled 'patron!' Literature in our days has only to assert its own dignity, to be true and faithful to the right, to avoid ribaldry, and preserve a noble and brave independence ; and then its importance to the state, as the minister of good, must be acknowledged. It is only when forgetful of great purpose and great power, that literature is open to be forgotten or sneered at. Still the indifference an Englishman feels towards genius, even while enjoying its fruits, was likely enough to check and chill the enthusiasm of Burke, and drive him to much mystery as to his early literary engagements. One of his observations made during his first visit to Westminster Abbey, while hopes and ambitions quickened his throbbing pulse, and he might have been pardoned for wishing for a resting-place in the grand mausoleum of England, is remarkable, as showing how little he changed, and how completely the youth

'Was father to the man.'

'Yet after all, do you know that I would rather sleep in the southern corner of a country church-yard than in the tomb of the Capulets. I should like, however, that my dust should mingle with kindred dust ; the good old expression, "family burying-ground," has something pleasing in it, at least to me.'

This was his last as it seems to have been his first desire ; and it has found an echo in many a richly dowered heart.

'Lay me,' said Allan Cunningham, 'where the daisies can grow on my grave'; and it is well known that Moore—

'The poet of all circles,'—

and, as a poor Irishman once rendered it—

The *darlint* of his own ;'

has frequently expressed a desire to be buried at Sloperton beside his children.

The future orator found the law, as a profession, alien to his habits and feelings, for at the expiration of the usual term he was not even called to the bar. Some say he desired the professorship of logic at the University of Glasgow, and even stood the contest ; but this has been disputed, and if he was rejected, it is matter of congratulation, that his talents and time wore not confined to so narrow a sphere. At that period his mind was occupied by his theories on the Sublime and Beautiful, which were finally condensed and published in the shape of that essay which roused the world to admiration.

Mr. Prior says, and with every show of reason, 'that Mr. Burke's ambition of being distinguished in literature, seems to have been one of his earliest, as it was one of his latest, passions.' His first avowed work was 'The Vindication of Natural Society ;' but he wrote a great deal anonymously ; and the essay on 'The Sublime and Beautiful,' triumphant as it was, must have caused him great anxiety ; he began it before he was nineteen, and kept it by him for seven years before it was pub-lished—a valuable lesson to those who rush into print and mistake the desire for celebrity, for the power which bestows immortality.

The literature which is pursued chiefly in solitude, is always of the best sort : society, which cheers and animates men in most employ-ments, is an impediment to an author if really warmed by true genius, and impelled by a sacred love of truth not to fritter away his thoughts or be tempted to insincerity.

The genius and noble mind of Burke constituted him a high priest of literature ; the lighter, and it might be the more pleasurable, enjoy-ments of existence, could not be tasted without interfering with his pur-suits ; but he knew his duty to his God, to the world, and to himself, and the responsibility alone was sufficiently weighty to bend a delicate frame, even when there was no necessity for labouring to live—but where an object is to be attained, principles put forth or combated, God or man to be served, the necessity for exertion always exists, and the great soul must go forth on its mission.

That sooner or later this strife, or love, or duty—pursued bravely—must tell upon all who even covet and enjoy their labour, the experience of the past has recorded ; and Edmund Burke, even at that early period of life, was ordered to try the effects of a visit to Bath and Bristol, then the principal resort of the invalids of the United Kingdom.

At Bath he exchanged one malady for another, for he became attached to Miss Nugent, the daughter of his physician, and in a very little time formed what, in a worldly point of view, would be considered an imprudent marriage, but which secured the happiness of his future life ; she was a Roman Catholic ; but, however unfortunate dissenting creeds are in many instances, in this it never disturbed the harmony of their affection.

She was a woman exactly calculated to create happiness ; possessing accomplishments, goodness of heart, sweetness of disposition and manners, veneration for talent, a hopeful spirit to allay her husband's anxieties, wisdom and love to meet his ruffled temper, and tenderness to subdue it—qualities which made him frequently declare 'that every care vanished the moment he sheltered beneath his own roof.'

Edmund Burke became a husband, and also continued a lover—and once presented to his lady-love, on the anniversary of their marriage, his idea of 'a perfect wife.'[88]

---

[88] This as a picture is outlined with so delicate a pencil, and coloured with such mingled purity and richness of tone, that we transcribe a few passages, as much in honour of the man who could write, as of the woman who could inspire such praise : —

"The character of —

'She is handsome, but it is beauty not arising from features, from complexion, or from shape. She has all three in a high degree, but it is not by these she touches a heart ; it is all that sweetness of temper, benevolence, innocence, and sensibility, which a face can express, that forms her beauty. She has a face that just raises your attention at first sight ; it grows on you every moment, and you wonder it did no more than raise your attention at first.

'Her eyes have a mild light, but they awe when she pleases ; they command like a good man out of office, not by authority, but by virtue.

'Her stature is not tall, she is not made to be the admiration of everybody, but the happiness of one.

'She has all the firmness that does not exclude delicacy—she has all the softness that does not imply weakness.'

*   *   *   *   *   *

'Her voice is a soft, low, music, not formed to rule in public assemblies, but to charm those who can distinguish a company from a crowd ; it has this advantage—*you must come close to her to hear it.*

'To describe her body, describes her mind ; one is the transcript of the other ; her understanding is not shown in the variety of matters it exerts itself on, but in the goodness of the choice she makes.

'She does not display it so much in saying or doing striking things, as in avoiding such as she ought *not* to say or do?

For a considerable time after his marriage Burke toiled as a literary man, living at Battersea or in town, now writing, it is believed, jointly with his brother Richard and his cousin William, a work on the 'European Settlements in America,' in two volumes, which according to tradition, brought him, or them, only fifty pounds then planning and commencing an abridgment of the 'History of England.'

Struggling, it may be with difficulties brought on by his generous nature, and which his father's allowance of two hundred a-year, and his own industry and perseverance could hardly overcome, the birth of a son was an additional stimulant to exertion, and, in conjunction with Dodsley, he established the *Annual Register*. This work he never acknowledged, but his best biographers have no doubt of his having brought forth and nurtured this useful publication. A hundred pounds a volume seems to have been the sum paid for this labour ; and Burke's receipts for the money were at one time in the possession of Mr. Upcott.

Long before he obtained a seat in Parliament he won the esteem of Doctor Johnson, who bore noble testimony to his virtue and talent, and what he especially admired, and called, his 'affluence of conversation.'

For a time he went to Ireland as private secretary to Mr. Hamilton, distinguished from all others of his name as 'single-speech Hamilton ;' but disagreeing with this person, he nobly threw up a pension of three hundred a-year, because of the unreasonable and derogatory claims made upon his gratitude by Hamilton, who had procured it for him.

While in Dublin he made acquaintance with the genius of the painter Barry, and though his own means were limited, he persuaded him to come to England, and received him in his house in Queen Anne Street, where he soon procured him employment ; he already numbered Mr., afterwards Sir Joshua, Reynolds amongst his friends ; and his corre-

---

     *   *   *   *   *   *

'No person of so few years can know the world better ; no person was ever less corrupted by the knowledge.

'Her politeness flows rather from a natural disposition to oblige, than from any rules on that subject, and therefore never fails to strike those who understand good breeding, and those who do not.'

     *   *   *   *   *   *

'She has a steady and firm mind, *which takes no more from the solidity of the female character, than the solidity of marble does from its polish and lustre.* She has such virtues as make us value the truly great of our own sex. She has all the winning graces that make us love even the faults we see in the weak and beautiful in hers?

spondence with Barry might almost be considered a young painter's manual, so full is it of the better parts of taste, wisdom, and knowledge.

Mr. Burke was then on the threshold of Parliament, Lord Verney arranging for his *début* as member for Wendover, in Buckinghamshire, under the Rockingham Administration ; another star was added to the galaxy of that brilliant assembly, and if we had space it could not be devoted to a better purpose than to trace his glorious career in the senate ; but that is before all who read the history of the period, and we prefer to follow his footsteps in the under current of private life.

He was too successful to escape the poisoned arrows of envy, or the misrepresentations of the disappointed. Certain persons exclaimed against his want of consistency, and gave as a reason that at one period he commended the spirit of liberty with which the French Revolution commenced, and after a time turned away in horror and disgust from a people who made murder a pastime, and converted Paris into a shambles for human flesh.

But nothing could permanently obscure the fame of the eloquent Irishman, he continued to act with such worthiness, that, despite his schism with Charles James Fox, 'the people' did him the justice to believe, that in his public conduct, he had no one view but the public good.

He outlived calumny, uniting unto genius diligence, and unto diligence patience, and unto patience enthusiasm, and to these, deep-hearted enthusiasm, with a knowledge, not only, it would seem, of all things, but of such ready application, that in illustration or argument his resources were boundless ; the wisdom of the Ancients was as familiar to him as the improved state of modern politics, science and laws ; the metaphysics and logic of the Schools were to him as household words, and his memory was gemmed with whatever was most valuable in poetry, history, and the arts.

After much toil, and the lapse of some time, he purchased a domain in Buckinghamshire, called 'Gregories ;' there, whenever his public duties gave him leisure, he enjoyed the repose so necessary to an overtaxed brain ; and from Gregories some of his most interesting letters are dated.[89] Those addressed to the painter Barry, *whom his liberality*

---

[89] Our cut exhibits all that now remains of Gregories—a few walls and a portion of the old stables. Mrs. Burke, before her death, sold the mansion to her neighbour, Mr. John Du Pré, of Wilton Park. It was destroyed by fire soon afterwards.

sent to and supported in Rome, are, as we have said, replete with art and wisdom ; and the delicacy of both him and his excellent brother Richard, while entreating the rough-hewn genius to prosecute his studies and give them pleasure by his improvement, are additional proofs of the beautiful union of the brothers, and of their *oneness* of purpose and determination that Barry should never be cramped by want of means.[90]

GREGORIES.

After the purchase of Gregories[91] Mr. Burke had no settled town-house, merely occupying one for the season. In one of his letters to Barry, he tells him to direct to Charles Street, St. James's Square ; he writes also from Fludyer Street, Westminster, and from Gerrard Street, Soho ; but traces of his 'whereabouts' are next to impossible to find. Barry was not the only artist who profited by Edmund Burke's liberality. Barret the landscape-painter had fallen into difficulties, and the fact coming to the orator's ears during his short tenure of power, he be-

---

[90] During Barry's five years' residence abroad he earned nothing for himself, and received no supplies save from Edmund and Richard Burke.

[91] Mr. Prior says in his admirable Life of Burke—'How the money to effect this purchase was procured has given rise to many surmises and reports ; a considerable portion was his own, the bequest of his father and elder brother. The Marquis of Rockingham offered the loan of the amount required to complete the purchase ; the Marquis was under obligations to him publicly, and privately for some attention paid to the business of his large estates in Ireland. Less disinterested men would have settled the matter otherwise—the one by quartering his friend, the other, by being quartered, on the public purse. To the honour of both a different course was pursued.'

stowed upon him a place in Chelsea Hospital, which he enjoyed during the remainder of his life.

Indeed, this great man's noble love of Art was part and parcel of himself ; it was no affectation, and it led to genuine sympathy with, not only the artist's triumphs, but his difficulties. He found time, amid all his occupations, to write letters to the irritable Barry, and if the painter had followed their counsel, he would have secured his peace and prosperity ; but it was far otherwise : his conduct, both in Rome and after his return to England, gave his friend just cause of offence ; though, like all others who offended the magnanimous Burke, he was soon forgiven.

He never forgot his Irish friends, or the necessities of those who lived on the family estate ; the expansive generosity of his nature did not prevent his attending to the minor comforts of his dependants, and his letters 'home' frequently breathe a most loving and careful spirit, that the sorrows of the poor might be ameliorated, and their wants relieved.

We ought to have mentioned before that Mr. and Mrs. Burke's marriage was only blessed by two sons ; one died in childhood, the eldest grew up a young man of the warmest affections, and blessed with a considerable share of talent ; to his parents he was every thing they could desire ; towards his mother he exhibited the tenderness and devotion of a daughter and his demeanour to his father was that of an obedient son, and mast faithful friend ; at intervals he enjoyed with them the pleasure they experienced in receiving guests of the highest consideration ; amongst them the eccentric Madame de Genlis, who put their politeness to the test by the exercise of her peculiarities, and horrified the meek and amiable Sir Joshua Reynolds by the assumption of talents she did not possess.

The publication of his reflections on the French Revolution, which, perhaps, never would have seen the light but for the rupture with Mr. Sheridan, which caused his opinions to be misunderstood, brought down the applause of Europe on a head then wearying of public life.

But, perhaps, a tribute Burke valued more than any, remembering the adage—an adage which, unhappily, especially applies to Ireland, "no man is a prophet in his own country," was, that on a motion of the provost of Trinity College, Dublin, in 1790, the honorary degree of LL.D. was conferred upon him in full convocation, and an address afterwards presented in a gold box, to express the University's sense of his serv-

ices. When he replied to this distinguished compliment, his town residence was in 'Duke Street, St. James.'

His term of life—over-tasked as it was—might have been extended
to a much longer period, but that his deeply affectionate nature, as time
passed on, experienced several of these shocks inseparable from even
moderate length of days ; many of his friends died ; among others, his
sister and his brother ; but still the wife of his bosom and his son were
with him—that son whose talents he rated as superior to his own, whom
he had consulted for some years on almost every subject, whether of a
public or a private nature, that occurred, and very frequently preferred
his judgment to his own.   This beloved son had attained the age of
thirty-four, when he was seized with rapid consumption.   When the malady was recognised and acknowledged, his father took him to Brompton,
then, as now, considered the best air for those affected with this cruel
malady.   'Cromwell House,' chosen as their temporary residence, is
standing still, though there is little doubt the rage for extending London
through this once sequestered and rural suburb, will soon raze it to the
ground, as it has done others of equal interest.

CROMWELL HOUSE.

We have always regarded 'Cromwell House,' as it is called, with veneration. In our earliest acquaintance with a neighbourhood, in which we lived so long and still love so well, this giant dwelling, staring with its whited walls and balconied roof over the tangled gardens which seemed to cut it off from all communication with the world, was associated with our 'Hero Worship' of Oliver Cromwell. We were told he had lived there (what neighbourhood has not its 'Cromwell House?')—that the ghastly old place had private staircases and subterranean passages— some underground communication with Kensington ;—that there were doors in the walls, and out of the walls ; and, that if not careful you might be precipitated through trap-doors into some unfathomable abyss, and encounter the ghost of old Oliver himself. Those tales operated upon our imagination in the usual way ; and many and many a moonlight evening, while wandering in those green lanes—now obliterated by Onslow and Thurloe Squares—and listening to the nightingales, have we watched the huge shadows cast by that solitary and melancholy-looking house, and, as we have said, associated it with the stern and grand Protector of England. Upon closer investigation, how grieved we have often been to discover the truth, for it destroyed not only our castles in the air, but their inhabitants ; we found that Oliver never resided there, but that his son, Richard, had, and was a rate-payer to the parish of Kensington for some time. To this lonely sombre house Mr. and Mrs. Burke and their son removed, in the hope that the soft mild air of this salubrious neighbourhood might restore his failing strength ; the consciousness of his being in danger was something too terrible for them to think of. He had just received a new appointment—an appointment suited to his tastes and expectations ; he must take possession of it in a little time. He was their child, their friend, their treasure, their all! Surely God would spare him to close their eyes. How could death and he meet together! They entreated him of God, by prayer, and supplication, and tears that flowed until their eyes were dry and their eyelids parched—but all in vain. The man, in his prime of manhood, was stricken down ; we transcribe, from an article in the *Quarterly Review,* on 'Fontenelle's Signs of Death,' the brief account of his last moments :—

'Burke's son, upon whom his father has conferred something of his own celebrity, heard his parents sobbing in another room at the prospect of an event they knew to be inevitable. He rose from his bed, joined his illustrious father, and endeavoured to engage him in a cheerful conversation. Burke continued silent, choked with grief. His son again made an effort to console him. "I am under no terror," he said ; "I feel my-

self better and in spirits, and yet my heart flutters, I know not why.
Pray, talk to me, sir! talk of religion ; talk of morality ; talk, if you will,
of indifferent subjects." Here a noise attracted his notice, and he exclaimed, "Does it rain!—No ; it is the rustling of the wind through the
trees." The whistling of the wind and the waving of the trees brought
Milton's majestic lines to his mind, and he repeated them with uncommon grace and effect : —

> 'His praise, ye winds, that from four quarters blow,
> Breathe soft or loud ; and wave your tops, ye pines,
> With every plant, in sign of worship, wave!'

A second time he took up the sublime and melodious strain, and,
accompanying the action to the word, waved his own hand in token of
worship, and sank into the arms of his father—a corpse. Not a sensation
told him that in an instant he would stand in the presence of the Creator
to whom his body was bent in homage, and whose praises still re-
sounded from his lips.'

The account which all the biographies of Burke give of the effect
this bereavement produced upon his parents is most fearful even to
read ; what must it have been to witness! His mother seems to have
regained her self-possession sooner than his father. In one of his letters
to the late Baron Smith, he writes—'So heavy a calamity has fallen upon
me as to disable me from business, and disqualifies me for repose. The
existence I have—*I do not know that I can call life.* * * Good nights to
you—I never have any.' And again—'The life which has been so em-
bittered cannot long endure. The grave will soon close over me, and my
dejections.' To Lord Auckland he writes—'For myself, or for my family (alas! I have none), I have nothing to hope or to fear in this world.'
And again in another letter—'The storm has gone over me, and I lie like
one of these old oaks which the late hurricane has scattered about me. I
am stripped of all my honours, I lie prostrate on the earth ; I am alone, I
have none to meet my enemies in the gate. I greatly deceive myself, if
in this hard season of life, I would give a peck of refuse wheat for all
that is called fame and honour in the world.'

There is something in the 'wail ' and character of these laments
that recalls the mournful Psalms of David ; like the Psalmist he endeavoured to be comforted, but it was by an effort. His political career was
shrouded for ever—the *motive* to his great exertions was destroyed—but
his mind, wrecked as it had been, could not remain inactive. In 1795 his
private reply to Mr. Smith's letter, requesting his opinion of the expedi-

ency of and necessity for Catholic Emancipation, got into public circulation ; and in that singular document, though he did not enter into the details of the question with as much minuteness as he would previously have done, he pleaded for the removal of the whole of the disabilities of the Roman Catholic body. From time to time he put forth a small work on some popular question. He originated several plans for benefiting the poor in his own neighbourhood. He had a windmill in his park for the purpose of supplying the poor with cheap bread, which bread was served at his own table ; and as if clinging to the memory of the youth of his son, he formed a plan for the establishment of an emigrant school at Penn, where the children of those who had perished by the guillotine or the sword amid the French convulsions, could be received, supported, and educated. He made a generous appeal to government for the benefit of these children, which was as generously responded to. The house appropriated to this humane purpose had been inhabited by Burke's old friend, General Haviland ; and after his death several emigré French priests sheltered within its walls. Until his last fatal illness Mr. Burke watched over the establishment with the solicitude of a friend and the tenderness of a father. The Lords of the Treasury allowed fifty pounds per month for its sustenance : the Marquis of Buckingham made them a present of a brass cannon and a stand of colours. When the Bourbons were restored in 1814 they relieved the government from this charge, and the institution was dissolved in 1820; in 1822 Tyler's Green House,' as it was called, was sold in lots, pulled down, and carried away : thus, Burke's own dwelling being destroyed by fire, and this building, sanctified by his sympathy and goodness, razed to the ground, little remains to mark the locality of places where all the distinguished men of the age congregated around 'the Burkes,' and where Edmund, almost to the last, extended hospitalities, coveted and appreciated by all who had any pretensions to be considered as distinguished either by talent or fortune.

It has frequently struck us as strange, the morbid avidity with which the world seizes upon the slightest evidence of abstraction in great men, to declare that their minds are fading, or impoverished : the public gapes for every trifle calculated to prove that the palsied fingers can no longer grasp the intellectual sceptre, and that the well-worn and hard-earned bays are as a crown of thorns to the pulseless brow. It was, in those days whispered in London that the great orator had become imbecile immediately after the publication of his *Letter to a Noble Lord ;'* and that he wandered about his park kissing his cows and horses.

A noble friend went immediately to Beaconsfield to ascertain the truth, and was delighted to find Mr. Burke anxious to read him passages from 'A Regicide Peace,' which he was then writing ; after a little delicate manoeuvring on his part, to ascertain the truth, Mr. Burke told him a touching incident which proved the origin of this calumny on his intellectual powers.

An old horse, a great favourite of his son's, and his constant companion, when both were full of life and health, had been turned out at the death of his master, to take his run of the park for the remainder of his life, at ease, with strict injunctions to the servants that he should neither be ridden, nor molested by any-one. While musing one day, loitering along, Mr. Burke perceived this worn-out old servant come close up to him, and at length, after some moments spent in viewing his person, followed by seeming recollection and confidence, he deliberately rested his head upon his bosom. The singularity of the action itself the remembrance of his dead son, its late master, who occupied so much of his thoughts at all times, and the apparent attachment, tenderness and intelligence of the creature towards him—as if it could sympathise with his inward sorrow—rushing at once into his mind, totally overpowered his firmness, and throwing his arms over its neck, he wept long and loudly.

But though his lucid and beautiful mind, however agonised, remained unclouded to the last, and his affections glowed towards his old friends as warmly as ever, his bodily health was failing fast ; one of the last letters he ever dictated was to Mary Leadbeater, the daughter of his old friend and master, Shackleton ; this lady was subsequently well known in Ireland as the author of 'Cottage Dialogues.' The first literary attempt we believe, made towards the improvement of the lower order of Irish, was by her faithful and earnest pen ; to this letter, congratulating her on the birth of a son, is a PS. where the invalid says :—'I have been at Bath these four months to no purpose, and am therefore to be removed to any own house at Beaconsfield tomorrow, *to be nearer to a habitation more permanent, humbly* and fearfully hoping that my better part may find a better mansion!'

It would seem as if he anticipated the hour of his passing away. He sent sweet messages of loving-kindness to all his friends, entreating and exchanging pardons ; recapitulated his motives of action on various political emergencies ; gave directions as to his funeral, and then listened with attention to some serious papers of Addison on religious subjects and on the immortality of the soul. His attendants after this were in the act of removing him to his bed, when indistinctly invoking a blessing on all around him, he sunk down and expired on the 9th of July, 1797, in the sixty-eighth year of his age.

'His end,' said his friend Doctor Lawrence, 'was suited to the simple greatness of mind which he displayed through life ; every way unaffected, without levity, without ostentation, full of natural grace and dignity, he appeared neither to wish nor to dread, but patiently and placidly to await the appointed hour of his dissolution.'

It was almost impossible to people, in fancy, the tattered and neglected churchyard of Beaconsfield as it now is—with those who swelled the funeral pomp of the greatest ornament of the British senate ; to imagine the titled pall-bearers, where the swine were tumbling over graves, and rooting at headstones. Seldom, perhaps, never, in England, had we seen a churchyard so little cared for as that, where the tomb of Waller[92] renders the surrounding disorder 'in a sacred place' more conspicuous by its lofty pretension, and where the church is regarded as the mausoleum of Edmund Burke. Surely the 'decency of churchyards' ought to be enforced, if those to whom they should be sacred trusts, neglect or forget their duty. That the churchyard of Beaconsfield, which has long been considered 'a shrine,' should be suffered to remain in the state in which we saw it, is a disgrace not only to the town, but to England ; it was differently cared for during Burke's life-time, and though, like that of the revered Queen Dowager, his Will expressed a disinclination to posthumous honours, and unnecessary expense, never were mourners more sincere—never did there arise to the blue vault of heaven the incense of greater, and more deepfelt sorrow, than from the multitude who assembled in and around the church, while the mortal remains of Edmund Burke, were placed in the same vault with his son and brother.

The tablet to his memory, placed on the wall of the south aisle of the church, records his last resting-place with the relatives just named ;

---

[92] Waller was a resident in this vicinity, in which his landed property chiefly lay. He lived in the family mansion named Well's Court, a property still in the possession of his descendants. His tomb is a table monument of white marble, upon which rises a pyramid, resting on skulls with bat's wings ; it is a peculiar but picturesque addition to the churchyard, and, from its situation close to the walk, attracts much attention.

as well as the fact of the same grave containing the body of his 'entirely beloved and incomparable wife,' who died in 1812, at the age of 76.

Deeply do we deplore that the dwelling where he enjoyed so much that renders life happy, and suffered what sanctifies and prepares us for a better world, exists no longer ; but his name is incorporated with our history, and adds another to the list of the great men who have been called into life and received their first and best impressions in Ireland ; and if Ireland had given nothing to her more prosperous sister than the extraordinary men of the past and present century, she merits her gratitude for the gifts which bestow so much honour and glory on the United Kingdoms.

THE TOMB OF EDMUND BURKE.[93]

---

[93] Our engraving exhibits his simple tablet, as seen from the central aisle of the church, immediately in front of the pew in which Burke and his family always sat.

Mrs. Burke, previous to her death, sold the mansion to her neighbour ; Mr. John Du Pré, of Wilton Park. Mrs. Haviland, Mr. Burke's niece, lived with her to the last, though she did not receive the portion of her fortune to which she was considered entitled. Her son, Thomas Haviland Burke, grand-nephew of Edmund, became the lineal representative of the family ; but the library and all the tokens of respect and admiration which he received from the good, and from the whole world, went with the property to *Mrs. Burke's* nephew, Mr. Nugent. Some of the sculpture which ornamented the house now graces the British Museum.

The mansion was burnt on the 23rd of April, 1813. The ground where it stood is unequal ; and some of the park wall remains, and fine old trees still flourish, beneath whose shade we picture the meeting between the mourning father and the favourite horse of his lost son.

There is a full-length portrait of Edmund Burke in the Examination Hall of the Dublin University. All such portraits should be copied, and preserved in our own Houses of Parliament, a meet honour to the dead, and a stimulant to the living to 'go and do likewise.' It hardly realises, however, the *ideal* of Burke ; perhaps no portrait could. What Miss Edgeworth called the 'ground-plan of the face' is there ; but we must imagine the varying expression, the light of the bright quick eyes, the eloquence of the unclosed lips, the storm which could gather thunder-clouds on the well-formed brow ;[94] but we have far exceeded our limits

---

[94] The late Queen Caroline, when Princess of Wales, requested the widow of Edmund Burke to let her have a cast taken from the bust of her husband, and the widow anxious for his honour—as Her Royal Highness said it should be one in a gallery she was about to form of British Warthies—presented the Princess with the original. The collection was never formed ; and at the sale of Her Royal Highness's effects at Connaught House, it was discovered amongst the rubbish, and put up for sale. There was a contest for it between Turnerelli, the sculptor, and Mrs. Thomas Haviland ; the lady bought her uncle's bust, and some time after Mr. Haviland presented it to the British Museum.'—Prior's *Life of Burke*.

without exhausting our subject and, with Dr. Parr, still would speak of Burke :—

'Of Burke, by whose sweetness Athens herself would have been soothed, with whose amplitude and exuberance she would have been enraptured, and on whose lips that prolific mother of genius and science would have adored, confessed—the Goddess of Persuasion.'

Alas we have lingered long at his Shrine, and yet our praise is not half spoken!

A Day at Chatsworth.

ERBYSHIRE is so entirely an English stronghold of interest and scenery, that it merits and pays the attention of all who, residing in our rich Prairie counties, scarcely imagine its variety, sublimity, and extreme loveliness. The hills, without approaching to the height or dignity of mountains, mimic Alpine scenery to perfection, in gaunt or fantastic peaks ; while the exquisitely toned woods, the dales, the folded "bluffs," the winding rivers, the wide moors, the ancient castles, the venerable mansions, the mysterious caverns, the hollows filled with tufts of trees, the brawling gulleys,—the lonely villages, surprising the traveller at some unexpected turn of a defile or rocky pass—the carts, laden with shining ore, the troops of miners with their safety lamps and quaint costume—the beautiful spars—very jewels of geology—the bubbling health-springs—are so many varied sources of deep and exciting interest.

Who would not visit the sweet hamlet of Hathersage, resting in the Bosom of the hills,—to seek out, in its green church-yard, the grave of Robin Hood's own bow-bearer, "brave Little John?" Who would not covet the repose of nature in Hope Dale, rich in all sylvan graces, through which generous Derwent bountifully flows? Who would not climb to where the castle of the Peverils frowned, for ages, from the rocky heights—proud, bold, and stern? Who, once having seen, would not long again to wander in Monsal Dale, the very Tempé of Derbyshire, where the foaming Wye seems to change its nature, and expands in silver sheets of living water to the loving meadows which slope to meet the kisses it bestows.

195

THE ENTRANCE GATES.

The antiquary may feed his very soul in Derbyshire. And it is never a profitless retrospect—this looking back into the past ; it tends to a higher appreciation of the liberty and prosperity we actually enjoy ; it deepens our interest in the beauties of nature, outliving as they do the changing thoughts and habits of the "peopled desert ;" it elevates us to the threshold of that Immortality which rises above all decay.

Bounding rivers intersect the county as if they had studied how to beautify it best. The Dove rises a little distance south of Buxton, and flowing generally through rocky channels, presents us with a miniature copy of the Gap of Dunloe. The Vale of the Dove is one of the sweetest of English valleys ; and the capricious character of the river adds to its charm : sometimes it inclines to the south, then to the east ; then rushing from the pyramidal mountain of Thorp Cloud, it goes westward, until it reaches the vale of Uttoxeter,—when, again turning to the east, it flows beneath the bold hill which displays the ruins of Tutbury Castle. Tutbury! one of the prisons of the unfortunate Mary of Scotland. The Wye becomes near Bakewell a tributary stream to increase the beauty of the queenly Derwent. After it has added the animation of river life to the magnificence of Chatsworth, the pleasant vale of Darley is brightened by these united streams ; and on they go until their channel is ingulphed between lofty rocks, which in their recesses enclose the romantic scenery of Matlock Dale—where

" * * * *All his force lost,
Gentle and still, a deep, and silent stream
He scarcely seems to move ; o'er him the boughs
Bend their green foliage, shivering with the wind
And dip into his surface."

THE BRIDGE ACROSS THE DERWENT.

We are so little proud of the beauties England, that the foreigner only hears of Derbyshire as the casket which contains the rich jewel of CHATSWORTH. The setting is worthy of the gem. It ranks foremost among the proudly beautiful of English mansions ; and merits its familiar title of "The Palace of the Peak." It was the object of our pilgrimage ; and we recalled the history of the nobles of its House. The family of Cavendish is one of our oldest descents ; it may be traced lineally from Robert de Gernon, who entered England with the Conqueror, and whose descendant, Roger Gernon, of Grimston, in Suffolk, marrying the daughter and sole heiress of John Potton, Lord of Cavendish in that county, in the reign of Edward II, gave the name of that estate as a surname to his children, which they ever after bore. The study of the law seems to have been for a long period the means of according position and celebrity to the family, Sir William Cavendish, in whose person all the estates conjoined, was Privy Councillor to Henry VIII., Edward VI., and Queen Mary ; he had been Gentleman-Usher to Wolsey ; and after the fall of the great Cardinal, was retained in the service of Henry VIII. He accumulated much wealth, but chiefly by his third and last marriage with Elizabeth, then the wealthy widow of Robert Barley, Esq., at whose instigation he sold his estates in other parts of England, to purchase lands in Derbyshire, where her great property lay. Hardwick Hall was her paternal estate, but Sir William began to build another residence at Chatsworth, which he did not live to finish. Ultimately, she became the wife of George Talbot, Earl of Shrewsbury ; she was one of the most remarkable women of her time—the foundress of the two noble houses of Devonshire and Newcastle. Her second son, William, by the death of his elder brother in 1616, became possessed of his large estates, and after being created Baron Cavendish, of Hardwick, was, in 1618, created Earl of Devonshire. It was happily said of him, "his learning operated on his conduct, but was seldom shown in his discourse." His son, the third Earl, was a zealous loyalist ; like his father remarkable for his cultivated taste and learning which was perfected under the superintendence of the famous Hobbes, of Malmesbury. His eldest son, William, was the first Duke of Devonshire ; he was the friend of Lord Russell, and one of the few who fearlessly came forth to testify to his honour on his memorable trial. Wearied of courts, he retired to Chatsworth, which at that time was a quadrangular building, with turrets in the Elizabethan taste ; and then, "as if his mind rose upon the depression of his fortune," says Dr. Kennett, "he first projected the now glorious pile of Chatsworth ;" he pulled down the south side of "that good old seat," and rebuilt it on a plan "so fair and august, that it looked like a model only of what might be done in after ages." After seven years, he added the other sides, "yet the building was his least charge, if regard be had to his gardens, water-works, statues, pictures, and the other finest pieces of Art and nature that could be obtained abroad or at home." He was highly honoured with the favour and confidence of King William III. and his successor Queen Anne. Dying in 1707, his son William, who was Lord Lieutenant of Ireland, spent the latter part of his life at Chatsworth, dying there in 1755. It is now the favourite country residence of his great grandson, the sixth Duke and ninth Earl of Devonshire—his seats being Chatsworth House and Hardwick Hall, Derbyshire ; Bolton Abbey, Yorkshire ; Chiswick House, Middlesex ; Lismore Castle, Waterford ; and Devonshire House in London.

We would avoid the semblance of adulation in speaking of the Duke of Devonshire ; but it is impossible to write of him without praise—as, in Ireland as well as in England, the best of landlords, the truest of men, and the most perfect of gentlemen—one who has made and retained more friends and fewer enemies than fall to the lot of most persons—gentle or simple ; one whose rank, high as it is among the highest, is butt "the guinea stamp."

His tastes are evidenced at Chatsworth ; they are of the purest and happiest order ; —and are to be found in the adornments of his rooms, the shelves of his library, the glorious Art-riches of his galleries, and the rare and beautiful exotic marvels of his gardens and conservatories.

THE GREAT CONSERVATORY.

Charles Cotton in his poem descriptive of the "Wonders of the Peak," thus wrote, two centuries ago, of the then Earl of Devonshire ; and surely no language can apply with greater force or truth to the Duke who is the descendant of that Earl, and now the master of princely Chatsworth :—

"But that which crowns all this, and does impart
A lustre far beyond the pow'r of Art,
Is the great Owner ; He, whose noble mind
For such a Fortune only was design'd.
Whose bounties, as the Ocean's bosom wide
Flow in a constant, unexhausted tide

Of Hospitality, and free access,
Liberal Condescension, cheerfulness.
Honour and Truth, as ev'ry of them strove
At once to captivate Respect and Love :
And with such order all perform'd, and grace,
As rivet wonder to the stately place."

Although by the courtesy of the Duke carriages are permitted to drive from the railway terminus at Rowsley, to the pretty and pleasant inn at Edensor, by a road which passes directly under the house, the stranger should receive his first impressions of Chatsworth from one of the surrounding heights. It is impossible to convey a just idea of its breadth and dignity ; the platform upon which it stands is a fitting base for such a structure ; the trees, that at intervals relieve and enliven the vast space, are of every rich variety, the terraces nearly twelve hundred feet in extent—"the emperor fountain" throwing its jet two hundred and seventy feet into the air ; far over-topping the noble avenue of majestic trees of which it forms the centre. The dancing fountain, the great cascade, even the smaller fountains (wonderful objects any where, except here, where there are so many more wonderful) sparkle through the foliage ; while all is backed by magnificent hanging woods, and the high lands of Derbyshire, extending from the hills of Matlock to Stoney Middleton. And the foreground of the picture is, in its way, equally beautiful ; the expansive view, the meadows now broken into green bills and mimic valleys, the groups of fallow deer, and herds of cattle, reposing beneath the shade of wide-spreading chestnuts, or the stately beech—all is harmony to perfection ; nothing is wanting to complete the fascination of the whole.

The enlarged and cultivated minds which conceived these vast yet minute arrangements, did not consider minor details as unimportant : every tree, and brake, and bush ; every ornament, every path, is exactly in its right place, and seems to have ever been there. Nothing however great, or however small, has escaped consideration ; there are no bewildering effects, such as are frequently seen in large domains, and which render it difficult to recall what at the time may have been much admired ; all is arranged with the dignity of order ; all however graceful, is substantial ; the ornamentation's, sometimes elaborate, never descend into prettiness ; the character of the scenery has been borne in mind, and its beauty never outraged by extravagance. All is in harmony with the character which Nature in her most generous mood gave to the hills and valleys : God has been gracious to the land, and man has followed in the path way He has made.

"A Day at Chatsworth!"—a month at Chatsworth would hardly suffice to count up its beauties ; but much may he done in a day, when eyes and ears are open, and the heart beats in sympathy with the beauties of Nature and of Art.   It is, perhaps, best to visit the gardens of Chatsworth first ; they are little more than half a mile to the north of the park ; and there Sir Joseph Paxton is building his new dwelling or rather adding considerably to the beauty and convenience of the old.   In the Kitchen-Gardens, containing twelve acres, there are houses for every species of plant, but the grand attraction is the house which contains the Royal Lily (Victoria Regia), and other lilies and water-plants from various countries.

THE ROCK-WORK.

It will be readily believed that the flower-gardens are among the most exquisitely beautiful in Europe : they have been arranged by one of the master minds of the age, and bear evidence of matured knowledge, skill, and taste ; the nicest judgment seems to have been exercised over even the smallest matter of detail, while the whole is as perfect a combination as can be conceived of grandeur and loveliness.   The walks, lawns, and parterres are lavishly, but unobtrusively, decorated with vases and statues : terraces occur here and there, from which are to be obtained the best views of the adjacent country ; "Patrician trees" at intervals form umbrageous alleys ; water is made contributory from a hundred mountain streams and rivulets, to form jets, cascades, and fountains, which—infinitely varied in their "play," ramble among lilies, or—it is scarcely an exaggeration to say—fling their spray into the clouds, and descend to refresh the topmost leaves of trees that were in their prime three centuries ago.

THE WELLINGTON ROCK AND CASCADE.

The most striking and original of the walks is that which leads through mimic Alpine scenery to the great conservatory ; here Art has been most triumphant ; the rocks which have been all brought hither are so skilfully combined, so richly clad in mosses, so luxuriantly covered with heather, so judiciously based with ferns and water-plants, that you move among, or beside, them, in rare delight at the sudden change which transports you from trim parterres to the utmost wildness of natural beauty. From these again you pass into a garden, in the centre of which is the conservatory, always renowned, but now more than ever, as the prototype of the famous Palace of Glass, which, in this *Annus Mirabilis,* received under its roof six millions of the people of all nations, tongues, and creeds. In extent, the conservatory at Chatsworth is but a pigmy compared with that which glorifies Hyde Park : but it is filled with the rarest Exotics from all parts of the globe—from "farthest Ind" from China, from the Himalayas, from Mexico ; here you see the rich banana, Eschol's grape, hanging in ripe profusion beneath the shadow of immense paper-like leaves ; the feathery cocoa-palm, with its head peering almost to the lofty arched roof ; the far-famed silk cotton-tree, supplying a sheet of cream-coloured blossoms, at a season when all outward vegetable gaiety is on the wane ; the singular milk-tree of the Caraccas ; the fragrant cinnamon and cassia—with thousands of other rare and little known species of both flowers and fruits.

THE ITALIAN GARDEN.

The Italian Garden—opposite the library windows, with its richly-coloured parterres, and its clustered foliage wreathed around the pillars which support the statues and busts scattered among them, and hanging from one to the other with a luxurious verdure which seems to belong to the south—is a relief to the eye sated with the splendours of the palatial edifice.

The water-works, which were constructed under the direction of M. Grillet, a French artist, were begun in 1690, when a pipe for what was then called "the great fountain" was laid down ; the height of twenty feet to which it threw water being, at that time, considered sufficiently wonderful to justify the hyperbolical language of Cotton—

"should it break or fall, I doubt we should
Begin to reckon from the second flood."

THE EMPEROR FOUNTAIN.

It was afterwards elevated to fifty feet, and then to ninety-four ; but
it is now celebrated as the most remarkable fountain in the world ; it
rises to the height of two hundred and sixty-seven feet, and has been
named the "Emperor Fountain," in honour of the visit of the Emperor of
Russia to Chatsworth in the year 1844. Such is the velocity with which
the water is ejected, that it is calculated to escape at the rate of one hundred miles per minute ; for the purpose of supplying it, a reservoir, or
immense artificial lake, has been constructed on the hills, above
Chatsworth, which is fed by the streams around, and the springs on the
moors, drains being cut for this purpose, commencing at Humberly

Brook, on the Chesterfield Road, two miles and a half from the reservoir, which covers eight acres ; a pipe winds down the hill side, through which the water passes ; and such is its waste, that a diminution of a foot may be perceived when the water-works have been played for three hours. Nothing can exceed the stupendous effect of this column, which may be seen for many miles around, shooting upwards to the sky in varied and graceful evolutions.

THE TEMPLE CASCADE.

From this upper lake the waterfalls are also supplied which are constructed with so natural an effect on the hillside, behind the water temple ; which reminds the spectator of the glories of St. Cloud. From the dome of this temple bursts forth a gush of water that covers its surface, pours through the urns at its sides, and springs up in fountains underneath, thence descending in a long series of step-like falls, until it sinks beneath the rocks at the base, and—after rising again to play as "the dancing fountain"—is conveyed by drains under the garden and park, —being emptied into the Derwent.[95]

---

[95] A quaint whim of the olden time is constructed near one of the walks ; it is the model of a willow-tree in copper, which has all the appearance of a living one, situated on

But we may not forget that our space is limited : to describe the gardens and conservatories of Chatsworth would occupy more pages than we can give to the whole theme ; suffice it that the taste and liberality of the Duke of Devonshire, and the skill and judgment of Sir Joseph Paxton, have so happily combined Nature and Art in this delicious region, as to supply all the enjoyment that may be desired or is attainable, from trees, shrubs, and flowers seen under the happiest arrangement of countries, classes, and colours.

The erection of the present house is thus narrated by Lysons ; the south front was begun to be rebuilt on the 12th of April, 1687, and the great hall and staircase covered in about the middle of April, 1690. The east front was begun in 1691, and finished in 1700; the south gallery pulled down and rebuilt in 1703.   In 1704, the north front was pulled down, the west front was finished in 1706, and the whole of the building not long afterwards completed, being about twenty years from the time of its commencement.   The architect employed was Mr. William Talman, but in May, 1692, the works were surveyed by Sir Christopher Wren.

On entering—the Lower Hall or Western Lodge contains some very fine antique statuary, and fragments which deserve the especial attention of the connoisseur.   Among them are several which were the treasured relics of Canova and Sir Henry Englefield, and others found in Herculaneum, and presented by the King of Naples to "the beautiful" Duchess of Devonshire.

A Corridor leads thence to the Great Hall, which is richly decorated with paintings by the hand of a famous Artist in his day—Verrio— who has been celebrated by Pope for his proficiency in ceiling-painting. The effect of the hall is singularly good, with its grated stair and triple arches opening to the principal rooms.   The sub-hall behind is embellished by a very graceful fountain, with the story of Diana and Actæon, and the abundance of water at Chatsworth enables it to be constantly playing, producing an effect seldom attempted within doors.

---

a raised mound of earth.   From each branch, however, water suddenly bursts, and also small jets from the grassy borders around.   It was considered a good jest some years age to delude novices to examine this tree, and wet them thoroughly by suddenly turning on the water above and around them.   This tree was originally made by a London plumber in 1693; but it has been recently repaired by a plumber in the neighbourhood of Chesterfield, under the direction of Sir Joseph Paxton.

THE ENTRANCE HALL.

A long Gallery leads to the various rooms inhabited by the Duke, the walls being decorated with a large number of fine pictures by the older masters of the Flemish and Italian schools. In the billiard-room are Landseer's far-famed picture of "Bolton Abbey in the Olden Time," with charming specimens of Collins, and other British painters.

The Chapel is richly decorated with foliage in carved woodwork, which has been erroneously attributed to Grinling Gibbons. It was executed by Mr. Thomas Young, who was engaged as the principal carver in wood in 1689; and by a pupil of his, Samuel Watson, a native of

Heanor, in Derbyshire, whose claim to the principal ornamental wood-carving at Chatsworth is set forth in verses on his tomb in Heanor Church. Over the Colonnade on the north side of the quadrangle, is a gallery nearly one hundred feet long, in which have been hung a numerous and valuable collection of drawings by the old masters, arranged according to the schools of art of which they are examples. There is no school unrepresented, and as the eye wanders over the thickly covered wall, it is arrested by sketches from the hands of Raffaelle, Da Vinci, Claude, Poussin, Paul Veronese, Salvator Rosa, and the other great men who have made Art immortal. To describe these works would occupy a volume ; to study them a life ; it is a glorious collection as gloriously set forth.

The old State-rooms, which form the upper floors of the south front, occupy the same position as those which were appropriated to the unfortunate Mary Queen of Scots during her long sojourn here. There is, however, but little to see of her period ; if we except some needle-work at the back of a canopy, representing hunting scenes, worked by the hand of the famous Countess of Shrewsbury, popularly known as "Bess of Hardwick."

The Gallery, originally constructed for dancing, and measuring ninety feet by twenty-two, has been fitted up by the present duke as a library. Among the books which formed the original library at Chatsworth, are several which belonged to the celebrated Thomas Hobbes, who was for many years a resident at Chatsworth old hall. The library of Henry Cavendish, and the extensive and valuable collection at Devonshire House, have also aided to swell its stores. Here the historian might revel, and the bookworm feast, during a life. Thin quartos of the rarest order, unique volumes of old poetry, scarce and curious pamphlets by the early printers, first editions of Shakespeare, early pageants, and the rarest dramatic and other popular literature of the Elizabethan era, may be found in this well-ordered and elegant room—not to speak of its great treasure, the *Liber Veritatis* of Claude.[96]

The Statue Gallery is a noble room, erected by the present Duke, and containing a most judiciously selected series of sculpture. The gem of the collection is the famous seated statue of Madame Buonaparte, the mother of Napoleon, by Canova. The same style of treatment charac-

---

[96] The Duke of Devonshire has privately printed a perfect fac-simile of this curious and valuable collection.

terises that of the Princess Pauline Borghese, by Campbell. Other works of Canova are here—his statue of "Hebe" and "Endymion sleeping ;" a bust of Petrarch's "Laura," and the famous "Lions," copied by Benaglia from the colossal originals on the monument of Clement XIV., in St. Peter's, Rome. Thorwaldsen is abundantly represented by his "Night and Morning," and his charming bas-reliefs of "Priam Petitioning for the Body of Hector," and "Briseis, taken from Achilles by the Heralds :" Schadow's "Filatrice," or Spinning Girl, and his classic bas-reliefs are worthy of all admiration. Our native school of sculpture appears to good advantage also in Gibson's fine group, "Mars and Cupid," and his bas-relief of "Hero and Leander"—Chantry's busts of "George IV. and Canning"—Westmacott's "Cymbal Plaery"—Wyatt's "Musidora," and many others.

THE SCULPTURE GALLERY.

It will be obvious that to enter into details concerning all the Art-riches of Chatsworth would be to occupy a whole Part—instead of a few pages—of our Journal ; and our visit to the mansion may conclude with a brief notice of one of its most interesting relics.

"Queen Mary's Bower" is a sad memorial of the unhappy Queen's fourteen years' imprisonment here.   It has been quaintly described as "an island plat on the top of a square tower, built in a large pool." It is reached by a bridge, and in this lonely island-garden did Mary pass many days of a captivity, rendered doubly painful by the jealous bickerings of the Countess of Shrewsbury, who openly complained to Elizabeth of the Queen's intimacy with her husband ; an unfounded aspersion, which Mary's urgent solicitations to Elizabeth obliged the Countess to retract, but which led to Mary's removal from the Earls custody to that of Sir Amias Pawlot.

QUEEN MARY'S BOWER.

Perhaps the crowning point of our excursion was a ramble to the Hunting-Tower on the hill above the house.   The ascent is by a road winding gracefully among venerable trees, planted "when Elizabeth was queen," and occasionally passing beside a fall of water, which dashes among rocks from the moors above. The tower stands on the edge of the steep and thickly wooded hill ; it is built on a platform of stone, reached by a few steps ; it is one of the relics of "old" Chatsworth, and is a characteristic and curious feature of the scene. Such towers were frequently placed near lordly residences in the olden time, for the purpose "of giving the ladies of those days an opportunity of enjoying the sport of hunting," which, from the heights above, they saw in the vales beneath.

THE HUNTING TOWER.

The view from the tower is one of the finest in England. The house and grounds below, embosomed in foliage, peep through the umbrage far beneath your feet ; the rapid Derwent courses along through the level valley. The wood opposite crowns the rising ground, above Edensor—the picturesque and beautiful village within whose humble church many members of the noble family are buried. The village itself may be considered as a model of taste—it resembles a group of Italian and Gothic villas, the utmost variety and the most picturesque styles of architecture being adopted for their construction, while the little flower-gardens before them are as carefully tended as those at Chatsworth itself.

Upon the hills above are traces of Roman encampments, and from the summit you look down upon the beautiful village of Bakewell, and far-famed Haddon Hall—the antique residence of the Dukes of Rutland, an unspoiled relic of the sixteenth century. Looking toward the north, the eye traverses the fertile and beautiful valley of the Derwent, with the quiet little villages of Pilsley, Hassop, and Baslow, consisting of tiny groups of cottages and quiet homesteads, speaking of pastoral life in its most favourable form. The eye following the direction of the stream is carried over the village of Calver, beyond which the rocks of Stoney Middleton converge and shut in the prospect, with their gates of stone ;—amid distant trees, the village of Eyam, celebrated for its mournful story of the plague, and the heroism of its pastor, is embosomed. The ridge of rock stretches around the plain to the right, and upon the moors are traces of the early Britons in circles of stones and tumuli, with various other singular and deeply interesting relics of the "far off past."

Turning to the south, the prospect is bounded by the hills of Matlock ; the villages of Darley-le-Dale, and Rowsley, reposing in mid-distance ; the entire prospect comprising a series of picturesque mountains, fertile plains, wood, water, and rock, which cannot be surpassed in the world for variety and beauty. The noble domain in the foreground forming the grand centre of the whole :

"This palace, with wild prospects girded round.
Where the scorn'd Peak rivals proud Italy."

It was evening when we ascended this charming hill, and stood beneath the shadow of its famous Hunting Tower. The sun had just set, leaving a landscape of immense extent sleeping beneath rose-coloured clouds ; the air was balmy and fragrant with the peculiar odour of the pine trees which topped the summit of the promontory on which we stood. We were told of Taddington Hill—of Beeley Edge—of Brampton Moor—of Robin Hood's bar—of Froggat Edge—until our eyes ached from the desire to distinguish the one from the other. There was Tor this, and Dale that, and such a hall and such a hamlet ; but the stillness by which we were surrounded had become so delicious that we longed to enjoy it in solitude.

THE MOORISH SUMMER HOUSE.

What pen can tell of the beams of light that played on the high-lands, when, after the fading of that gorgeous sunset the valley became steeped in a soft blue-grey colour, so tender, and clear and pure, that it conveyed the idea of "atmosphere" to perfection. Then, as the shadows, the soothing shadows of evening, increased around us, the woods seemed to melt into the mountains ; the rivers veiled their course by their misty incense to the heavens—wreath after wreath of vapour creeping upwards ; and as the distances faded into indistinctness, the bold headlands seemed to grow and prop the clouds ; the heavens let down the pall of mystery and darkness with a tender, not terrific, power ; earth and sky blended together, softly and gently ; the coolness of the air refreshed us, and yet the stillness on that high point was so intense as to become almost painful. As we looked into the valley, lights sprung up in cottage dwellings ; and then, softly on a wandering breeze, came at intervals the tolling of a deep bell from the venerable church at Edensor ; a token that some one had been summoned to another home—perhaps in one of those pale stars that at first singly, but then in troops, were beaming on us from the pale blue sky.

While slowly descending from our eyrie, amid the varied shadows of a most lustrous moonlight our eyes fell upon the distant wood which surrounded Haddon Hall ; its massive walls, its mouldering tapestries, its stately terrace, its quaint rooms and closets, its protected though decayed records of the olden time, its minstrel gallery—were again present to our minds ; and it was a natural and most pleasing contrast—that of the deserted and half-ruined house, with the mansion happily inhabited, filled with so many Art-treasures, and presided over by one of the best gentlemen that monarch ever ennobled and a people ever loved.

The Village of Eyam.

ERBYSHIRE has been long and deservedly celebrated for the variety and beauty of its scenery. No English county possesses these qualities in a more remarkable degree ; for while the scenery in some districts is of the most luxuriantly pastoral character, in others it is wild and barren—presenting a total contrast— singularly impressive and magnificent. These very distinct characteristics sometimes closely combine, and we have the grandeur of rocky scenery coupled with the most luxuriant vegetation, as in Dove Dale, the beauties of which have been celebrated from the days when Izaak Walton fished there, with his friend Cotton, who sang "The Wonders of the Peak," and the beauties of the charming river Dove. A greater poet, who brought travelled experience to the scene, has also strongly testified to its charms. Byron in a letter to Moore asks him :—"Have you ever seen Dove Dale? there are some scenes in England equal to anything in Switzerland." Moore afterwards lived at Ashbourne, within a mile or two of the Dale, for about two years, and while there wrote his most beautiful poem "Lalla Rookh." The county is indeed a fit residence for a poet for like the poetic mind :—

By turns 'tis soft, by turns 'tis wild—

a character it assumes from the nature of its surface, which is singularly undulating, and at varied altitudes, so that a walk of a few miles may not unfrequently display a change indicative in a very marked degree of varied temperature in the high and low lands. Thus reaping may have been completed in the valleys, and the grain secured, while the corn is yet green on the mountains—the husbandmen there awaiting another month to ripen the harvest. The highest point is about Castleton, where the head of Mam Tor is frequently enveloped in clouds, and from the summit of which may be distinctly traced the geological character of the county, the eye detecting the series of *plateaux* which step by step stretch onward toward the low land in which the capital city of the county stands. This mountain range takes its rise near the village of Ashover, and is continued thence through the Peak of Derbyshire, Westmoreland, and Cumberland into Scotland, increasing in grandeur and sublimity in its course, and has been dignified by Camden and others with the appellation of "the English Apennines."

VILLAGE OF EYAM.

The visitor to Chatsworth, "the Palace of the Peak," is in the midst of the hill scenery which gives beauty to the county, and at the foot of the rocks which contribute to its grandeur, some few miles distant in the district known as "the High Peak." From the terrace in front of this noble residence ; or better still, from the antique hunting tower on the hill above, the eye commands a view up the valley of the Derwent, where :—

"Deep and low the hamlets lie,"

of Pilsley, Hassop, and Baslow, sheltered on one side by the lofty ridge of mountains denominated Froggat Edge, whose sterile and rugged edges cut sharply against the sky, toward the village of Calver, where the hills meet on the other side of the Derwent, which runs rapidly along its stony bed with a sound beautifully realising Coleridge's lines :—

"A noise as of a hidden brook
   In the leafy month of June ;
That to the listening woods all night,
   Singeth a quiet tune."

Beyond Calver the mountains rapidly close in, until at Stoney Middleton they leave but a narrow gorge for the travellers who journey toward the Peak. Here the rocks have the appearance of perpendicular walls, and, in some instances, the regular tower and turret-like forms they assume, have nearly as much the effect of an old castellated building when viewed from a distance, as the famed group of rocks on Stanton Moor, that go by the name of Mock Beggar Hall, from its similarity to a baronial residence, which might lead a beggar out of his path in quest of Charity. Half way up the dale,[97] a chasm in the rock leads by a steep ascent to the village of Eyam, which occupies the table-land on the summit of these cliffs, and above which again rise the green hills. The situation of the village has been truthfully and happily described by Mary Howitt :—

"Among the verdant mountains of the Peak,
There lies a quiet hamlet, where the slope
Of pleasant uplands ward the north-winds bleak
Below, wild dells romantic pathways ope ;
Around, above it, spreads a shadowy cope
Of forest trees : flower, foliage, and clear rill
Wave from the cliffs, or down ravines elope ;
It seems a place charmed from the power of ill
By sainted words of old :—so lovely, lone, and still."[98]

---

[97] Middleton Dale is not without its history and its legends : traces of Roman occupancy have been frequently discovered and the bath is believed to have been originally established here by them. It is two degrees higher than the warmest springs at Matlock. The high perpendicular rock which forms the first grand opening to Middleton Dale is known as the Lover's Leap, from the circumstance of a love-stricken damsel of the name of Baddeley precipitating herself from the summit, in 1760, and falling from the fearful height comparatively uninjured, the shrubs and bushes catching her garments and breaking her fall. It was in passing through this dale in 1743 that the attention of Lord Duncannon was attracted by the beauty of the spar which his horse accidentally trod upon. He procured a larger piece, and had it formed into a vase by Mr. H. Watson of Bakewell, and thus originated a manufacture now extensively carried on of the beautiful fluor spar, provincially known as Blue John.

[98] These lines are from an exquisite little poem—"The Desolation of Eyam,"—published in a small volume of verse by William and Mary Hewitt nearly thirty years ago, when the gifted authors resided at Nottingham. The poem powerfully describes the ravages of the pestilence at Eyam, and the noble disinterestedness of its pastor.

The enduring celebrity of this unpretending village, which attracts the foot of the pilgrim from afar, is due to its having been the centre of the ravages of the great plague of 1665, and the scene of the more than Roman fortitude, the Christian devotion and self-sacrifice, of its pastor, the Rev. William Mompesson, who by his influence and example confined the plague to this one spot, and tended, encouraged, and lived among his people, until God was pleased to "stay" it.[99]

The plague was introduced into this remote district, (according to Dr. Mead, who notes the circumstance in his Narrative of the Great Plague in London), through the medium of a box of clothes sent to a tailor who resided there. "The person who opened the box, from whence the imprisoned pestilence burst forth, was its first victim ; and the whole of the family, with the solitary exception of one, shared the same fate. The disease spread rapidly, and almost every house was thinned by the contagion. The same roof in many instances, sheltered at the same time, both the dying and the dead. Short indeed was the space between health and sickness, and immediate the transition from the death-bed to the tomb. Wherever symptoms of the plague appeared, so hopeless was recovery, that the dissolution of the afflicted patient was watched with anxious solicitude, that so much of the disease might be buried, and its fatal influence destroyed. In the church-yard, on the neighbouring hills, and in the fields bordering the village, graves were dug ready to receive the expiring sufferers, and the earth with an unhallowed haste was closed upon them, even whilst the limbs were yet warm."[100] A clear idea of the ravages made here by this awful scourge may be gathered from the fact, that out of a population of three hundred and thirty persons who then inhabited Eyam, two hundred and fifty-nine fell victims to death.

When the pestilence first appeared, the clergy-man, Mr. Mompesson, was residing here with his wife and two children. The alarmed villagers communicated the fearful fact at once to their minister and friend. After the first shock, he speedily made up his mind as to the proper course to pursue ; he determined to confine the plague, if possi-

---

[99] The village has not wanted good or gifted ministers since the days of its renowned pastor. The Rev. Mr. Seward lived long here, and his accomplished daughter Anna Seward was born here, and yearly made a pilgrimage to her natal home. The Rev. P Cunninghame succeeded Mr. Seward ; he was a man of considerable poetic powers, and greatly devoted himself to bettering the condition of the cottagers around him.

[100] Rhodes's Peak Scenery, Pt 1 1818.

ble, to the bounds of his own parish, and to remain therein with his flock, as a true pastor should, and thus literally become "the priest, the physician, and the legislator of a community of sufferers." He was at this time a young man, his wife was in her twenty-seventh year ; and for her safety and for that of his two children he was deeply anxious ; he therefore at once imparted the melancholy news to her, explained the determined nature of his own self-sacrifice, and urged her immediate flight with the children while life and health remained. But he addressed a spirit as bold as his own, as truly imbued with knowledge of Christian duty, as determined to act with fortitude and resignation to death. She sent her children to a temporary home of safety, *but she refused to go herself ;* him whom she had sworn to love and cherish she would not desert in his hour of need ; the marriage vow of consolatory companionship, "till death doth part," she would keep to the letter, and resolutely with Christian fortitude cast away all fear, and prepared for a duty, although it was rendered doubly repulsive by the terrors which surrounded it.

These noble spirits by their example upheld the hopes of their poor parishioners ; they flew not from their homes when their pastor showed his faith and determination ; they trusted in him, and obeyed his behests ; he was their guide, their monitor in life and death. By this means the plague was pent in the narrow limits of the village, and the county— or perhaps we may say the country generally—was saved from similar ravages. Such was his influence over the villagers that at a time when, of all others, men listen least to argument and most to fear, he was implicitly obeyed in all things ; his character and example drew a moral *cordon*—"a charmed circle"—round Eyam which none attempted to pass, even though to remain within it was to hazard death almost inevitably. He arranged that food should be left at stated spots around the village, that troughs filled with water should be placed near the boundary line of communication, to receive and purify the purchase money used in the perilous traffic ; and thus all danger be avoided of spreading contagion. In his labours he was much assisted by the Earl of Devonshire, who was at the time residing at Chatsworth, where he also remained, undeterred by fear, during the whole time the plague was ravaging Eyam, doing all in his power to second the exertions of its noble pastor.

Mompesson felt more than ever the necessity of religious comfort and observances, and wished that his flock should unite in prayer to

God, and listen to the certain hope of salvation as they had done heretofore. But to assemble where they used in the village church would be to
woo the embraces of Death. He therefore fixed on a spot where he had
often enjoyed the beauty of retirement in happier hours, and there determined to assemble his hearers. It is a deep dell, close to the village,
formed by the fissures of the rocks as they descend toward Middleton
Dale, its craggy sides covered with trees, and a small stream trickling
along the midst. Half-way down the doll a rock projects from the mass
of foliage, and at a little height from the base is a small cavernous arch
about twelve feet high. This Mompesson chose for his pulpit ; it was
sufficiently high to command a view of the little dell ; its arched roof
concentrated and threw forth his voice to his hearers on the hill opposite.

> "A pallid, ghost-like, melancholy crew,
> Seated on scattered crags, and far-off knolls,
> As fearing each the other."

And thus was God's service conducted at Eyam during the plague,
and the spot is still sacred to the villagers, who term it *Cucklet Church.*

PULPIT ROCK.

The pastor's home was soon visited by the angel of death. His noble wife fell stricken by the pestilence : she died in the month of August,

and her death is thus feelingly told by her husband in a letter to Sir George Saville, the patron of the living at Eyam—"This is the saddest news ever my pen could write. The destroying angel having taken up his quarters within my habitation, my dearest wife has gone to her eternal rest, and is invested with a crown of righteousness, having made a happy end. Indeed had she loved herself as well as me, she had fled from the pit of destruction with the sweet babes, and might have prolonged her days, but she was resolved to die a martyr to my interest. My drooping spirits are much refreshed with her joys, which, I think, are unutterable."

MOMPESSON'S TOMB.

Her tomb is in front of the village church, near the entrance to the chancel. On one end is sculptured a winged hour-glass, and inscription, *Cavete, nescitis horam ;* on the other a skull and the words *Mors mihi lucrum.* At each corner, and a little in advance of the tomb, are placed four chamfered stone pillars, and close beside is an antique Runic cross.[101]

---

[101] This very beautiful cross has suffered from time and neglect : at one period it was thrown down in a corner of the churchyard and broken in three pieces. It was seen in this condition by the great philanthropist John Howard ; it was to the interest be showed in it, and to his recommendation, we owe its preservation. It was rescued from the docks and thistles which had nearly overgrown it, the shaft again set up in the churchyard, and the upper part of the cross placed on it, but the intervening portion (about two feet of the shaft) had been broken to pieces. It is an exceedingly interesting relic of early Christianity, and has been elaborately sculptured on all sides, with interlaced ornament and sacred figures.

When death had thus deprived him of his wife the pastor's hope of his own life failed him, and in the letter we have just quoted, he speaks of himself to Sir George as "your dying chaplain," and assures him "this paper is to bid you a hearty farewell for ever." He recommends his children to his care, in memorable words which all parents should echo, "I am not desirous that they should be *great,* but *good.*" In writing to his children, he says, "I do believe, my dear hearts, upon sufficient ground, that she was the kindest wife in the world ; and I do think from my soul, that she loved me ten times more than herself. Further I can assure you, my sweet babes, that her love to you was little inferior to hers for me. For why should she be so desirous of living, but that you might have the comfort of my life ;"—he adds a touching story of her death bed, when on refusing all sustenance or cordials, "I desired her to take them for your dear sakes. Upon the mention of your dear names, she lifted herself up and took them, which was to let me understand, whilst she had strength left, she would embrace any opportunity she had of testifying her affection to you."

RILEY GRAVESTONES.

At this time the plague raged fearfully at Eyam ; the churchyard was overcrowded, and in the fields and hills adjoining the village, its once-happy inhabitants found their graves. Some twenty years ago, the neighbouring fields contained the graves and monumental tablets of the dead ; but they are all now obliterated by the hand of the husbandman, except one group, known as "the Riley Gravestones," which are situated about half a mile from the village on the hill-side ; a wall has been erected round the stones that remain, but many whose resting-places were not distinguished by such marks, are not included within this humble enclosure. One square tomb and six head-stones record the resting-places of an entire family ; and show how fearfully sudden the plague swept all away. The first who died was Elizabeth Hancock,[102] on August 3rd, 1666; the father died on the following day ; the three sons died together on the 7th of that month ; another daughter on the 9th, and another the day following ; leaving one boy only as the representative of the family.[103]

EYAM CHURCH.

It was during the August and September of this year, that the plague raged uncontrolled ; early in November, it ceased, leaving unscathed the pastor Mompesson, who on the 20th of November writes— "The condition of this place has been so sad that I persuade myself it did exceed all history and example ; I may truly say that our place has become a Golgotha, the place of a skull : and had there not been a small remnant of us left, we had been as Sodom and been made like unto Go-

---

[102] A descendant of this family—Mr. Joseph Hancock—was the originator, in 1750, of the art of plating copper with silver which he practised at Sheffield, and which gave "Sheffield plate" an European celebrity, and the town employment and wealth ever since.

[103] Miss Seward relates that five of the villagers employed in the summer of 1757 in digging near these grave-stones, dug up some linen or woollen cloth ; the men all sickened of a putrid fever, and three of the five died ; the disorder was contagious, and proved mortal to numbers of the inhabitants of Eyam.

morrah. My ears never heard such doleful lamentations, and my eyes never beheld such ghastly spectacles. Now blessed be God, all our fears are over, for none have died of the infection since the 11th of October, and all the pest-houses have been long empty."

He now resumed his duties in the village church, the quaint and simple edifice where so many had listened whose ears were now closed by pestilential death. But he did not remain long amid the scenes his labours have consecrated ; his noble disinterestedness procured him many friends, who sedulously laboured to advance him in the Church ; the rectory of Eakring in Northamptonshire was presented to him, probably by his friend Sir George Saville, in whose neighbourhood it was situated. But such was the fear the people there still felt after the scourge of Eyam had been recorded, that they dreaded his coming among them, and a hut was erected for him in Rufford Park, where he stayed till all fear had subsided.

His friends afterwards succeeded in obtaining for him the prebends of York and Southwell, and had he been ambitious the highest ecclesiastical preferments might have been attained. He was offered the Deanery of Lincoln, but being more anxious to serve his friend than himself, he transferred his influence and interest to the witty and learned Dr. Fuller, author of "The Worthies of England," &c., who was accordingly inducted. He still resided at Eakring, and died there March 7th, 1708, in the seventieth year of his age.

It has been well said that a fervent piety, a humble resignation, a spirit that under circumstances peculiarly afflicting could sincerely say 'not my will but Thine be done,' a manly fortitude and a friendly generosity of heart, were blended together in the character of Mompesson."[104]

As Miss Seward emphatically observes, "his memory ought never to die ; it should be immortal as the spirit which made him worthy to live." We travel far to see costly tombs and "storied urns" of kings and conquerors, but is not a pilgrimage to such a grave as his a more worthy labour? for he has indeed triumphed over death, and "of such is the kingdom of heaven."

---

[104] Rhodes Peak Scenery.

The Grave of Grace Aguilar.

ILGRIMAGES, pilgrimages!" exclaimed a German friend whose family had been shorn of its "olive branches" by so many hurricanes, that, although still in the prime of life, his head was bowed and his hair grey :—"Pilgrimages! what is life but a pilgrimage over graves!"

The older we grow, the better we comprehend the force of this sad truth ; life is indeed a pilgrimage over graves ; but how different are the ideas and emotions they suggest or excite!

In pent up cities, the graves cluster round ancient churches ; congregations after congregations are pressed into festering earth until the enclosure becomes a charnel house ; yet they prove how devoutly later occupants have longed to rest in death with the loved in life. The nameless mounds are hardly shrouded by broken turf ; records, on the cankering, crumbling head-stones, are almost obliterated some are closely bordered and capped by heavy stones, as if rich inheritors dreaded a resurrection ; others there are, where the dock and the nettle are matted around rusty railings, as though no hand remained that ever pressed, in friendship or affection, the hand which moulders beneath ; others' again, are marked by broad headstones, new and well lettered, the black on the pure white setting forth a proud array of virtues, of which the co-mates of the departed never heard ; a few dingy and heavy monuments stand apart, and look down with civic haughtiness on humbler graves. Repulsive specimens of bad taste are these elaborate monuments often ; in their ornaments so unmeaning, their clumsy dignity so intrusive, so coarsely ostentatious—the epitaphs so earnest in saying *by whom* the carved stones were erected!

Our village churchyards, lying away amid glorious trees, or tranquil valleys, or sleeping on the sloping hills, where "birds sing, lambs bleat, and ploughboys whistle,"—however picturesque they may appear in the distance, have frequently the same uncared-for aspect as those within the city. We love the living, but we seem to care little for the dead. However much we may muse on crossing "the churchyard," or indulge in poesy, where

> "The rude forefathers of the hamlet sleep ;"

our places of burial, with the exception of cemeteries, which are as yet too new to show what they may become, bear but slight testimony to the "love that lives for ever." The contrast is humiliating when we visit other lands and mark the attention paid to graves of relatives and friends. A certain sum is annually set apart by the peasants in many districts of France, for visiting and decking the resting-places of those whom Death has taken ; the fresh garland is hung on the simple cross, and the prayer earnestly repeated for the soul's peace ; and these tributes continue for years and years, long after the bitterness of sorrow has passed away.

We have seen an aged woman with white hair strewing flowers on her mother's grave, though forty years had passed since the separation of the living from the dead ; and once, attracted by the beauty of a girl who had been decking, and then praying, beside a nameless grave, we asked for whom she mourned—although the word "mourned" had little association with her bright face and sunny smile.

She answered, none of her people slept there ; she had nothing of herself to do with graves ; it was Marie's mother's grave, and Marie had gone far away—to England. Marie was her friend, and she had promised her that she would deck that grave, and pray beside it ; and all for the love she bore her friend. We asked if she was certain Marie would return :

"No, there was no certainty, but she would watch the grave and deck it, and say the prayers Marie would have said, all the same ; she loved Marie, and had promised her." There was something very tender in this friendly fidelity, this tending the dead for the sake of the living— the living, dead to her.

For ourselves, the place of tombs has rarely been one of sorrow ; we have loved to visit the last dwellings of those who have gone home before us. We have thought of the enjoyment of re-union ; and dwelt upon the delight of an eternity of harmony and love—that "perfect love which casteth out fear." We have speculated on seeing Milton in the company of angels—on recognising Bunyan with the faithful—on be-

holding Fenelon at the "right hand," and Mendelssohn among the chosen! Knowing that God is a more merciful judge than man, we believe
that there we shall see many faiths prostrate in adoration of the one great
LORD, who is for all, and "above all and in us all." We have looked to
the higher nature, the divine essence, of those we have honoured ; and
when noble deeds have been done, or lofty genius has triumphed, we
have listened with more than doubt to the insinuations of those who, in
former, as in present, times, aim to detract from the excellence it is not
given them to understand. We do not cater for the prejudices of sects or
parties, but simply desire to lay our tribute of homage on the graves of
those who seem to us most worthy, and have been most useful. We
have enjoyed the high privilege of knowing many remarkable people
who have passed from among us during the last twenty years,—having
won for themselves a glorious immortality by the exercise of talents
which, in any other country, would have led to national distinctions.
Yet they are well remembered! and to them be *all* the glory of success.
The memory of these—great lights, great authors, great statesmen, great
philosophers, great warriors, —is still

"Green in our souls."

But there were some stars of lesser magnitude who, if longer
spared among us, would have become luminaries of power ; some who
were summoned, when, according to our finite views, they had arrived
at the period for their faculties to expand, and they were about to reap
the harvest of long years of labour and of care ; such was Mrs. Fletcher,
better known as Miss Jewsbury, one of the chosen friends of Mrs. He-
mans, who passed away in a foreign land, far from all who loved her.

And such was GRACE AGUILAR—a Jewess, of mind so elevated,
heart so pure, and principles so just and true, as to deserve a lofty seat
among those "Women of Israel," whose lives were so beautifully rendered by her delicate and powerful pen. It seems Quixotic in this day of
sunshine of civil and religious liberty, to attempt to combat the prejudices which, we are gravely told, do not now exist against the Jewish
community ; yet it is impossible to observe society and not perceive that
whatever political disabilities may be removed from them, individual
prejudice against those from whom our blessed Saviour sprung, and who
gave birth to the apostles of the Christian faith, is as deeply seated, as in
the days when faggot and fire were the ministers employed for their
conversion.

How can it be that we, in our age, look down with cold, or scornful eyes upon this once "chosen people"—chosen when the material world was in its youth—those children of Israel, whose history is the foundation of our faith! We read *our* Bible, which is *their* Bible ; our code of conduct is based upon *their* commandments, which are *our* commandments ; *our* salvation is gained by the Jewish sacrifice of the lamb without spot or blemish ; *our* apostles, the promulgators of the fulfilment of the Old Testament prophecies and the founders of the New, were Jews. We are especially blessed in triumphing in a hope fulfilled—while to them the promise is yet to come ; they linger and wait century after century for what they lost, and we won ; this is their sorrow, and hard to bear is their punishment—but it should not detract from the honour and glory which was, and is, theirs from ages past. The condemnation we give them is unworthy of us, and undeserved by them—*They brought no wrath upon us by their blindness ;* and we should remember the time will come when we shall be gathered—Jews and Gentiles—together from the four quarters of the globe, from the east and from the west, from the north and from the south, "And there shall be one fold and one shepherd." But of what do we, in these days, chiefly accuse the Jews?—of being a Mammon-making, and a Mammon-loving people?—Ought we not to look to ourselves in that matter, and remember the old saying about houses of glass, and throwing of stories. There are but too many evidences of late before the world, of the Mammon-worship of *our own* people, to render any bowing down to the molten image remarkable in the children of Israel ; yet it is marvellous how those who think and reason on all new things, give in to old prejudices without question or examination—clinging with child-like tenacity to foul traditions, as if they were established truths.

We no longer politically outrage a people who have been, at all times, LOYAL, peaceable, and industrious ; we do not confine them to any particular quarter of our great city ; nor drive them out of it like rabid dogs ; we suffer them to make money and keep it, and we borrow it for our own wants ; we allow them to worship as they please—but by denying them a cordial fellowship with us, we restrict their improvement in all Arts but the one of money-making ; —and they, unable to attain distinction except through their gold, naturally cling to that which gives them what all men covet—Power.

At our first introduction to Grace Aguilar we were struck, as much by the earnestness and eloquence of her conversation, as by her delicate and lovely countenance. Her person and address were exceedingly pre-possessing ; her eyes of the deep blue that look almost black in particular lights ; and her hair dark and abundant. There was no attempt at display ; no affectation of learning ; no desire to obtrude "me and my books" upon any one, or in any way ; in all things she was graceful and well bred. You felt at once that she was a carefully educated gentlewoman, and if there was more warmth and cordiality of manner than a stranger generally evinces on a first introduction, we remembered her descent,[105] and that the tone of her studies, as well as her passionate love of music and high musical attainments had increased her sensibility. When we came to know her better, we were charmed and astonished at her extensive reading ; at her knowledge of foreign literature, and actual learning—relieved by a refreshing pleasure in juvenile amusements. Each interview increased our friendship, and the quantity and quality of her acquirements commanded our admiration. She had made acquaintance with the beauties of English nature during a long residence in Devonshire ; loved the country with her whole heart, and enriched her mind by the leisure it afforded ; she had collected and arranged conchological and mineralogical specimens to a considerable extent ; loved flowers as only sensitive women can love them ; and with all this was deeply read in theology and history. Whatever she knew she knew thoroughly ; rising at six in the morning, and giving to each hour its employment ; cultivating and exercising her home affections, and keeping open heart for many friends. All these qualities were warmed by a fervid enthusiasm for whatever was high and holy. She spurned all envy and uncharitableness, and rendered loving homage to whatever was great and good. It was difficult to induce her to speak of herself or of her own doings. After her death it was deeply interesting to hear from the one of all others who loved and knew her best (her mother), of the progress of her mind from infancy to womanhood ; it proved so convincingly how richly she deserved the affection she inspired.

Grace Aguilar, the only daughter of Emanuel and Sarah Aguilar, was born at the Paragon, in Hackney, in June 1816;[106] for eight years

---

[105] Grace Aguilar's family fled to England to escape Spanish and Portuguese persecutions, and some of them found homes and fortunes in the West Indies. Her mother's name was Diaz Fernandes.

[106] Her family were of the tribe of Judah. Of the original twelve tribes two only are at present known ; the tribe of Judah, the fourth son of Jacob and Leah, and the tribe of Benjamin, the youngest son of Jocob and Rachel. The other ten tribes revolted from Rehoboam A.M. 2964, when there were two separate kingdoms, A.M. 3205, when the ten

she was an only child, and after that period had elapsed, two boys were added to the family. Grace was of so fragile and delicate a constitution, that her parents took her to Hastings when she was four years old, and at that early age she commenced collecting and arranging shells, learning to read almost by intuition, and when asked to choose a gift, always preferring "a book." These gift-books were not read and thrown aside, but preserved with the greatest care, and frequently perused.

From the age of seven years this extraordinary child kept a daily journal, jotting down what she saw, heard, and thought, with the most rigid regard to truth ; indeed, after visiting a new scene, her chief delight was to read and ponder over whatever she could find relating to what she had observed. Her parents were both passionately fond of the beauties of nature, and she enjoyed scenery with them, at an age when children are supposed to be incapable of much observation. Her mother, a highly educated and accomplished woman, loved to direct her child's mind to the study of whatever was beautiful and true ; before she completed her twelfth year she wrote a little drama called "Gustavus Vasa ;" it was an indication of what, in after life, became her ruling passion.

The first history placed in her hand was that of Josephus ; increasing, as it was certain to do, her interest in her own people. In 1828, after various English wanderings, the family, in consequence of Mr. Aguilar's impaired health, went to reside in Devonshire. The beauty of the scenery which surrounds Tavistock inspired her first poetic effusions, and she became passionately fond of her new power ; yet her well-regulated mind prevented her indulging in the exercise of this fascinating talent, until her daily duties and studies were performed.

A life spent, as was that of Grace Aguilar, affords little incident or variety ; it is simply a record of talents highly cultivated, of duties affectionately fulfilled, and, as years advanced, of the formation of a great purpose persevered in with stoic resolution, until, supported by pillows, and shaken by intense suffering, the trembling fingers could no longer hold the pen. It cannot fail to interest those at all acquainted with her writings, to learn how she mingled the most intense faith and devotion to her own people, with respect for the teachers of Christianity. Well as

---

tribes were made captives by Shalmaneser, king of Assyria. The ten tribes have never since been heard of ; but the Israelites believe they are in existence, and will be gathered "from all the nations whither the Lord our God hath scattered them." The Spanish and Portuguese Jews are of the tribe of Judah. The German Jews are of the tribe of Benjamin.

we knew her, we were quite unacquainted with her religious habits ;
though the odour of sanctity exhaled from all she did and said, she never
assumed to be holier than others ; never sought discussion ; never, in
her intercourse with Christians, though sometimes sorely pressed, gave
utterance to a hard word or an uncharitable feeling ; even when roused
to plead with eloquent lips and tearful eyes the cause of her beloved Israel.

It is a beautiful picture to look upon—this young and highly endowed Jewish maiden, nurtured in the bosom of her own family, the
beloved of her parents, —themselves high-class Hebrews, —gifted with
tastes for the beautiful in Art and Nature, and a sublime love for the
true ; leaving the traffic of the busy city, content with a moderate com-
petence, soothed by the accomplishments, the graces, and the devotion
of that one cherished daughter, whose high pursuits and purposes never
prevented the daily and hourly exercise of those domestic duties and
services, which the increasing indisposition of her father demanded more
and more.

Stimulated by the council of a judicious friend, who, while she admired the varied talents of the young girl, saw, that for any *great purpose,* they must be concentrated, Grace Aguilar prayed fervently to God
that she might be enabled to do something to elevate the character of her
people in the eyes of the Christian world, and—what was, and is, even
more important—in their own esteem. They had, she thought, been too
long satisfied to go on as they had gone during the days of their tribula-
tion and persecution ; content to amass wealth, without any purpose beyond its possession ; she panted to set before them "The Records of Israel," to hold up to their admiration "The Women of Israel," those heroic women of whom any nation might be justly proud. Here was a
grand purpose,—a purpose which made her heart beat high within her
bosom. She knew she had to write *against* popular feeling ; —she had
the still more bitter knowledge that the greater number of those for
whom she contended, cared little, and thought less, of the CAUSE to
which she was devoted, heart and soul. But what large mind was ever
deterred from a great purpose by difficulties! The young Jewish girl,
with few, if any, literary connections ; with limited knowledge as to how
she could set those things before the world ; treasured up her intention
for a while, and then imparted it to that mother who she felt assured
would support her in whatever design was high and holy. Her mother
exulted in her daughter's plan, and had faith in that daughter's power to

work it out : she believed in her noble child, and thanked the God of Israel, who had put the thought into her mind. Mrs. Aguilar knew that Grace had not made Religion her study only for her own personal observance and profit. She knew that she embraced its *principles* in a widely-extended and truly liberal sense ; the good of her people was her first, but not her sole, object. The Hebrew mother had frequently wept tears of joy and gratitude when she observed how her beloved child carried her practice of the holy and benevolent precepts of her faith into every act of her daily life—doing all the good her limited means permitted— finding time, in the midst of her cherished studies, and still more cherished domestic duties, and most varied occupations, to work for and instruct her poor neighbours ; and, while steadily venerating and adhering to her own faith, neither inquiring nor heeding the religious opinions of the needy, whom she succoured or consoled. Her young life had flowed on in bestowing and receiving blessings, and now, when her aspiring soul sought still higher objects, how could her mother, knowing her so well, doubt that she would falter or fail in her undertaking! Proofs have been for some time before the world that she did neither.

She first translated a little work from the French, called "Israel Defended ;" she tried her pinions in "The Magic Wreath," and, feeling her mental strength, soared upwards in the cause of her people ; she wrote "Home Influence," and "The Spirit of Judaism." But the triumphant spirit was, ere long, clogged by the body's weakness. In the spring of 1838, she was attacked by measles, and from that illness she never perfectly recovered. Soon, she commenced the work that of itself is sufficient to create and crown a reputation—"The Women of Israel." But while her mental powers increased in strength and activity, she became subject to repeated attacks of bodily prostration ; and her once round and graceful form was but a shadow. The physician recommended change of air and scene ; and sometimes she rallied, but there was no permanent improvement. Music was still, as it had ever been, her solace and delight ; but she was obliged to relinquish her practice of the harp, and to exercise her voice but seldom ; still her spirit cried "On, on," and every hour she could command was devoted to her pen.

"The Records of Israel," "The Women of Israel," and "The Jewish Faith," separately and together, show how, heart and soul, she laboured in the cause she had so emphatically made her own. The first publication relating so particularly to her own people, met with but a cool reception from the English Jews but in America (where the Hebrews enjoy perfect equality with their Christian brethren) they hailed this rising star with joy, and looked anxiously for its meridian. Letters and congratulations came to her across the Atlantic ; and those who had read only her fugitive pieces, were astonished at the concentrated zeal and pious energy which animated her when writing of the Hebrews.

A little "History of the English Jews," published by the Messrs. Chambers, is perhaps superior to her other writings in style and finish— the sentences are more condensed—the information more full of interest. It was, we believe, her last labour of love, and she greatly rejoiced in its publication. When it was finished, she had resolved to visit the German baths, and enjoy, as much as her increased debility permitted, the society of her eldest brother, who at that time was studying music (the art in which he now so much excels) at Frankfurt. Her youngest brother was at sea. There were times, even before her departure for Germany, that she felt as if her days were numbered ; but this feeling she studiously concealed from her mother, and bore her sufferings with the sweet and placid patience which rendered it a privilege to see her and to hear her speak. At times she really thought she might be spared a little longer to comfort her mother, to witness the distinction certain to reward her brother, and enjoy the reputation which now rushed upon her, especially from her own people, both here and in America.

Devotedly attached to her friends, she bitterly regretted that she could not take leave of them all ; but her weakness increased daily ; propped up by pillows she still continued to write, until her medical advisers expressly commanded that she should abstain from this—her "greatest and last luxury." She obeyed, though expressing her conviction that writing did her good, not harm ; she frequently said that when oppressed by care, anxiety, and pain, her favourite pursuit drew her from herself and she firmly believed that writing relieved her headaches, —and this at a period when she had grown too ill even to listen to music. But, all—all her sufferings were borne with angelic patience, as the will of her Heavenly Father and she would console her mother with words of cheerfulness and hope.

We have said her life had in it nothing to render it remarkable ; surely we are in error ; her patient, industrious, self-sacrificing life, was remarkable not only for its sanctity, its talent, and its high purpose, but for its earnest and beautiful simplicity, and perfect *womanliness.*

When the period of her departure for Germany had arrived, her friends found it difficult to bid her farewell ; for they thought it would be the last time they should ever press that thin attenuated hand ; but the brightness of her eyes, the hopefulness of her smile, made them hope against hope. She left England on the 16th of June, 1847, lingered in the brilliant city of Frankfurt for a few weeks, and then went to the baths at Langen Schwalback. She persevered in her use of the baths and mineral waters, but they afforded no relief ; she was seized one night with violent spasms, and the next day was removed to Frankfurt. Convinced that recovery was now impossible, she calmly and collectedly awaited the coming of death : and though all power of speech was gone, she was able to make her wants and wishes known by conversing on her fingers. Her great anxiety was to soothe her mother ; though her tongue refused to perform its office, those wasted fingers would entreat her to be patient, and trust in God. She would name some cherished verse in the bible, or some dearly-loved psalm, that she desired might be read aloud. The last time her fingers moved it was to spell upon them feebly, *"Though he slay me, yet will I trust in Him ;"* when they could no longer perform her will, her loving eyes would seek her mother and then look upwards, intimating that they should meet hereafter. Amen!

Her death occasioned deep regret among the Hebrews both in Europe and America ; foreign tabernacles poured forth their lamentations, private friends gave voice to their grief in prose and poetry, and the various journals of both hemispheres spoke of her with the respect and admiration else deserved. But to those who really knew Grace Aguilar, all eulogium falls short of her deserts ; and she has left a blank in her particular walk of literature, which we never expect to see filled up! Her loss to her own people is immense ; she was a golden link between the Christian and the Jew ; respected and admired alike by both, she drew each in charity closer to the other ; she was a proof ; living and illustrious, of Jewish excellence and Jewish liberality, and loyalty, and intelligence. The sling of the son of Jesse was not wielded with more power and effect against the scorner of his people, than was her pen against the giant Prejudice.

We have dwelt more than may be thought necessary on Grace Aguilar's championship of her own people, because *that* distinguishes her from all other female authors of our time ; and when writing of the "fold of Judah," there is a tone of feeling in all she has published which elevates and sustains her in a remarkable manner. In conversation, the mention of her people produced the same effect. Sometimes she seemed as one inspired ; and the intense brightness of her eyes, the deep tones of her voice, the natural and unaffected eloquence of her words, when referring to the past history of the Jews,—and the positive radiance of her countenance when she spoke of the gathering of the tribes at Jerusalem, could never be forgotten by those who knew this young Jewish lady. In time, as we have said, her own people estimated her as she deserved. She received a very beautiful address from some of the "women of Israel" before she left this country for Germany. Among her works of a more general nature, "Home Influence" is perhaps the most popular ; and its sequel, "The Mother's Recompense," though only lately published, was written as far back as the year 1836. "The Vale of Cedars" is a tale of Jewish faith and Jewish suffering, founded on singular facts that came to her knowledge through some of her own people : the arrangement of the story was difficult as it is always difficult to embellish what is simple and dignified, without destroying its effect and beauty — but, as we have said, whenever Grace touched upon her own people, she wrote and spoke as one inspired ; she condensed and spiritualised, and all her thoughts and feelings were steeped in the essence of celestial love and truth. We are persuaded that had this young woman lived in the perilous times of persecution, she would have gone to the stake for her faith's sake, and died praying for her murderers. And this heroism was not only for the great trials of life ; she was also a heroine in her endurance of small sufferings, and petty annoyances, deeming it sinful to manifest impatience, and thinking it right to be afflicted.

Grace Aguilar had earnestly desired that we should have met her at Frankfurt ; and the only letter we received from her after her arrival there, was full of the pleasant hope that we should meet again—in that cheerful city ; this was however impossible ; but when we knew that we should see her no more in this world we promised ourselves a pilgrimage to her grave : and over all the plans which mingled with our dreams of the splendid churches and vast cathedrals we were to see in Germany, would come a vision of Grace Aguilar's quiet grave in the Jewish burying ground of Frankfurt-on-the-Main ; and all the reality of the animated handsome city, its merchant palaces in the *Zeil,* and *Neue Mainzer Strasse,* its old *Dom,* so full of interest, with its fine monument of Rudolph of Sachsenhausen, beside which you cannot but recall the time when St. Bernard preached the crusade within its walls,—not even when we stood alone beneath the roof of St. Leonhard's Church, and knew that there once stood the Palace of CHARLEMAGNE,—not there—nor anywhere—could we forget that we had vowed a pilgrimage to the grave of "the lost star of the house of Judah."

How wild and inharmonious is the mingling of sights, as you whirl through continental cities! Heroic monuments—dark and deep dungeons—magnificent palaces—pictures—flowers—instruments of torture—delicious operas—all crowded together into a few short days!

We had not failed to remember that the brilliant city of Frankfurt was the cradle of the Rothschilds ; and it had been suggested that before we visited the Jews' burying-ground, we should see "the Jews' Quarter," to look upon the house where the "very rich man was born," and where his mother chose to live to the end of her many days, preferring, wise woman that she was, to dwell to the last amongst her own people ; yet living, we believe, long enough to know that her grandson represented in Parliament the first city of the modern world : and so became a practical illustration of the altered position of the Jews in the middle of the nineteenth century—sheltered under the vine and fig-tree that flourishes in England.

In few of the German cities did the Jews endure more persecution than in the *free* city of Frankfurt. During the past century the gates of the quarter to which they were confined, were closed upon them at an early hour, and egress and ingress were alike denied. In 1796 Marshal Jourdan, in bombarding the town, knocked down the gate of the Jews, quarter ; and laid several houses in ruin ; they have not since been replaced. Another tyrannical law, not repealed until 1834 restricted the number of Hebrew marriages in the city to thirteen yearly. It would seem, however that like the mother of the Rothschilds the people continue to dwell in their own quarter from choice, not necessity ; and well it is for the lover of the picturesque and for the antiquary that they do so. A ramble in the Jews quarter at Frankfurt might well repay a journey from London ; it is like going back to the fourteenth century, and meeting the people you read of in history far gone. Imagine the narrowest possible streets through which a carriage can drive flanked at either side by houses so high that the blue sky above becomes an idea rather than a reality ; story after story, with windows of ancient construction, small and narrow enclosed by iron gratings, from which frequently depended portions of many-coloured draperies ; garments for sale, which might have been of the spoil of the Egyptian ; strong swords and all kinds of weapons, rust-worn ; bunches of keys, whose handles would drive an antiquary distracted by their elaborate workmanship ; dresses of all countries and all fashions, fez caps, and old but costly turbans.   The rich balconies of the most exquisite design, however timeworn ; the *jalousies,* sometimes within, sometimes without the windows ; the Atlantes, supporting entablatures ; lost none of their effect from being half draped by a scarlet mantle or variegated scarf of Barbary.   Numbers of the houses were profusely ornamented at intervals by ball-flowers in the hollow moulding ; and balustrades, supporting carved copings.   Then above the doors, some of which evidently led to an inner court or a mysterious-looking passage, was inserted the most exquisitely wrought ironwork, sufficiently beautiful to form a model for a Berlin bracelet ; while from a stealthy passage peered forth the half shrouded face and illuminated eyes of dazzling brightness, of some ancient Jewess, whose long, lean, yellow fingers grasped the strong, but exquisitely moulded handle of the entrance.   The doors (except the very modern ones) were all of great strength, frequently studded with nails, and the bolts, now worn and rusty, had withstood many a rude assault.   We passed beneath small oriel windows, supported by richly carved stone brackets, grey and mouldering ; and beside bay windows, of pure gothic times ; and when we gazed up—up—up—story after story, we saw what appeared to us more than one Belvedere, doubtless erected by some wealthy Jew as a place from whence he could overlook the city it was forbidden him to tread, or to enjoy pure air, which certainly he could not do in the densely close street beneath.   Many of the brackets supporting a solitary balcony were of beautiful design, though the greater number were defaced and crumbling.   We also passed several of the fan-shaped windows, so characteristic of the early German style, and here and there a quaint and fantastic *gurgoyle ;* from the mouth of one depended a bunch of soiled but many-coloured ribands.   What a vision it seems to us now—that wonderful Jews' quarter of the bright and busy city of Frankfurt!—a vision of some far-off Oriental Pompeii, repeopled in a dream! Never did we look upon faces so keen and withered, beards so black, or eyes so bright ; once we saw a curly-headed child, half naked in its swarthy beauty, throned, like a baby-king, upon a pile of yellow cushions ; and once again, as we drove slowly on, a tall young girl turned up a face of scornful beauty, as if she thought we pale-faced Christians had no business there, —and those two young creatures were all we clearly observed of youthful beauty within the "Quarter."

The avenues in the outskirts of German towns contribute greatly to their interest, —they protect from both sun and wind.   We drove leisurely along that which leads to the Cemetery of Frankfurt, and turned up a narrower road, that we might enter the walled-off portion of ground appropriated as the Jews' Burying-ground. Nothing can exceed the beauty of the view from the gate of entrance. The city is spread out in the valley like a panorama ; the brightest sunshine illumined the scene ; a girl was seated beneath the branches of a spreading tree in the distance ; she was a garland-weaver, and there she spent her days weaving garlands, which the living bought from her to place on the graves of their departed friends. The gates were open. Mrs. Aguilar had told us that HER grave was near the wall of the Protestant burying-ground—and there we found it.

The head-stone which marks the spot, bears upon it a butterfly and five stars, and beneath is the inscription—

"Give her of the fruit of her hands, and let her own works praise her in the gates."—PROV. Chap. xxxi., 31

Our pilgrimage was accomplished. It was, though in a foreign city, a pilgrimage to an English Shrine—for it was to the grave of an English woman—pure and good. On the 16th of September, 1847, at the early age of thirty-one, Grace Aguilar was laid in that cemetery, far from the England she loved so well—the bowl was broken, the silver cord was loosed!

We cannot conclude this tribute to the memory of one we loved, respected, and admired, without extracting a portion of an address presented to her by several young Jewish ladies, before her departure for Germany. Had the gift which accompanied it been of the richest and rarest jewels, and offered by the princes of this earthly world, it could not have been as acceptable as it was, coming from the hearts and hands of the maidens of her own faith.

We would simply add that the address is a proof ; if proof were needed, that Jewish ladies not only feel and appreciate what is refined, and high, and holy, but know how to express their feelings beautifully and well. Its orientalism does not detract from its pure and sweet simplicity :—

"DEAR SISTER,—Our admiration of your talents, our veneration for your character, our gratitude for the eminent services your writings render our sex, our people, our faith,—all these motives combine to induce us to intrude on your presence, in order to give utterance to sentiments which we are happy to feel, and delighted to express. Until you arose, it has, in modern times, never been the case, that a woman in Israel should stand forth, the public advocate of the faith of Israel, that with the depth and purity which is the treasure of woman, and the strength of mind and extensive knowledge that form the pride of men, she should call on her own to cherish, on others to respect, the truth as it is in Israel. You, Sister, have done this, and more. You have taught us to know and appreciate our own dignity ; to feel and to prove that no female character can be more pure than that of the Jewish maiden,—none more pious than that of the woman in Israel. You have vindicated our social and spiritual equality in the faith ; you have, by your excellent example, triumphantly refuted the aspersion that the Jewish religion leaves unmoved the heart of the Jewish woman,—while your writings place within our reach those higher motives, those holier consolations which flow from the spirituality of our religion, which urge the soul to commune with its Maker, and direct it to His grace and His mercy, as the best guide and protector here and hereafter."

We can say nothing of Grace Aguilar more eloquently or beautifully true ; it is the just acknowledgement of a large debt from the Women of Israel to a holy and good sister, who, having done much to destroy prejudice, and to inculcate charity, merits the thanks of the true Christian as much as of the conscientious Jew.

Chertsey and its Neighbourhood.

I.

THE DWELLING OF THOMAS DAY.

HOROUGHLY to appreciate England the stranger must leave its mighty Babylon ;—to understand the rich treasures of her actual beauty, he must quit the iron-shod highways of her traffic, and away, from even her country towns, into her villages ; abandon himself heedless of the passing hours, to the wonderful fertility and loveliness of her bye lanes, her high and fragrant hedgerows, her unrivalled parks, timbered with gigantic trees, and clothed in tints of ever-varying underwood. He must sit beneath the shadows of her church steeples, when the bells are ceasing to chime for morning service, and the sons and daughters of the village crowd to render the homage of consecrated prayer to the Almighty : he must inhale the rich perfume of her cottage gardens ; he must survey the swelling and folding hills, the placid and fertilising rivers ; he must loiter, again and again, in her lanes, creeping close to the hedges to permit the richly-laden waggons to pass on ; he must pause beside the entrances of her suburban villas,—and, stranger that he is! wonder at the marvellous order, and regularity, and neatness of every arrangement ; seeing that flowers grow, and turf is levelled, and arbours are twined as they are in no other country of the world : so that hill and dale, wood and park and field, castle and cottage, look one universal garden, where tillage seems as a garlanded pastime, and the wildest luxuriance of nature is tempered—perhaps too much tempered—into beauty.

In Scotland—stern, rigid, right-hearted Scotland—mountains, and streams, and lakes, and magnificent rocky passes abound ; but there is little richness to repose upon, little that gives assurance of the abounding, overflowing prosperity of England,—*too little,* for our taste, of the garden-like aspect, so suggestive of home and home delights. In de-populated Ireland there are the unfilled outlines of everything great and nothing accomplished,—except by nature ; the amazing fertility of the soil contrasting painfully with careless farming and ruined "cabins." The bewildering beauty of Killarney and the loveliness of the county Wicklow, steep the soul in sadness, because of the misery that clothes a fine cordial-hearted people in rags, and the unfortunate policy which still trails them through the "slough of despond" in which so many have perished : thus our spirits are blighted, and our sense of the beautiful is dulled by sorrow for sufferings we cannot alleviate.

How our English hearts rejoice when we pass the liquid barrier of our sea-girt isle, into the fertile, peaceful, rich, and glowing beauty of dear old England! How do we gladden at the reality of our return HOME! How we joy in the noble trees, the park-like meadows, the deli-cious lanes and hedge-rows,—the abundance of rural delights, which are fraught with a thousand times the enjoyment we derive from any foreign travel in the "mere country."

The overpowering and wonder-working provincial cities of Eng-land—filling space with the magnitude of their utilities—afford subject-matter for the philosopher and the "man of business ;" but for ourselves, we love the pastoral employments of England, we shun the power-loom, the railroad, and the steam-engine, and when we desire enjoyment we seek it

> "In cool grot and mossy cell,"

by dimpled brooks, where, through the woodland lacings of the trees, the blue arch of heaven reminds us of a future home, and the sunbeams, as they dapple the rich sward beneath, tell of bright pathways to eternity.

Of late, the world has given itself up, soul and body, as it were, to railway travelling ; we cannot project a journey of twenty miles without inquiries as to the "next station," and an immediate reference, not to the county map, but the almost unintelligible almanac of the railway, more perplexing in its "ups" and "downs" than the most intricate rule in alge-bra ; but which we regard, nevertheless, as an oracle, regulating our movements and our time thereby. We make no appeal from the laws of the steam-king ; we relinquish the independence of posting ; we are content to stop alike at the most convenient, or inconvenient distances from our object, provided we stop at a "station." We give our freedom, our comfort, our WILL in all matters of movement to the despot STEAM!

We only use our horses to pay visits, and our carriages as make-shifts—
"where there is no train!" We submit our motives to the locomotive, and
yield us, a willing sacrifice, in helpless listless multitudes, to the wholesale traffickers in steam and iron. Happily for us, our little innocent
railroad terminates, as we have said, peacefully enough at Chertsey ; it
arrives at its shady terminus in anything but an ostentatious manner,
and, to confess a truth, has made our tardy carriers wondrous civil, and
reduced the price of coal,—it leaves us plenty of highways and by-ways,
it has not displaced an inch of the old abbey meadows, or interfered with
the sacred groves of St. Anne's Hill. It seems, as we have before said,
rather ashamed of disturbing our rural ways at all, seeing it has so very
little to do ; its puffs are reduced to sighs, and its whole bearing is really
so unobtrusive that we scarcely object to its neighbourhood, and if it
were drawn by a horse instead of an engine, we believe it might even
look in keeping with the crowned head of St. George's Hill and the
mimic pine forest, through which, when detached from its parent train,
it creeps along its own particular "siding" from the Weybridge Station.
Leaving it, therefore, in peace, we proceed musingly on this our pilgrimage towards THE DWELLING OF THOMAS DAY.

Thomas Day! the eccentric and accomplished author of "Sand ford
and Merton," the friend of Lovell Edgeworth,—Thomas Day, who
planted the dark woods of Anningsley, which sweep round the bend of
Timber Hill, skirting the wild village of Brocks, the still wilder common
of Woking, and separated only by the hill from the Saxon holding of
Ottershaw! We take the lower road of St. Anne's Hill, fringed as it is
with laurels and over-hanging shrubs ; and ever and anon a peep at a
grotto, a temple, or an undulating lawn realises Arcadia. Away rapidly,
yet without the assistance of steam, through a road shaded by picturesque trees, and commanding a view of Fox's Hills, until we come to a
railing, inclosing a modern Elizabethan cottage, suggestive of far more
comfort than belonged to the period. The name—Almner's Barns—reminds us of the appropriation of the estate to the almoners of Chertsey
Abbey, becoming, in progress of time, vested in the crown at the period
of the suppression of religious houses. Tradition says that for a long,
long time, this estate was occupied by the Wapshott family, both as ten-
ants to the abbots of Chertsey, and to the crown ; the same tradition,
leaning to the marvellous, declares that these old heritors of the soil had
continued to cultivate the same spot of earth from generation to generation, ever since the reign of Alfred, by whom the farm on which they
resided was granted to Reginald Wapshott, their ancestor. This is a cu-

rious legend in farm history : tradition moreover adds that the ancestor of the Wapshotts was standard-bearer to Alfred, but turned his sword into a ploughshare, and became a farmer. There is, we are told, abundant proof that for at least five hundred years the Wapshotts rented this property, but during the period that the crown estates in Chertsey were held by his late Royal Highness the Duke of York, the rental of Almner's Barns was considerably increased ; and, after a heart breaking struggle to retain the farm of his ancestors, the last of this humble but time-honoured family, resigned what he felt he could not profitably or honestly retain. It is exceedingly interesting to converse with the aged, but clear-headed and firm-hearted man—the representative of the ancient yeoman-farmer race—who still resides in our pensive little town of Chertsey ; he is an admirable specimen of the hale old English farmer, who guided his own plough and gloried in his teem. He speaks freely of his long and lost inheritance, and believes that his ancestor was *warrener,* not armour-bearer, to Alfred.

He argues "that none of his descendants were inclined to cultivate the art of war, but that all were peace-loving, industrious farmers, and that if their ancestors had been war-like, the war spirit would have descended to some among them." At all events, whether the story of the standard be true or not, it is certain that the same family has occupied the same farm for several hundred years—never above, and never below, the rank of yeomen-farmers. Mr. Wapshott told us it was remarkable that his father died the very day they received notice to leave Almner's Barns, "which," he added, "was a most happy change for him, as he continually said the government would never turn the family out :" adding, "but I knew better." The measure was very unpopular in the neighbourhood where the Wapshotts were much respected.[107] England

---

[107] A newspaper of the period just before the Wapshotts compulsory flitting from their inheritance, gave the following sketch of this "farming family :"—"In the parish of Thorpe, between Chertsey and Egham, there resides a family, the most ancient perhaps in Europe, though by no means the most conspicuous.

"While disease, the sword, and sometimes the gallows or the guillotine, have reduced or extinguished so many families, while the revolutions in human affairs have elevated some, and sunk others in obscurity, through all the vicissitudes of Church and State, the peaceful family of Wapshott has continued to cultivate the same spot of earth, ever since the time of king Alfred. The storms which swept away such multitudes during the contests of York and Lancaster, passed harmless over this obscure dwelling. The Saxon, Danish, or Norman conquests, affected them not, and every king, from Alfred to George III., inclusive, may see the same space of a few acres, freely yielding its produce to the laborous hands of a Wapshott.

of late has deserted ancestral for Mammon worship, but this fine intelligent old man is still a subject of interest and an object of great respect in his native district.

KITCHEN IN ALMNER'S BARN.

He tells us there has long been a saying in Surrey that no Wapshott was ever very rich or very poor, and that he, the last of his race, will go to the grave in strict fulfillment of the adage. He dwells upon his ancestors fondness for field sports—it may be they were too fond of them, and maintained large hospitality in a warm country fashion, dining and supping as they did on a long oak table, the servants "below the salt" the farmer's family and friends at the upper end, and that concluded, they assembled within the walls of the great chimney which is still, as you see, in a degree preserved at Almner's Barns ; and while the mistress and her daughters spun or worked, and the servants were busied according to the season, the song was sung, the story told, and the events of the neighbourhood talked over. We cannot but think it melancholy that these old heritors have passed for ever from their holding ; it is the

---

"This family never experienced any elevation, and its humility is such as to exempt it from danger of depression. * * * * * The pride of ancestry, which swells in the bosom of a Courtenay, a Howard, or a Russell, is unknown to the lowly bosom of a Wapshott, whose blood flows on in an uncontaminated stream from the remotest ages : —he tills the same land that was ploughed by his grandfathers, and then sinks into the same grave.

'Doomed to the spot on which he grew,

He seeks his native bed.'

going out of a singular race, the extinguishing of a great fact in rural history ; and shining and pleasant as Almner's Barns looks now, and though we wish all good to its present possessor, we regret that it has passed into his hands.

Leaving Almner's Barns we turn up "Hardwick Court Lane," passing several tangled-looking cottages, and the green where once a fair was held ; (after the lapse of twenty years, forgotten! with all its revels, its buying and selling, and cheating and winning, as if it had never been!) this pretty lane brings us out opposite the noble park of Botleys—the finely built and richly wooded seat of Robert Gosling, Esq.—which we skirt, shaded by its umbrageous trees on one side, and those of Bretlands on the other, and leaving the tiny villa of Marylands to the right. On, along this wide and well-kept road, until we arrive at the old Saxon village of Ottershaw ; on—and up Timber Hill, pausing on its summit to inhale the pure fresh breeze, and take in, at a glance, the beauty and variety of the surrounding country. To the left crouching beneath the shelter of the pine wood, is the lodge and gate of ANNINGSLEY and the enjoyment of a wild wood drive is indeed refreshing, when, however high and hot the sun, the shadows of those perfumed trees lie closely upon beds of moss and waves of fern and heather.

LODGE GATE, ANNINGSLEY.

What a delicious wood it is! wild and wandering—untrimmed and prodigal of its own peculiar beauty ; such deep-toned red-brown stems to the lofty firs, whose dark green spines mat above our heads, where the summer breeze makes such reed-like music that we could fancy it the court of Pan himself. We hear the bleating of the lambs in the far-off meadows, and the soft tinkling of the sheep-bell ; the whistle of the blackbird, the loud daring song of the missel-thrush, and the soft whispering "coo" of the little brown dove,—"Brown Bessy," as the boys call her. The insect world revel in this shady place,—the stag-beetle and the greedy dragon-fly are of enormous size, and wood-lizards and stony-eyed frogs rove among the moss, while the "game" rustle about the spiral fern. We remember, last spring, seeing piles of fir-trees—shorn of their boughs—heaped outside the gates, and we trembled lest the wood had been despoiled of its greatest beauty,—"cleared," or "trimmed," or "untangled,"—but no, the hand of the spoiler had not impaired the character of the dark woods of Anningsley, and the only regret we feel is when they are left behind, and we reach a short tract of cultivated land through which the drive passes to the house.[108]

ANNINGSLEY.

[108] At the time when Mr. Day purchased this estate, there were at least 20,000 acres of land lying waste in its immediate vicinity. It lies about three miles south of Chertsey, but the district was as little visited, and the people as ignorant as if in the wilds of the New Forest. It was among such unpropitious circumstances the philosopher seated himself to improve the soil and its inhabitants.

The house, we can hardly tell how, looks put away in a corner, though there is no corner to put it in ; but it is exactly the sort of house we should have imagined Mr. Day, in his eccentricity, would have desired. Something shy and mysterious, commodious and unpretending ; peeping, rather than looking, at the wild solitary world beyond, and loving uncultivated, rather than cultivated, nature,—even at the time that his fine mind and benevolent heart were acting together for the good of present and future generations.

Some years ago it was our privilege, while visiting Edgeworthstown, to hear much of this singular man, from Maria Edgeworth, who loved to speak of her father's friends. It was pleasant to hear her talk of the author of "Sandford and Morton," as she talked of every one, developing a character in a sentence, and touching the foibles of humanity with rays of her own light and good nature until they almost brightened into perfections. Much of her power and innate cheerfulness she inherited from her father, who, though very different from Mr. Day, was his chosen friend from the time when Mr. Edgeworth was pursuing his mingled path of philosophy, amusement, and mechanics, at Hare Hatch, where Mr. Day, who then lived with his father and mother at Bear Hill, in Berkshire, called upon him and sought his acquaintance.[109] "To the day of his death," Mr. Edgeworth has written, and the characters are well drawn, "we continued to live in the most intimate and unvarying friendship,—a friendship founded upon mutual esteem, between persons of tastes, habits, pursuits, manners, and connections totally opposite. A love of knowledge and a freedom from that admiration of splendour which dazzles and enslaves mankind, were the only essential points in which we entirely agreed. Mr. Day was grave, and of a melancholy temperament ; I, gay, and full of 'constitutional joy.' Mr. Day was not a man of strong passions ; I was. He delighted, even in the company of women, to descant on the evils brought upon mankind by love ; and yet he could not avoid frequently tempting his fate, and what was still more extraordinary, he expected, that with a person neither formed by nature, nor cultivated (at that time) by art, to please, he should win some female

---

[109] Day was born, in 1748, in Wellclose-square, London, and received the first rudiments of his education at the Charter-house, completing his acquirements at Corpus Christi College, Oxford. He studied for the law, and was called to the bar, but the pursuit was ungenial to his tastes, and his fortune being ample, he studied to indulge it by a connection with the first literary men of the day, in whose friendship and correspondence he found the greatest pleasure, and to one of whom—Rousseau—he dedicated his "Dying Negro."

wiser than the rest of her sex, who should feel for him the most romantic and everlasting attachment,—a paragon!—who should forget the follies and vanities of her sex for him—who

'Should go clad like our maidens in grey,
And live in a cottage on love.'"

Mr. Edgworth says that Mr. Day's exterior was not prepossessing : "He seldom combed his raven locks, though he was remarkably fond of washing in the stream." Gentlemen seldom agree with ladies in their estimates of manly beauty ; we think Mr. Day's portrait decidedly handsome, though the want of *self-esteem,* which must have been a prominent organ in Mr. Edgeworth's development, was evidently deficient in that of Mr. Day ; he doubted his own success, and consequently did *not* succeed. His matrimonial views were a strange mingling of sacrifice and selfishness. Mr. Edgeworth states, that "for an object which should resemble the image of his fancy, he could give up fortune, fame, life,—everything but virtue ;" but he expected the lady to do the same, to yield up to his her habits, and even tastes, down to the selection of a glove or a ribbon. Love will do this, and more, spontaneously ; but love is impatient of dictation. He attached himself to Mr. Edgeworth's sister, but the lady was not to be intreated, and, after this disappointment—the herald of othera,—Mr. Day put in practice a scheme which had long occurred to his imagination : he resolved to rear up two girls as equally as possible, under his own eye, hoping they might be friends in childhood, and that before they grew to be women he might be able to decide which of them would be most agreeable to himself as a wife. The first selected was a beautiful orphan child, from the orphan school at Shrewsbury, whom he called Sabrina Sydney ; he then took another from the Foundling Hospital in London, whom he called Lucretia. He first placed these wards at a widow's house, in some court near Chancery Lane, and immediately applied himself to their education. For our own part, we think the plan might have succeeded had they been younger, but they were eleven and twelve years old, and, of course, their feelings and habits were already, in a great degree, formed. His romantic scheme occasioned inquiry and curiosity ; to avoid both, he determined to take them to France, where, as they were perfectly unacquainted with the language, their minds would be more under his control. He resided some time at Avignon. Whatever surprise his mode of life or opinions might have excited, his simplicity and purity of conduct, his strict morality, uncommon generosity, and excellent understanding, removed.

He entertained an unconquerable horror of the empire of fashion over the minds of women : simplicity, perfect innocence, and attachment to himself were the only qualifications at that time which he seemed to desire in a wife ; he was Rousseau-mad, but afterwards recanted the opinions he had endeavoured to practise. After the lapse of a few months he returned to England and parted with Lucretia, finding her either stupid or unwilling to learn, or unlearn, what he desired. He gave her three or four hundred pounds, placed her under proper protection, and, after a time, she married some small shopkeeper in London.

Everyone who knew Mr. Day was desirous of seeing how the second part of this philosophic romance would terminate. Sabrina was most engaging and amiable ; her guardian took a pleasant house at Stow Hill, near Lichfield, and steadily pursued his plan. All the ladies of the neighbourhood took notice of the girl, and attributed only the most honourable motives to Mr. Day. There he first met Honora Sneyd, whose personal and mental charms, developed beneath the loving care of the poet, Anna Seward, and her accomplished family, had power to attract the affections of three distinguished men,—Major Andre, Thomas Day, and Richard Lovel Edgeworth ; subsequently Honora became the wife of the latter, but not until after Major Andre's departure for America, and it is doubtful if she ever responded to the affection which the unfortunate officer felt for her to the last hour of his existence, and which drew forth the beautiful monody on his death from Miss Seward's pen. Sabrina, failing to realise her guardian's dream, he at last placed her at a school ; she was wilful, perhaps, touching the colour of a ribbon, or the arranging of her hair, and his feeling towards her fluctuated considerably at last. He provided for her with his usual liberality, and remained her friend until his death.[110]

Perhaps Mr. Day's new-found love for Honora Sneyd had much to do with his final rejection of Sabrina ; he offered this beautiful woman his hand, in a voluminous letter, telling her *honestly* what he expected, which men seldom do until *after* marriage. He was next led captive by the charms of Elizabeth Sneyd, a younger sister of the conquering Honora ; but again his want of self-esteem overthrew his wooing ; he abso-

---

[110] It was singular that when no longer very young, Sabrina was wooed and wed by a barrister, a Mr. Bicknel, who was the companion of Mr. Day when he selected her from among the orphans of Shrewsbury.

lutely went to France, and, in the simplicity and gravity of his heart, determined

(*"Such is the power of mighty Love,"*)

to cultivate those graces which he despised, in the hope they would aid his course of love.

Mr. Edgeworth says, in his Memoirs, "It was astonishing to behold the energy with which he persevered in these pursuits. I have seen him stand between two boards, which reached higher than his knees, from a desire to make them straight ; these boards were adjusted with screws, but the screwing was in vain. I could not help pitying my philosophic friend pent up in durance vile, for hours together, with his feet in the stocks, a book in his hand, and contempt in his heart."

And yet, after all this martyrdom, besides "doing" dancing, and fencing, and riding, on his return he was refused by the fair Elizabeth. Surely any loving, wise, woman could have been happy with—and, as the phrase goes, "managed"—such a man. A man who has sufficient honesty to talk common sense to a woman before marriage, pays the highest possible compliment to her intellect, and proves that he desires her friendship and companionship as well as her love. Mr. Day talked loudly of mans prerogative ; simply because he felt the kindliness of his own nature, he feared he should yield too much, be too heavily bound by the chains he sought. At last, and after, in a right noble hearted manner, promoting his friend Richard Lovell Edgeworth's marriage with Honora Sneyd, Mr. Day was united to Miss Milnes, of Wakefield, in Yorkshire ; a lady of charity and benevolence as unbounded as his own ; and the only objection he ever made to this accomplished lady, was, that she possessed a large fortune! No wonder that Thomas Day, the author of "Sandford and Merton," should be called "eccentric."

Maria Edgeworth said Mr. Day "talked like a book," and she believed (to use her own expression) "that he always thought in the same full-dress style." He wrote as fast as his pen could move ; this arose from the early care he had bestowed upon his native language. His poem of the "Dying Negro" was in advance of our abolition of the slave trade ; and it is believed that Doctor Darwin wrote more than one of the stanzas in that touching poem. The history of his authorship of "Sandford and Merton" was bound up with the Edgeworths.

Mr. Edgeworth and his charming wife, Honora, felt the lack of a particular class of books to follow "Mrs. Barbauld's Lessons," and commenced, without any intention of publication, the first part of "Harry and Lucy, or Practical Education," as it was called in the title-page to the first copies, printed literally for their own children. Mr. Day, much pleased with Mr. Edgeworth's plan, offered to assist him, and, with this intention, began "Sandford and Merton," which was first designed as a short story to be inserted in "Harry and Lucy."

The illness and death of Mrs. Honora Edgeworth interrupted the progress of the little volume, and Mr. Edgeworth, for a long time, could not endure to think of what her loss had rendered so painful. Meanwhile, Mr. Day wrote on rapidly, and finished, and published, his delightful book. While this floated on the full tide of popularity,—for a period of twenty years, or more,—"Harry and Lucy" remained *perdu* at Edgeworthstown. Miss Edgeworth used to say that all her dear father's literary ambition was for her, and that he at last gave her the first part of "Harry and Lucy" for a portion of her "Early Lessons." Well for the world was it that he did so!

We have heard that Mr. Day underrated "Sandford and Merton," and fancied his poems, and some political tracts he wrote, of far higher consequence. But while they are forgotten, the bright story-book of our own childhood will endure ; and were it "got up" in the modern fashion now, and republished, with a few erasures, and the illustrations it so frequently suggests, its popularity would revive, and it would be welcomed wherever the highest and best sentiments of our morel nature are cultivated.

It was deeply interesting, while driving through the very wood at Anningsley, which, in 1789, Mr. Day was occupied in planting, to read one of his letters to Mr. Edgeworth, where he confesses, nearly at the commencement, that he is out of pocket 300*l.* a-year by his farm! He says the soil he has taken is barren,—"the most completely barren in England,"—adding, "I consider the pleasure of everything to lie in the pursuit and, therefore, while I am contented with the conveniences I enjoy, it is a matter of indifference whether I am five, or twenty years in completing my intended plans. I have, besides, another very material reason, which is that it *enables me to employ the poor.*" This last consideration was ever uppermost in his mind ; with all his eccentricity and affected stoicism, his nature was essentially benevolent brave, and thoroughly independent. While he fancied him-self a misanthrope, he was exerting his time and faculties, and expending an ample fortune, for beneficent purposes, relieving, to the utmost of his power, all the wants of his fellow-creatures. Some one has said, that whoever plants a tree is a patriot ; although Mr. Day's marriage was unblessed—or unplagued—with children, he delighted in planting those beautiful woods for same future inheritor of the stubborn land.

It may be that our quotations seem somewhat tedious, but we write of one who, in that respect like his friend Richard Lovell Edgeworth, was singularly in advance of his period ; in our childhood we revered the author of "Sandford and Merton" next to the author of "Early Lessons," and never pass beneath the trees he planted without the memory of old feelings creeping into our very heart. Amongst many blessings we thank GOD that he keeps our "memory green," and that our enthusiasm is as genuine as when we first trembled with reverence in the presence of some of those great thinkers whom we hope to meet HEREAFTER. Anningsley, with its varied shadows and mysterious woods, is to us a place of deep interest. Though it is difficult to identify the rooms which were, or were not occupied by Mr. and Mrs. Day, the house and land have not departed from the family.[111] The joyful voices of happy children echo through the woods, and tempt one almost to forget that on the confines of that very wood the author and philosopher breathed his last on the 28th of September, 1789. His death is but another lesson of the uncertainty of life, which we too often calculate on, as if it were eternity. Mr. Day held a theory that whenever horses were vicious or unruly it was simply because they had been harshly treated. Having reared a favourite foal he determined to "break it" himself ; he mounted the colt, but his horsemanship was not sufficiently good to enable him to keep his seat, when the animal plunged, and eventually threw him, and struck him with his heels so severe a blow on his head that it terminated his existence.[112]

Mrs. Day was inconsolable ; she loved her husband with all the enthusiasm of young romance ; never was there a more devoted wife. She loved sufficiently to forget his peculiarities in her admiration of his virtues ; and she placed the following epitaph over his remains, in Har-

---

[111] The present owner of Anningsley is the Hon. James Norton, in right of his wife the grand-niece of Mr. Hay.

[112] The accident was the more sad, as it occurred when Day was paying an act of affectionate duty which he never omitted, a visit to his aged mother. She resided at Bear Hill, near Wargrave, in Berkshire, and he was on his journey thither when his horse threw him, and he died on the spot.

grave Church, Berkshire. The epitaph had been written by Mr. Day for the monument of a friend, but it was well applied to himself :—

> "Beyond the reach of time, or fortune's power,
> Remain cold stone, remain, and mark the hour,
> When all the noblest gifts which heaven ere gave,
> Were centred in a dark untimely grave!
> Oh! taught on Reason's boldest wings to rise
> And catch each glimmering of the open skies!
> Oh gentle bosom! oh unsullied mind!
> Oh, friend of truth, to virtue, to mankind!
> Thy dear remains we trust to this sad shrine,
> Secure to feel no second loss like thine."

Chertsey and its Neighbourhood.

II.

*T*HE walk from Chertsey to Weybridge is as pleasant a walk as can be desired ; especially on a morning of May, when the weather is cool, and the sun is playing at bo-peep through the fleecy clouds, which yield shade and refreshment to the teeming earth. Those who have no desire to pass through the pretty scattered village of Addlestone (where, here and there, an ambitious "villa residence" intimates that the Londoners are appreciating its salubrity and convenience) may still desire to prolong their walk by rendering homage to the CROUCH OAK, one of the most superb trees in England, which deserves a pilgrimage to its leafy shrine from any genuine lover of nature.[113] But if this has been already seen, it is pleasanter to wander up Woburn Hill than to pass over the Addlestone railway. The hill is deliciously sheltered from wind, and rain, and heat, by the outspreading foliage of the beautiful trees of Wo-

---

[113] In Brayley's excellent "History of Surrey," we are told that, "tradition states that this oak, in former ages, was considered to mark the boundary of Windsor Forest in this direction, and Queen Elizabeth is said to have dined beneath its shadow. Its girth at 2 feet from the ground is 24 feet. At the height of 9 feet, the principal branch, in itself as large as a tree, shoots out almost horizontally from the trunk, to the distance of 48 feet, and is known to have been 8 or 10 feet longer about twenty years ago. Before the enclosure of the manor of Chertsey-Beomond in 1808, this oak stood on the open common ; but it is now surrounded by a railing, and connected with the grounds of Captain De Visme. It forms, however, no part of his estate, and has been thus inclosed in order to preserve it from a practice accelerating its decay, namely, that of having the bark peeled off by ignorant females, from an opinion that, taken internally, it operates as a love charm! The name of *crouch* oak may possibly have been given to this tree from the low, crouching form of its chief branches." There is also a tradition that Wickliffe preached under it.

burn (the seat of the Hon. Locke King); and the public road, after crossing Fordwater Bridge, continues between the trickling Bourne and the Basing-stoke Canal, until it crosses the bridge, where the Wey, (dividing the parishes of Weybridge and Chertsey) the canal, and the Bourne, unite in one considerable body of water.

THE CROUCH OAK.

We are told that some rare aquatic plants border the meandering Bourne, and render a stroll along its banks a rich treat to the botanist. The entrance to the village of Weybridge has something of a foreign aspect, owing, perhaps, to its lofty trees and an uninterrupted avenue of limes, between quaint houses that are dimly seen beyond their walled-in gardens. But there are two roads, which, as it were, gird the village and spread out in different directions ; one, leading to the common and station, passes the chapel where the remains of Louis Philippe are for the present interred, and which is rendered still more sacred by the sorrows and tears of a royal, but exiled, family, living not far off—at Claremont—and those of many illustrious pilgrims from their native land. The chapel commands a beautiful view over the breezy heath, bounded by the bold headland of St. George's Hill. We were courteously admitted beneath a domed porch, (where the turning of a wheeled gate rings a soft-sounding bell), and conducted through a picturesque and exquisitely-kept garden to the little chapel, where the exiled family of France frequently assemble. We then descended to the crypt, containing two tombs—that of the founder of the chapel, a devout man (ac-

cording to his faith), and that of the first King of the French who maintained peace in France for eighteen years, and preferred the abdication
of his Throne to the shedding of his people's blood.[114] There was an
earnestness and fullness of sorrow within that crypt, which we have not
often felt in the midst of elaborate tombs and the pomp and pageantry of
death. The perfect and entire silence—the loneliness of the situation—
the rays of light pouring directly through the windows upon the
founder's tomb, while that of the KING occupied what may be called the
centre of the crypt, elevated two steps above the floor, and reaching to
the far end of the vault. There is something inexpressibly grand in the
simplicity of this last refuge of a great man and a mighty monarch. Our
hearts were filled with memories of the past ; when we saw him in the
radiance of his power—the venerated Ruler of a nation—combining the
holiest virtues of domestic life with the dignity and duties of his high
position. We remembered his vicissitudes—his large attainments—his
suavity and royal bearing—

    "All crushed into that small and silent tomb."

Great he was in adversity, and great in prosperity : for he had
learned the "uses" of both. Hereafter, he will receive gratitude from
France, and justice from History. In him the Arts of Peace had their
patron and protector : his choicest rewards were accorded to men of
genius : his recognition of *mind* was ever ready and cordial : and to have
been useful to his country—or to any country—was the surest road to
those public honours of which he was the wise and liberal distributor.

It is, therefore, a privilege to render homage at the grave of the illustrious exile : for it is homage less to the greatness of the monarch,
than to the virtues of the man!

---

[114] The chapel is a very small building, capable of giving accommodation to fifty persons only ; its ground-plan is, however, cruciform.

TOMB OF LOUIS PHILIPPE.

A crown and sceptre are carved at the head, and these few words :—

DEPOSITÆ JACENT
SUB HOC LAPIDE
DONEC IN PATRIAM
AVITOS INTER CINERES
DEO ADJUVANTE TRANSFERANTUR RELIQUÆ
LUDOVICI PHILIPPI
PRIMI FRANCORUM REGIS
CLARMONTII IN BRITANNIA
DEFUNCTI DIE AUGUSTI XXVI.
ANNO DOMINI MDCCCL.
ÆTAT. LXXVI.

REQUIESCAT IN PACE.[115]

---

[115] Under this stone lie buried the remains of Louis Philippe, first King of the French ; until, by God's assistance, they may be transferred into his country, among the ashes of his ancestors. He died at Claremont, in Great Britain, on the 26th of August, 1850, in the 76th year of his age. —May he rest in peace.

Upon the steps were placed several garlands, such as decorate the tombs in Pere-la-Chaise, and two vases of flowers.[116] "These," said the attendant, "were placed here by the Queen." A robin poured forth its wealth of song close to the window. A saintly requiem could not have moved us more ; it was so wild and tender—such clear, gushing music ; there was no other sound upon the clear, frosty air. We did not move until the chaunt was finished. We ascended into the outer world, and heard the key turned upon the door of that lonely crypt.

INTERIOR OF BRADSHAW'S HOUSE.

The other road, after passing the new church, leads beneath the lime avenue more directly to the most interesting part of Weybridge,— the entrance to Oatlands Park. The manor of Weybridge anciently belonged to the Abbey of Chertsey ; Henry VIII. obtained possession of Oatlands, and Queen Elizabeth is said to have shot with a crossbow "in the paddock." Anne of Denmark, the wife of James I., took to cultivate silk-worms at Qatlands, and had there a silk-worm room. The youngest son of Charles I. was born there, and was hence styled Henry of Oatlands ; it had previously been settled by the unfortunate Charles, as a dower-land, on Henrietta Maria. The house and domain were much injured during the interregnum, but, after the Restoration it was returned

---

[116] Wreaths of *immortels* are placed in front, upon which we noticed two inscriptions formed in dark flowers—"Regrets Eternels," "Au meilleur des Rois," and the dates "1827-1851."

to the queen in its dilapidated and dismantled state. It has confessed to
many masters, and, amongst others, to the Earl of Lincoln, who formed
the gardens at Oatlands.[117] This first gateway leads from the park to
Walton-on-Thames ; another, designed by Inigo Jones, and which
formed an entrance to the terrace, was not long ago sold for 10*l*, pulled
down, and removed. It was a fine work, and a real loss to the place.
The Duke of Newcastle built the far-famed grotto within the park, and
after the park and grotto[118] became the property of the Duke of York, the
duchess indulged her feeling and her fancy by the erection of some sixty
monuments to the memory of her dogs. These are placed at intervals
round what was once an ornamental piece of water, stored with gold and
silver fish. But her grace's love of the animal creation was only one of
the phases of her benevolence ; she was a singularly amiable and kind-
hearted princess, and there are those in Weybridge, to this day, who
speak of her charities with intense gratitude. It was deemed necessary,
by some, to erect a monument to her memory, and those who designed
to do honour to her excellent qualities also desired to be as sparing as
possible of their pecuniary resources. In times long past the column
which was known as the "Seven Dials', in London, had been removed,
and conveyed, for some forgotten purpose, to a place in our neighbourhood, called "Sayes Court,"—a handsome, well-wooded residence,
whose gables and chimneys form a picturesque object from Crockford

---

[117] There is a curious bird's-eye view of the old palace at Oatlands, as it appeared
about the time of Elizabeth, in Manning and Bray's "Surrey," and which is reproduced on
a smaller scale in Brayley's County History. Many of its features closely resemble
Hampton Court, particularly its square gate-towers, flanked by octangular turrets. The
buildings were exceedingly irregular, the entrance-court a waste walled space of great size,
with stabling and offices on each side, a central path leading to the principal gate-way,
through which a square enclosed court of an oblong form was reached, surrounded with
dwellings ; beyond this, another gate, of very similar construction, led to some smaller
courts, and a confused triangular assemblage of buildings, seemingly constructed in "most
admired disorder," with characteristic turrets and gables. The garden wall still exhibits
traces of the old palace in a brick gateway, evidently of the time of Henry VIII., and some
remains of vaulted cellars are preserved in other parts of the grounds.

[118] The grotto is reported to have been constructed by a father and his two sons, who
were occupied many years in its formation, at a cost to the Duke of Newcastle of about
40,000*l*. It is entirely composed of minute pieces of spar, coral rock, minerals, and shells,
and consists of various apartments and winding passages. The upper room has a domed
roof, from which hang stalactites of satin spar, and here George IV., when Prince of
Wales, gave one of his luxurious *petites soupers* to a select party of his friends. It was
also a favourite retiring-room of the Duchess of York, and the Chinese chairs and other
furniture remaining are those she used, the cushions being covered with her needlework.

Bridge, which spans the stream of the Bourne, on the New Haw and
Pyrford roads,—there it lay, for many years, amongst the *débris* of long
grass and architectural fragments, and from thence it was again removed
and set up at Weybridge ; the original direction as to the locality of the
Seven Dials[119] being cast away where it still is, close to a public-house
on the green, and the graduated spire crowned by a coronet, while an
inscription is introduced upon the pedestal, expressive of an admiration
which deserved a better monument.[120]

THE WEY BRIDGE.

Oatlands Park is, however, *now* only "Oat-lands Park" by courtesy ; its glory has departed, and it has been let in lots for building. Its
noble trees are removed or retained at the pleasure of those who erect
Swiss cottages, or trim, bright, glazy villas, amid the silent groves,
where once the deer browsed, and the squirrel played, and which often
echoed the hunting-horn of royalty. The views over the valley of the
Thames are most beautiful, and Windsor Castle towers in the distance.
There are many trees, vistas, and glimpses of scenery which still delight

[119] The stone, although marking the "*Seven* Dials," is hexagonal ; and it is clear that it
must have been originally cut with six sides only. Indeed, it is recorded that one of the
dials served for two streets, opening into one angle ; it is engraved in our initial letter.
The marks are plainly discernible where the indexes of the various dials were placed, and
portions of the metal with which they were secured is still remaining.

[120] A new church has lately been erected at Weybridge, and when a spire is added
thereunto, it will be handsome both inside and out. But here Chantrey's monument to the
excellent Duchess is thrust into a corner, with all the other tablets and monuments removed
from the old church—much to the disgust of all who conceive that God's temple ought to
be adorned by the beautiful works of men's hands.

COLUMN AT WEYBRIDGE.

the lover of nature, but the once great palace is now park-less, and we cannot but regret that, however desirable for "building ground," such a noble heritage should be "lotted" and cut up for mere utility ; it is one of the signs—alas, too many!—that the *poetry* of life is fast fading from among us.

The ascent to St. George's Hill, from either gate, is sufficiently easy for man or horse. The view, from the "view point," is more extensive on one side than from its neighbouring hill of St. Anne's ; its sides are more precipitous, it is altogether grander and bolder ; it stands proudly above the landscape, as if conscious of its Roman encampment,[121] of its woods, enriched of late by so many rare trees, of its historic and antiquarian importance ; it

[121] Though constantly described as a Roman camp, and even sometimes called "Cæsar's camp," the irregularity of its form would lead the judicious antiquary to give it an earlier date, and ascribe it to a British origin. Brayley considers it "one of those hill fastnesses from which our rude ancestors were driven by the superior discipline and weapons of the Roman soldiers. The discovery of some ancient urns at Silvermere (at the foot of the hill), a few years ago, may be referred to as corroborative of this opinion." These urns were discovered in a grave mound, and were of unbaked clay, ornamented with a double zig-zag round the rim, and are decidedly of British manufacture. The area of the camp encloses nearly 14 acres of ground ; the vallum and ditches are perfectly distinct the latter very deep in many places. The ground plan is exceedingly irregular, taking in the crest of the hill, and on the south side is an embankment enclosing the declivity, as if the original camp had been thus added to, or strengthened. On St. Anne's Hill are traces of similar entrenchments, which were, no doubt, formed by the early inhabitants of the country, who would naturally choose such commanding and elevated situations for their fortresses. Coway Stakes is about a mile and a half distant from St. George's Hill, and here Camden and other writers affirm that Cæsar crossed the Thames, in pursuit of Cassivellaunus.

hardly bends its leafy crown to imperial Windsor ; it commands a grand view of the Surrey hills, and mingles Alpine and English scenery together ; it is delicious to inhale the breeze, so fresh and pure, that rushes over the valley ; and pleasant to rest, after the fatigue of the ascent, on the seats so kindly set apart and sheltered from the sun, by the considerate liberality of its noble proprietor, the Earl of Ellesmere ; it was also pleasant during the feverish summer of 1851, to show the foreigner such a view, so rich in English beauty, and to hear his exclamations of delight and astonishment.

WALTON CHURCH.

WALTON is another village, quite within a walk of CHERTSEY, even if you skirt the Thames from Weybridge, and leave Oatlands to the right ; you then obtain a better view of the double bridge of Walton, and see to advantage the sweep of Lord Tankerville's villa. Walton is a pleasant village to live in, and, having a station of its own, and being near the Thames, it has many summer attractions for those whose duties limit them to a "convenient distance" from London.

Its church[122] contains several interesting monuments, and the intelligent clerk, who is not a little proud of the structure, turns up a piece of matting, and shows the flat grey stone, inscribed to the memory of the once famous astrologer, Lilly, who resided five and forty years in Walton ;[123] but the leading attraction of Walton Church is the monument executed by Roubiliac, by order of Grace, Countess of Middlesex, to the memory of her father, the Lord Viscount Shannon, commander of the forces in Ireland.[124] Those who remember the doings in England during the Commonwealth, will not fail to people the churchyard of Walton with a singular assembly when, a few Sundays after the execution of Charles I., a soldier bearing a lighted candle in his hand, having failed to compel the rector of Walton to resign his pulpit to him, mounted a tombstone, and preached one of those extraordinary discourses, so common in that wonder-working age.

We read the other day of a Tuscan city, where every house in which a remarkable person had been born was marked by an inscription : we render genius no such homage here. A man of singular wit talent and learning, Doctor Maginn, died and was buried at Walton, little more than ten years ago. There is no stone inscribed with his name ; and we wandered over many half-obliterated mounds before even the sexton could point out to us the spot where he had been dropped into his grave[125]—

"Alas, poor Yorick!"

There are some curious monuments within the church, and five brasses in memory of a certain John Selwyn, one of himself another of his wife ; one where, mounted on the back of a stag, he is in the act of stabbing it in the throat, and another of no less than "eleven olive

---

[122] The church is a very ancient structure ; It consists of a nave and side aisles, with a chancel beyond. Four pointed arches spring from massive columns on each aide of the nave, which were probably constructed in the twelfth century ; but the church has undergone so many changes, that its other antique features are lost, or masked by more modern work.

[123] The stone has been removed from its proper place, over the grave of Lilly, which was on the left aide of the communion table. It was placed there by his friend, the visionary antiquary, Elias Ashmole, who records that this "fair black marble stone" cost him 6*l.* 4*s.* 6*d.*

[124] He was nephew to the famous Robert Boyle, and "volunteer when a youth at the battle of the Boyne."

[125] We have also sought in vain for the house in which Admiral Rodney was born, though it is known he was born at Walton.

branches," all belonging to the said John Selwyn, a forester of Oatlands, in the reign of Elizabeth, famous for his deeds of daring ; a fifth containing the inscription to their memories.[126] This parish is also endowed with an instrument for the control of female eloquence, which would in no degree receive homage from the "Bloomers" of the present day. It is of curious construction, and, when fixed on, one part enters the mouth, and prevents articulation. It originally bore the following inscription, and the date 1633, but only faint traces now remain of either.

> "Chester presents Walton with a bridle,
> To curb women's tongues that talk too idle."[127]

Ashley Park, seated with so much dignity upon its stately lawn, commands the admiration of all wayfarers, and is *said* to have been inhabited by Oliver Cromwell. But the most interesting relic of *his* times is the house of the President Bradshaw. Its effect is much injured by a narrow street of small houses, built in such a way as effectually to prevent the whole from being seen at Once.[128] The house within is divided

---

[126] These five plates are evidently a series, forming only one memorial to Selwyn and his family, and originally inserted in a grave-stone. The most curious plate is that representing Selwyn stabbing the stag, and it is still more remarkable as it is a *palimpsest* (or brass engraved on both aides), with some variations of the same incident, which has been explained as being, probably, an incorrect version of the exploit, turned face downward, and a more correct one done on the same plate, to save expense. Selwyn was under-keeper of the park at Oatlands in the reign of Elizabeth, and was remarkable for his skill in horsemanship ; upon one occasion, during the heat of the chase, he leaped from his horse upon the back of the stag, and, keeping his seat gracefully, notwithstanding all efforts of the affrighted beast, guided it towards the Queen, and drawing his *couteau de chasse*, plunged it in its throat, and it fell dead at her feet.

[127] It is said that this bridle was presented by the individual whose name it bears because he had lost an estate "through the instrumentality of a gossipping, lying woman." Its construction and mode of fastening is shown in our cuts, which exhibit the bridle unfastened, and as it would appear when closed over the head ; when locked, a flat piece of iron projects into the mouth, and effectually keeps down the tongue, a triangular opening in the bar above admits the nose, and allows the machine to fit tightly on the head. One of a precisely similar kind is described by Brand in his "history of Newcastle-upon-Tyne," and Dr. Plott engraves another in his "History of Staffordshire," "which being put upon the offender," he tells us, "by order of the magistrate, and fastened with a padlock behind, she is led round the town by an officer, to her shame, nor is it taken off till after the party begins to show all external signs imaginable of humiliation and amendment." The town council of Lichfield still possess one of these bridles, another is at Beau desert the seat of the Marquis of Anglesey ; but the most curious is at Harnstall Ridware, in Staffordshire, which has apertures for the eyes and nose, giving the face a grotesque appearance, and towering above it like the cap of a grenadier.

[128] There is a very good engraving of the exterior of this house before the street was built, in Brayley's "Surrey." It was then an exceedingly picturesque object. The best

and subdivided into small tenements, where old and young are mingled together as in one large family ; one aged woman, who stood in the middle of the room on the ground floor, which exhibits the most considerable remains of the original fittings up in its carved chimney-piece, pannelled wainscoting, and strong beams, said "it was a great house once, but full of wickedness, and no wonder the spirits of its inhabitants troubled the earth to this day," but all others were silent as to sights or sounds belonging to the world of shadows. Many doubtless, were the consultations held within these mouldering walls, touching the fate of England, and it is not a matter of wonder that the superstitious who are in its immediate neighbourhood should sometimes there "see visions and dream dreams." [129]

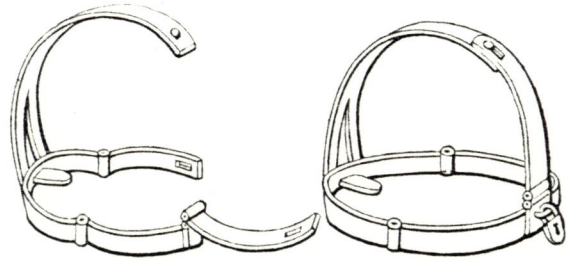

THE SCOLD'S BRIDLE.

These "visions" and "dreams" are, of course, less frequent now that the house of the Regicide is, as it were, "shored up" by streets, where a ghost of any respectability would find it impossible to wander, even on the darkest night. In old times, the "good old times," the house must have been isolated, and far away from any dwelling of equal size or pretension ; it was surrounded by a garden, and there is a rumour of a subterranean passage, leading, one report says, to the Thames, another states to the palace at Oatlands, another to Ashley Park. In old times (whether deserving the epithet of "good" or not is a question), these underground passages and caves were necessary alike for the preservation of property and life, and we believe there are still numerous excavations immediately round our old mansions, which have been either

---

notion of its original appearance may be obtained from an examination of the room we engrave, which is now the only unspoilt portion of this once important and interesting house.

[129] Tradition affirms that in this house was signed the death-warrant of the unhappy King Charles I.

intentionally walled in, or have become choked up by the *débris* of time ; it is somewhat remarkable that, even when discovered and inspected, so little traces have been found of those who sought protection and shelter within their gloomy sanctuary. It is trite enough to say what tales their walls could tell, but it is impossible to look into them without wishing "these walls had tongues."

Chertsey and its Neighbourhood.

III.

YRFORD is certainly a good long walk from Chertsey, and is, unfortunately for the lovers of the picturesque, but little known. It cannot be called a hamlet there are too few houses, and neighbourhood it has none. The walk moreover is flat and lonely. We pass through Addlestone, over Crockford or Crokford bridge, then over the canal bridge, and under that of the South Western Railway. The country is rough and wild ; gravel pits, whose sides are wreathed with fern and heather, patches of fir plantation, with here and there a farm-house swarming with black pigs, lowing calves, and noisy poultry ; a cottage half hidden by its abundant orchard ; more heather, more fir plantation, more black pigs and poultry, and the roads mottled by the restless shadows of the waving birch trees, whose branches hang with pensile grace, above the hedge rows : as we draw nearer to our destination the trees and hedges mingle, forming a bower above our heads.

And what was Pyrford, or Piford, or Pyreford? truly it has its histories! of old, old, it belonged to the Abbey of Westminster, then to the Abbey of Sheen, then Elizabeth reclaimed it for the crown, then Edward Lord Lincoln, Lord high Admiral of England at that time, built himself a fair house at "Pyriford," but after all this expenditure it would seem as though he had only a life interest in the place, for we find Elizabeth visiting "John Wolley" at "Pirford," the same "John Wolley," who succeeded the learned Roger Ascham, as her Majesty's Latin secretary ; in the eventful course of years it had many masters whose names only live in church books, upon old tombstones, or in forgotten county histories. Evelyn in his Diary speaks of Mr. Denzil Onslow's seat at "Purford," and Aubrey calls it a delightful place, "three miles about," and tells how it "is a fair house standing near the river Wey, and that

267

from the lodge you may overlook the ruins of Newark Abbey, the seven streams running by it, and the rich meadows, watered by them." He tells of avenues of elms and birches, of a decoy pool, "with four tunnels," of the great lake of Sheerwater, "two miles about." Alas! all these are gone! the house has been pulled down, the decoy suffered to go to ruin, the lake drained and filled up, population (thin as it seems) and cultivation have overspread the solitude of conservatism, and though the present "Ladie farm" looks perfectly innocent of aristocratic associations, crouching amid evergreens and roses, its ample byre filled with the

     "Lowing herd,"

yet many a

     "Yeoman and bowman bold,"

have claimed hospitality and received a welcome on the self-same spot. Yes, there is Pyrford Church, or as we believe it is more correct to call

PYRFORD CHURCH.

it, chapel. Ascending the path which leads to its humble gate, you pass the pretty little school (unless you like to tarry and hear the pleasant music of young voices), and the gate which leads to the Vicarage, and you exclaim "What a fine old yew tree!" You are interested by the number of "green graves," purely brightly green, where the grasshopper hops and the white moth glistens in the sunbeam. The church is very small and very old. There is nothing to "notice" in the interior, the pews of oak irregularly placed generally, are old and worm-eaten. The building simply consists of a nave and chancel, with a low tower, surmounted by an ordinary spire rising from the roof of the former. What a primitive-looking old church it is! it belongs so entirely to the past, that you wonder how it has been preserved! and that rude old spire seems so perishing! you look from the Porch, through the trees across to the Vicarage. What a lovely spot, the spot of all others suited for the residence of a country clergyman ; and, happily, a good man is there! You gaze upon it with delight and think the report of the beauty of Pyrford no exaggeration, but you are only on the threshold of its beauty.

RUINS OF NEWARK PRIORY.

Move slowly, and carefully through the long grass—carefully! least you tread upon those nameless but hallowed graves ; you now know, that the withered looking little church, stands upon a commanding mount. You can hardly believe that such is the case—the ascent has been so gradual ; now you are close to the hollow tree that for ages has

sentineled the pathway-pass to the rich valley outspread at your feet—
THERE! Look at it with loving eyes, where it reposes in the sunshine,
while a soft warm mist half shrouds the distant hills, and seems to unite
them to the heavens ; they are not so grand or so harsh as mountains,
Oh, no! our Surrey Hills pretend to nothing so ambitious or so cold ; but
we are very grateful to them for giving what we so often want a
background to our pictures. To the left are the ruins of Newark Abbey,
which the artist would clothe with ivy—though, perhaps, grim and grey
as they are, they contrast better with the deep bright green by which they
are surrounded.[130] We will not believe that in old times monks blessed
with such a residence, ever disturbed the peace of the fair nuns of Ockham :[131] there is a wicked old ballad which prates of this, but it is
doubtless a fable ; these however are the ruins, which, with their surrounding scenery, composed of rivers and rivulets, foot bridge and
fords, plashy pools and fringed tangled hollows, trees in groups or
alone, cattle-enjoying the freshness and food of this happy valley, or
gathering round the wide spreading trees, chewing their cud or tossing
their tails at the intruding flies, while there the beauty of the herd remains perfectly motionless as if conscious of her importance in so lovely
a landscape ; these, and a hundred other pleasant things—the floating of
the rooks beneath the fleecy clouds, the cooing of the ringdoves in the
nearest copse, the impassioned song of the wondrous nightingale from a
bough somewhere in the verdant ravine beneath your feet the coming
and going effects of the shadows, now deepening the tone of a clump of

---

[130] The old Priory of Newark was inhabited by canons regular of the order of St.
Augustine, and was founded about the time of Richard Cœur de Lion, by Ruald de Calva,
and his wife, Beatrice de Sandes. The church was dedicated to the Blessed Virgin and St.
Thomas of Canterbury, and was well endowed with lands by himself and successors ; the
canons gradually increasing in wealth and lands, and privileges, until the time of Henry
VIII., when it was surrendered to the rapacity of that sovereign by the principal, Richard
Lyppescomb, who gained thereby a pension of 40l., and grants to seven other canons
belonging to the foundation. The priory church is now so much ruined, that scarcely any
of the facing stones remain ; the walls are about 3 feet thick, and exhibit little more than
the core of flint, cemented with grout and rubble ; the country folks and road contractors
formerly came here as to a stone quarry for materials to repair walls and roads, and the
wonder is that anything remains of this once important edifice.

[131] At Ockham, in the adjoining parish, was a nunnery, and the tradition goes that a
communication between that building and Newark Abbey was formed by a subterranean
passage, which passed beneath the river. It is needless to call attention to the fact, which
must have fallen under the observation of all who investigate old buildings, of the fre-
quency with which such tales of subterranean passages are narrated, and their general
absurdity.

ENTRANCE GATE, BYFLEET.

hawthorn in the foreground, almost into blackness, then spangling the meadow with diamonds ; now flying over hill and valley, then lingering on the ruins until they seem steeped in some dark dream of the past ; while all the time the purring river keeps circling in little eddies round the supports of the footbridge, and taking frothy leaps over huge stones which make-believe to intercept its course from that cavern of foliage from whence it issues to fertilise the meadows of Newark Abbey! Aye, look, and look again, enjoy it ALL—for it is a blessed enjoyment, one forbidden by no law, moral or divine—to enjoy the loveliness of wood and water, hill and dale, with which the Almighty has decked as with a garland, our blessed English land. But your pleasant task is not ended until you descend the ravine and reach the footbridge, then look up at the old church, and if you have pencil and paper, and do not sketch it on the instant, you will never be an artist!

Between this lovely spot and Woking, somewhere near the healthy heathy common which hears the same name, once stood the mansion of Sir Edward Zouch, and there, it has been written, he often received the visits of his patron James I. The king went thither from his palace of Oatlands, and according to Mr. Manning a tradition prevails that a turret, still existing on a hill to the north of the house, was built for the purpose of exhibiting a light, as a beacon for the guidance of messengers, who resorted to the king at night. We could gossip through a goodly quarto did we speak of all the places deserving remark in our neighbourhood, but one other has an especial interest for us, and we at least found it worthy a visit, though it lies quite away from the very pretty village which bears its name—we mean Byfleet Park. Byfleet[132] is an admirable village for the artist—a treasure-house of long barns, whose roofs are overgrown with moss—its dwellings so well cared for, half farm half cottage houses, its trees so nobly grown, and more than one or two stately venerable mansions opened upon by solid gateways, and protected by massive railings or walls covered with ivy—it lies low certainly, but that makes vegetation more luxuriant—and what more beautiful to gaze upon than the green ravines and bold promontory of St. George's Hill. But the road to Byfleet Park—a royal chase until purchased from the crown by the late Lord King—leads through a narrow road, then passes the entrance to the mill, where the Wey dividing its waters circles round an island, which we are told is the very paradise of gardens ; then forward—ploughed land on one side, and on the other the Wey, now broad, now narrow ; seen through the copse, and glancing beneath the tall trees, it shines in the sun like liquid silver. Lovely, capricious river that it is! seldom retaining the same aspect or breadth for half a mile.

The house, as you approach it, has a singularly lonely and deserted appearance ; standing so straight and narrow against the clear sky, it looks like something left as a monument of the past : two piers of carved stones are flanked by high walls, and the hall-door is reached by a flight of high narrow stone steps, divided and time-worn ; it has been for some time used as a farm-house, or rather occupied by the person to whom a portion of what was so long royal property, has been let by its present "lord and master," the Hon. Locke King, M.P.

---

[132] About the middle of the last century the rectory of Byfleet was held by the Rev. Stephen Duck, who was originally an agricultural labourer, but his poetic talents attracted the notice of Caroline, consort of George II., and though his poetry is forgotten, it procured him the notice and education which led to the living of Byfleet ; not long did he enjoy it, for in a fit of melancholy insanity he drowned himself at Reading. There is another instance of elevated circumstances near this, but with a happier result. When the house of James Kirkpatrick Escott, Esq., at Ongar Hill House, was building, Sir George Soane worked at its walls, as a bricklayer's boy. There is a monument in Byfleet Church to the memory of the amiable and accomplished Joseph Spence.

The kind courtesy of its occupant permitted us to enter, and the cold lonely aspect of the house was at once changed to one capable of

every comfort. Above the fire-place, in the entrance-hall, is a coat of arms ; but the stair-case has been barbarously painted over, though evidently of oak ; the rooms are panelled, and "beautified" (?) by paint, they are lofty and cheerful, the walls are thick, and as the roof has no gutters, the dryness of the house is a proof of its solidity ; in one of the bedrooms, a beautifully carved slab of stone-work forms the front of the chimney-piece, and a little attic which commands a delicious view of the windings of the Wey, and St. George's Hill, was once richly panelled and gilt, but the taste of the times has encrusted it with

CHIMNEY, BYFLEET HOUSE.

whitewash ; our fair guide disclaimed any act or part in this tragedy, which she assured us was perpetrated before her husband became tenant of the farm.

A portion of these walls was most likely of those which heard the stormy wailings of Henry VIII., when the huge baby was (so runs the legend) sent to nurse at Byfleet Park. They have been "modernised," the greater part rebuilt and patched up with the old decorations, probably during the reigns of William or Anne ;[133] yet still here is the very spot from whence Edward II. dated letters for the arrest of the Knights Templar.

---

[133] This is very perceptible, both within and without ; the traces of modernisation on the *facade* do not conceal the few enrichments of an earlier period, while withinside, there is much carved work, and decorated panelling.

Passing to the back of the house, the view as *home scenery* is all that can be desired. If wings were added to the present house it would form a charming dwelling, for nature has decked the site with exceeding care. The bridge, leading to Byfleet Mill, would delight the "water-colour men" who like brilliant and broad effects ; the Wey in that spot

creates little bays, and picturesque "aites" crowded with such charming water-foliage, broad leaves, spiry rushes, and floating islands of forget-me-nots repeating the blue sky of heaven. There is a wild looking keeper's lodge on an eminence, which we were assured commanded a delicious view, and from which the mill and the mill-house on its flowery island were seen to great advantage, but the autumn sun was going down, and warned us to return. At the back of the dwelling, where the inequalities of the turf seem as if much that was mysterious lay beneath its surface, a subterraneous communication, perhaps with the house, has been discovered ; the entrance is arched, and farther on a hole has been dug

TOMB OF DENHAM.

into it, proving its continuance it might or might not be worth the trouble of excavation, but it is difficult to resist the desire to investigate a subterraneous passage of any kind, and the more impracticable it seems the more the desire increases ; we could not learn that any relics of old times have been found there, but when they are found in our neighbourhood they are seldom preserved with care.

We might extend our walks with profit and enjoyment as far "Windsor Way," as we have done in the opposite direction. The church at EGHAM (some three miles off or thereabouts) contains several monuments, of which any church might be proud. Among the more remarkable and interesting are two to the Denham family, one representing a body in the act of rising from the grave, the other telling palpably how Judge Denham married two wives, and loved them both so well, that in the monument they figure, one on his right hand, the other on his left, one pressing a naked infant in her arms, whose life was her death, while beside the other kneels the quaint little figure of Sir John Denham, the poet of "Cooper's Hill," in baby boyhood ; having seen these memorials of the poet's family, it will be pleasant to prolong our walk over the plashy lowlands that lead to the surpassing loveliness of "Cooper's Hill," and the heroic field of Runnymede,—heroic inasmuch as

"Peace hath her victories as well as war!"

Cooper's Hill still overlooks the glorious river,—Denham's "theme," which he longed to make his "example"—

"Though deep, yet clear ; though gentle, yet not dull ;
Strong without rage ; without o'erflowing, full."

The hill yet remains, famous for its beauty, as it has ever been :

"—his shoulders and his sides
A shady mantle clothes ; his curled brows
Frown on the gentle stream, which calmly flows,
While winds and storms his lofty forehead beat—
The common fate of all that's high and great!"

Its vicinity to Egham, where repose the poet's ancestors, adds interest to the theme of his song.[134]

The Company of Basket-makers (if there be such a London company) have claimed a large portion of the field—where the barons, "clad in complete steel," assembled to confer with King John upon the great charter of English freedom, by which, Hume truly but coldly says, "very important liberties and privileges were either granted or secured to every order of men in the kingdom to the clergy, to the barons, and to the people"—the Basket-makers, we say, have availed themselves of the

---

[134] Sir John Denham, the poet of "Cooper's Hill," was born in Dublin in 1615—his father being then Chief Baron of the Irish Exchequer. The poet was an uncompromising loyalist, and was actively engaged in the Civil Wars ; and he relates that some lines written by him coming accidentally under the notice of Charles I., the king advised him to "write no more," alleging that "when men are young, and have little else to do, they might vent the overflowings of their fancy that way ; but when they were thought fit for more serious employments, if they still persisted in that course, it would look as if they minded not the way to any better." "Cooper's Hill" obtained a rapid popularity : Dryden described it as "the exact standard of good writing ;" and "Denham's strength" was lauded by Pope.

low lands of Runnymede to cultivate osiers ; piles and stacks of "withies" in various stages of utility, for several hundred yards shut out the river from the wayfarer, but as he proceeds they disappear, and Cooper's Hill on the left, the rich flat of Runnymede, the Thames, and the groves of Time-honoured Ancker-wycke, on its opposite bank, form together a rich and most interesting picture. It is now nearly an hundred years since it was first proposed to erect a triumphal column upon Runnymede ; but we have sometimes a strange antipathy to do what would seem unavoidable ; the monument to the memory of Hampden is a sore proof of the niggardliness of liberals to the liberal ; but all monuments to such a man or to such a cause must appear poor ; the names "Hampden" and "Runnymede" suffice ; the green and verdant mead, encircled by the coronet of Cooper's Hill, reposing beneath the sun, and shadowed by the passing cloud, is an object of reverence and beauty, immortalised by the glorious liberty which the bold barons of England forced from a spiritless tyrant.

RUNNYMEAD.

Though Cooper's Hill has no claim to the sublimity of mountain scenery, its peculiar situation commands a broad expanse of country. It rises abruptly from the Runnymede meadows, and extends its long ridge in a north-westerly direction ; the summit is approached by a winding road, which from different points of the ascent progressively unfolds a gorgeous number of fertile views, such as no other country in the world can give—

> "Of hills and dales, and woods, and lawns, and spires,
> And glittering towns, and silver streams."

We have heard that the views from KINGSWOOD Lodge—the dwelling of the hill—are delicious, and that its conservatory contains an exquisite marble statue of "Hope." On the west of Cooper's Hill is the interesting estate of ANCKERWYCKE PURNISH. Anckerwycke has been for a series of years in the possession of the family of Harcourt. There is a "meet" of three shires in this vicinity,—Surrey, Buckinghamshire, and Berkshire. The views from the grounds of ANCKERWYCKE, are said to be of exceeding beauty, and the kindness of its master makes eloquent the poor about his domain. All these things, and the sound of the rippling waters of the Thames, and the song of the myriad birds which congregate in its groves, and the legends[135] sprung of its antiquity, all contribute to the adornment of the gigantic fact that HERE, on Runnymede, King John, sorely against his will, signed MAGNA CHARTA!

How that single fact fills the soul, and nerves the spirit ; how proudly the British birthright throbs within our bosoms! We long to lead the new Napoleon, the absolute Nicholas, the frank, hospitable, and brave, but sometimes over-confident American, to this green sward of Runnymede, and tell them, that HERE was secured to the Englishman—a LIBERTY *which other nations have never enjoyed!* Here, in the thickset beauty of yon little island, was our CHARTER granted. As to how we have kept it, and how enlarged it, "by God and our country" we may be tried! But surely there is stern truth as well as true poetry in that passage of our Anthem which tells us that

> "The nations not so blessed as thee
> Must in their turn to tyrants fall,
> Whilst thou shalt flourish great and free,
> The pride and envy of them all!"

There has been much dispute as to whether the Charter was signed upon the Mead or on the Island called *"Magna Charta Island,"* which forms a charming feature in the landscape, and upon which is built a

---

[135] There is much interest attached to a fine old yew tree, beneath whose shadow tradition says Anna Boleyn met Henry VIII. There is a legend, also, that a dove conveyed a bough of that yew tree in its bill to Germany, where a convent was built to protect the relic of Anckerwycke ; but Germany was abandoned after a time for Spain, where the tree now flourishes, it having been transplanted by the monks.

little sort of *alter-house*, so to call it. We leave the settlement of such matters to wiser and more learned heads ; but we incline to the idea that the cowardly king would have felt even the mimic ferry a protection, and been glad of the silvery barrier between him and his people. The island looks even now *exclusive,* and as we were impelled to its shore, we indulged the belief that the charter was really there signed by the king. There was a poetic feeling in whoever planted the bank of "For-get-me-not" just at the entrance to the low apartment which was fitted up to contain the *charter stone,* by the late Simon Harcourt, Esq., in the year 1835. The inscription on the stone is as fellows ;—"Be it remembered, that on this island, in June, 1215, JOHN, KING OF ENGLAND, SIGNED THE MAGNA CHARTA, and in the year 1834, this building was erected in commemoration of that great and important event by George Simon Harcourt, Esq., Lord of the Manor, and then High Sheriff of the county."[136] The windows are ornamented with stained glass, including portraits of King John, &c., &c., and small shields of the arms of the associated Barons are painted on the upper part of the surrounding walls. The lower panels are of old carvings, in the taste of the *rénaissance,* and on one side is a copy of the great charter in a brass frame. A gentleman rents the island from Mr. Harcourt, and has commenced building what we think, when finished, will be a Gothic cottage in excellent keeping with the history of the place. This joins the altar-room, but does not interfere with it, nor with the privilege so graciously bestowed on the public by Mr. Harcourt,—permitting patriots or fishermen to visit the island, and pic-nic in a tent prepared for the purpose, under the shelter of some superb walnut trees.

Though our varied pilgrimage draws to a close, let not our friends imagine there is

"No more to see, no more to tell."

There is much within a walk of our little pensive town, which we have not recorded, but which we hope we may induce others to record hereafter.

Our Surrey Hills and our Surrey Vales are, in truth, beautiful ; but their beauty is enhanced by the many associations of glory that are inseparably and for ever linked with them.

---

[136] That is, of Buckinghamshire.

Especially, and above all, be it remembered, that from every ascent to which, in this Pilgrimage, we have made reference, we obtain a view of Royal WINDSOR, perpetually reminding us, that while, on the one hand, we "hold fast" the liberties that have been obtained for us by arms or eloquence, on the other we are preserved alike from the evils that Despotism creates, and the perils that arise out of Democracy. And surely, while we raise our hearts to God in thankfulness that the land about us is free as well us fertile, we may waft a blessing towards that regal dwelling, whence, over all the kingdom and its dependencies, a holy and happy influence issues, teaching goodness by example alike to the high and to the humble, and showing that nowhere, either in palace or in cottage, are the duties of life more wisely or more purely performed than they are in the Royal Family of England.

Chertsey and its Neighbourhood.

IV.

"Come now toward Chertsey."
Richard the Third.

NE of the most pleasurable sensations of life,
arises from the consciousness of an increasing
attachment, not only to the land we live in,
but to our own immediate neighbourhood.
We confess to the possession of a large organ
of inhabitiveness ; and can sympathise with
the cat, the beaver,—even with the crow,
who prefers repairing his old rickety nest to
building a new one. "Exile!" has ever
seemed to us the most fearful of all punishments ; and
the power to augment the enjoyments and endear the
associations of "home," one of earth's greatest blessings ; but when that
"home" is placed in a locality, where time and its memories sanctify the
beauties of nature, and every walk or drive is suggestive of something
which recalls either history or legend, the interest increases daily, until
we seem to claim actual acquaintance with those whom we can summon
from amid the shadows of the past. So much has been done, so many
scenes have been enacted, such numberless great men have lived and
died within this small but mighty England, that every rood of ground, so
to say, has its story ; and it needs but small imagination to derive profitable instruction from highways and byways in any shire of our island.

The county of Surrey, so closely connected with London, is rich to
overflowing in all sorts of memories, both of persons and events ; and
the little quaint and quiet town of Chertsey, with its "grants," and
"fairs," and "markets,"—which, to judge by its usual state of sleepy
tranquillity seem to be rather fanciful than real—that very discreet little

town could tell of the gorgeous and gloomy past, as much as, or perhaps more than, many of its ancient neighbours within a day's drive of the Metropolis. Had the old Abbey stones (out of which, according to tradition, the walls of sundry of its now meek looking houses were raised)—had they but tongues, how they could discourse of gone-by years—when a visit to Chertsey was an undertaking ; although now, the distance between the city and the town is just an hour.

We hear as we enter our house (in Addlestone, one of its tributary villages) the curfew-bell, tolling as in "the good old times," when people dared not "show" in the street after its last peal had sounded. The curfew has endured in spite of all "reforms"—at once a relic and a reminder of ancient days, when it rung, as it does now, from Michaelmas to Lady-day, at eight of the evening. The worthy sexton first "rings up," that is to say, raises the bell ; he then rings for a few minutes, and stops a little while ; after which he tolls the number of the day of the month ; on the first day of the month, he strikes the bell once, and on the last day thirty or thirty-one times.'[137]

Chertsey is described in county histories as a "neat market town on the north side of Surrey, twenty miles from London ;" it is singularly "neat" and clean and quiet ; nothing within our memory has occurred to disturb its tranquillity. The name was written occasionally in old chronicles, *Cirolesege, Certessege,* or *Ceroti Insula.* Its situation may he said to be insular ; the Thames and Abbey river being on one side,

---

[137] The generally received opinion that the ringing of the curfew-bell and the consequent compulsory extinguishing of fire and candle, was imposed on the English by William the Conqueror as a badge of servitude, is open to considerable doubt, inasmuch as a similar law existed in Europe as a necessary safeguard at a period when houses were constructed of wood, and huddled together in walled towns. It is even stated that Alfred the Great, one of our most popular and humane sovereigns, introduced the usage. That it was neither so odious nor unpopular as the Poet Thomson vividly describes it to have been, (and from whose lines probably most persons form their idea) is apparent from the fact of private individuals in the middle ages frequently leaving sums of money toward defraying the expenses of ringing it, and keeping it in repair. In flat, marshy, and dangerous places it was an useful guide by night to the traveller, and many instances are on record of life and property saved by its welcome tones. It is still sounded in London as well as in very many of our country towns. The curfew or *couvre-feu* itself was an instrument so contrived that it covered in and extinguished the whole of the wood fire on the hearth when it was raked to the back of the chimney. It was made of metal sometimes ornamented. They are among the rarest of our domestic antiquities, being of that class which when out of fashion is soonest consigned to the melting-pot. Horace Walpole had one at Strawberry Hill ; another is engraved in Hone's "Every-day-book ;" and a third in the Journal of the British Archæological Association.

and on the other a small stream, now known as the Bourne, which comes in a leisurely dreamy way from Virginia Water, and crosses Guildford Street on its unmurmuring journey to the Thames.

Chertsey has also a branch railroad—our especial own—from Weybridge, with a station at the ambitious village of Addlestone. The railroad partakes of the nature of the neighbourhood ; not being by any means busy or boisterous, and having in an out-of-the-way corner of the pretty quiet town, a little low shed-looking terminus which seems as if it had no business there, and inclines to apologise for its intrusion ; yet this absence of puff and noise on the part of the railroad, this intense quiet, is in admirable keeping with the present character of the peaceful locality ; the town lies low, the Thames, bright and full bosomed as it flows, is enriched on either side by the greenest and most verdant meadows. In the season you are certain to see many contemplative brothers of the angle engaged at their "idle industry," either along the banks or in unpicturesque boats—boats which sleep lazily amongst rushes, until the first of June calls them from their rest. But to write more seriously, nowhere, within twenty miles of London (except in the immediate neighbourhood of Richmond) does the bland and beautiful Thames appear more queenly, or sweep with greater grace through its fertile dominions, than it does at Chertsey. It is, indeed, delightful to stand on the bridge in the glowing sunset of a summer evening, and turning from the refreshing green of the Shepperton Range, look into the deep clear blue of the flowing river, while the murmur of the waters rushing through Laleham Lock, give a sort of Spirit-music to the scene. On the right, as you leave Chertsey, the river bends gracefully towards the double bridge of Walton ; and to the left it undulates smoothly along, having passed Runnymede and Staines, while the almost conical hill of St. Anne's attracts attention by its abrupt and singular form, when viewed from the vale of the Thames.

Nor must we forget that, about a mile on the Walton side, from our favourite bridge, (Old Camden tells us so) are the "Cowey Stakes," marking the spot where Cæsar crossed the Thames.

Were the peasantry of Surrey and Middlesex as imaginative as their Irish brethren of Killarney, what legends would have grown out of this tradition ; how often would the "noblest Roman of them all" have been seen by the pale moonlight leading his steed over the waters of the rapid river—how many would have borne testimony to the fact that Cassivelaunus himself had been heard during the stillness of some particular

Midsummer night working at the rude defence which can still be traced
beneath the blue waters of the Thames. What hosts of pale and ghastly
spectres would have risen from those tranquil banks, and from the deepest hollows of the rushing current and—like the Huns, who almost live
on the inspired canvas of Kaulbach, —fought their last earthly battle,
again, and again, in the Spirit-world, amid the stars! But ours is no region of romance ; even remnants of history, which go beyond the com-
monest capacity, are rejected as dreams, or put aside as legends. But
history has enough to tell to interest us all ; and we may be satisfied with
the abundant enjoyment we have in delicious rambles, through the lanes
and up the hills, along the fair river's banks, and among the many traditional ruins of ancient and beautiful Surrey.

Never was desolation more complete than in the ruin of the Mitred
Abbey of Chertsey ; hardly one stone remains above another to tell
where this stately edifice—since the far-away year 664—grew and
flourished, lording it with imperial sway over, not only the surrounding
villages, but extending its paternal wings into Middlesex and even as far
as London.[138] The abbey was of the Benedictine order, and founded,
almost as soon as the Saxons were converted from Paganism, by Erkenwalde, afterwards Bishop of London ; but it was finished and chiefly
endowed by Frithwald, Earl of Surrey.[139]

The endowment prospered rarely ; the establishment increased in
the reputation of wealth and sanctity ; that it was "thickly populated" is
certain, for when the abbey was sacked and burnt by the Danes, in the
ninth century, the abbot, and ninety monks, were barbarously murdered
by the invaders.

Standing upon the site of their now obliterated cloisters and towers,
their aisles and dormitories, cells and confessionals, seeing nothing but
the dank, damp grass, and the tracings of the fishponds—stagnant pools
in our day—it is almost impossible to realise the onslaught of these wild
barbarians panting for plunder, the earnest defence of men who fought
(the monks of old could wield either sword or crozier) for life or death,

---

[138] Stowe, in his account of the ward of Queenhithe, says, "There is one great mes-
suage sometime belonging to the abbots of Chertsey, in Surrey ; and was their home
wherein they were lodged when they repayred to the Citie."

[139] Sir Edward Coke tells us, that *Saint* Erkenwalde was a younger son of Anna, king
of the East Saxons, and was first Abbot of Chertsey (which he had founded) and afterwards Bishop of London.

the terrible destruction, the treasures and relics, and painted glass, and monuments, the plunder of the secret almerys,[140] the intoxicated triumph of these rude northern hordes let loose in our fair and lovely island ; what scenes of savagery, where now the jackdaw builds, and the blackbird whistles, and the wild water-rat plays with her brood amongst the tangled weeds!

The fierce sea-kings being driven back to their frozen land, King Edgar ; willing to serve God after the fashion of his times, refounded the Abbey of Chertsey, dedicating it to St. Peter, and vying with Pope Alexander in augmenting its privileges and its wealth.[141]

Some of the abbots took great interest in home improvements, planting woods, conducting streams, enlarging ponds—building, now a mill, now a dove-cot, according to the wants of the abbey or their own fancies. Henry I. granted them permission to keep dogs, that, according to the old chronicle, they might take "hare, fox, and cats." King John, in the first year of his reign, gave them ample confirmation of all their privileges which, it would seem, they had somewhat abused, for we find that the sovereign seized their manors of Egham and "Torp" (Thorp)[142]

---

[140] In the ancient Rites of Durham, frequent mention is made of the Almerys, for different purposes : —"Within the Frater House door is a strong ambrie (almery) in the stone wall, where a great mazer, called a grace-cup, did stand, which did service to the monks every day, after grace was said, to drink it round the table."

[141] Chertsey was one of the mitred abbeys, whose head was also a baron or military tenant of the crown, holding his lands by barony. It was founded in the year 666 by Frithwald, the King of Mercia's viceroy for Surrey. He endowed it largely with nine hides of land well populated ; and shortly afterwards larger possessions, so that the monks increased in worldly wealth, and obtained the Pope's confirmation of their possessions. The Danes burnt their home and killed ninety of the monks ; but Edward the Confessor reinstated them, and granted them Chertsey itself, Egham, Thorp, Chobham, and some adjacent villages, so that they again waxed rich ; at the Conquest William I. munificently confirmed all to them free from any tax, and gave them entire jurisdiction over their lands, indulgences which were ratified by his successors, who added many rich gifts ; so that the abbey became one of the wealthiest and most powerful in the country, remaining in quiet possession of its riches until the dissolution by Henry VIII.

[142] In the parish of Thorpe are two pieces of land called "great and little custom pieces." The former supplies six loads of made hay every year for the use of the queen's deer in Windsor Park, to be ricked there ; and Mr. Bennett, lord of the manor of Thorpe, and vicar of the parish, delivers it regularly. If the crop of the great custom piece is insufficient to supply the quantity, it is made up from the little custom piece. In return, Mr. Bennett may claim an annual buck and a fawn or two, and the right of turning out four horses in Windsor Park ; the latter claim is never exercised. This information has been courteously supplied to us by Mr. Bennett.

on account of a servant of the abbot's having killed "Hugh de Torp."
Oh, rare "old times!" The abbot was mulcted in a heavy fine. Then,
while Bartholomew de Winchester was abbot, from 1272, until 1307,
during the reign of our first Edward, complaints were made to Pope
Gregory X. that the possessions of the abbey were alienated to civilians
and laymen, whereupon the pope issued a bull ordering such grants to be
revoked.

It is worthy of note, that the Chertsey monastery sheltered, for a
time, the remains of the pious, but unfortunate, Henry VI.

> "Poor key-cold figure of a Holy King,
> Pale ashes of the house of Lancaster."

and the reader of Shakespeare will recall the scene in which Richard
meets the Lady Anne on her way to Chertsey with her husband's body.

This poor king's remains had a claim to be well received by the
monks of Chertsey Abbey, for he had granted to the abbot the privilege
of holding a fair on St. Anne's-hill, then called Mount Eldebury, on the
feast of St Anne's (the 26th of July): the fair has changed its time and
quarters as well as its patron, and is held in the town on the 6th of
August, and called Black Cherry Fair. Manning, in his history of Surrey, says, that the tolls of this fair were taken by the abbot, and are now
taken by the owner of the site of the Abbey House ; thus the memory of
King Henry VI. is commemorated in the town of Chertsey to this day,
by the sale of black cherries in the harvest month of August!

Centuries passed over those magnificent abbeys, whose ruins in
many places add so much beauty to our fertile landscapes ; they grew
and grew, and added acre to acre, and stone to stone, and knowledge to
knowledge ; but most they cherished the knowledge which blazed like a
lamp under a bushel, and kept all but themselves in darkness ; they
preached no freedom in Christ to the Christian world, they abolished no
serfdom, they taught no liberty, they enslaved even these who in their
turn enslaved their "born thralls," and saw no evil in it. Oh, rare old
times! Better is it for us that the site of Chertsey Abbey should be
scarcely traceable now-a-days than that it should be as it was, with its
proud pageants and pent-up learning!—Yet we have neither sympathy
nor respect for that foul king, who, to serve his own carnal purposes,
overthrew the very faith which had hallowed his throne. But he did not
attack and storm the Abbey of Chertsey, as he did other religious
houses. He came to them, this Eighth Harry, with a fair show of kind-

ness, saying that "to the honour of God, and for the health of his soul, he proposed and most nobly intended to refound the late Monastery, Priory, or Abbey of Bisham in Berks, and to incorporate and establish the Abbot and Convent of Chertsey, as Abbot and Convent of Bisham, and to endow them with all the Manors late belonging to Bisham." How the then Abbot John Cordrey, and his brethren, must have shivered at the conditions ; how they must have grieved at quitting their cherished home, their stews and fish-ponds, their rich meadows of Thorpe, over-looked by the woods of Eldebury hill, their nursing ground where their calves and young lambs were stowed in luxurious safety in the pleasant farm of Simple Marsh at Addlestone![143]

REMAINS OF CHERTSEY ABBEY.

---

[143] The farm of Simple Marsh was the endowment of the sacristan of the Abbey, and its high and healthy situation was doubtless appreciated by the monks, who must have suffered from the low and swampy situation of their abbey. In 1614, Francis Maurice, and Francis Philips had a grant of Simple Marsh ; it came soon after into the possession of my Lord Castlemaine. There is a fine oak on the farm now, that could tell a tale of years long past, but there is not a tree in the Royal forest so fine as the "Crouch oak," which once marked the boundary of Windsor forest, and beneath whose branches Wickliff is said to have preached.

But their star was setting, and they were forced to comply with hard conditions ; here they are in one terrible sentence.

"The abbot and convent of Chertsey, give, sell, grant and confirm, to the king their house and all manors belonging to them."

The total destruction of the Abbey must have amazed the whole country. An earthquake could hardly have obliterated it more entirely. Aubrey, writing in the year 1673, says "of this great Abbey, scarce anything of the old building remains, except the out walls about it. Out of this ruin is built a 'fair house,' which is now in possession of Sir Nicholas Carew, master of the Buckhounds." Dr. Stukeley alludes to this house, in a letter written in 1752; he speaks of the inveterate destruction, and of "the gardener" carrying him through a "court" where he saw the remains of the church of the Abbey. He says the "east end reached up to an artificial mount along the garden wall ; that mount and all the terraces of the pleasure garden, to the back front of the house, are entirely made up of the sacred *rudera* or rubbish of continual devastations. Bones of abbots, monks, and great personages, who were buried in large numbers in the church and cloisters which lay on the south side of the church, were spread thick all over the garden, *so that one may pick up whole hands-full of them every where amongst the garden stuff.*" Brayley mentions in his pleasant History of Surrey, that this artificial mount, was levelled in 1810, and its materials employed to fill up a pond. Many human skulls and hones were found intermixed with the chalk and mortar of which it had been formed. Fragments of old tiles were also frequently found, and are still sometimes turned up. No trace even of the "Abbey house" is left ; it was purchased in 1809 by a stockbroker, who in the following year sold the materials—and so ends the great monastic history of Chertsey. Where are now its spiritualities in Surrey?—its temporalities in Berkshire and Hampshire?—its revenues of Stanwell, and rents of assize?— its spiritualities in Cardiganshire? Alas! alas! they have left no sign, except on the yellow parchment—of rare value to the antiquary.

Those who desire, like ourselves, to investigate what tradition has sanctified, will do well to turn down a lane beyond Chertsey Church,[144]

---

[144] Chertsey Church is of old foundation ; the only external traces of antiquity are in the tower, which has remained through all changes, the upper part being repaired and heightened by bricks. Within, the chancel is old but has been altered to adapt it to the new work with which it is conjoined. The body of the old church being greatly decayed, and of too narrow dimensions for the necessities of the parish, it was determined to rebuild it in

which leads directly to the Abbey bridge, and there amid tangled hedge rows and orchards, stands the fragment of an arch, partly built up, and so to say, disfigured by brick-work, and an old wall, both evidently portions of the Abbey. In the wall are a great number of what the people call *"black stones,"* a geological formation, making them seem fused by fire. Layers of tiles were also inserted in this wall, and where the cement has dropped away they can be distinctly traced ; there is also an ivy, very aged indeed ; it is so knotted and thick that it seems to grew through the stones, the soil has so evidently encroached on the wall that it is most probably rooted at the foundation. The pleasant market garden of Mr. Roake covers the actual ground on which the Abbey stood. The workmen frequently turn up broken tiles and human bones, and there is no doubt that by digging deeper much would be discovered that might elucidate the history of the past. At the farther end of the market garden a vault has been discovered which is of considerable length and breadth ; but the water rises so high in it (except after a long continuance of dry weather has sealed the land springs) that it is impossible to get to the end without wading. An enormous quantity of richly-coloured and decorated encaustic tiles have been found here ; some are preserved in our local museum. But the most interesting remains in this place are the "stews," or fish-ponds, which run parallel to each other ; like the bars of a gridiron ; these ponds do not communicate one with the other, nor has the water any outlet : a little care and attention might make them valuable for their old purposes ; but they are deplorably neglected. Occasionally you see the fin of some huge fish, whose slow movement partakes of the character of the stagnant water he has inhabited for years ;—who can tell how many?

"The Abbey River," as it is still called, travels slowly along its way, fertilising the meadows and imparting life and freshness to the

---

1806, but the expense being considerably greater than the architect's estimate, the tower and chancel were incorporated with the new work. Of the six bells contained in its tower one is said to have belonged to the abbey ; it has round its verge an inscription in early English letters each an inch in height as follows : —

"Ore : mente : pia. pro : nobis : Virgo : Maria."

In a few of the windows are fragments of stained glass, but there are none of the relics of antiquity within it which give such a charm to many of our country churches. Close to the altar rails is a bas-relief by Flaxman representing the Saviour raising the daughter of Jairus. It is a group of seven small figures treated in the simple and severe style of the sculptor.

placid scene. The denizens of Chertsey have planted orchards, and in a few instances gardens on its banks. One, the garden of Mr. Herring, is a model of neatness, almost concealed by its roses and carefully tended shrubs. We wandered from orchard to orchard, amid the trees and over the uneven ground ; all was so still and lonely that it required the suggestions of an active imagination to believe it had ever been the scene of contention by flood and field. From the Abbey Bridge the richness of the meadow scenery is exceedingly refreshing, the grass is deep and verdant, as it cannot fail to be, lying so low, and fertilised by perpetual moisture.

During their wide-spreading magnificence, the abbots of Chertsey, erected a picturesque chapel, on the lovely hill of St. Anne : this was done somewhat about the year 1334.   Orleton, Bishop of Winchester, granted an indulgence of forty days, to such persons as should repair to, and contribute to the fabric and its ornaments.

THE GOLDEN GROVE.

There is nowhere a more delightful road, than that which leads from the "Golden Grove," rendered picturesque by its old tree,[145] the plantations of Monksgrove on one side, and those of the once residence

---

[145] The little inn is somewhat romantically styled the "Golden Grove ;" before it, is a large tree, the branches of which spread luxuriantly at about eight feet from the ground, and support a railed platform, fitted round the central stem, upon which are a table and seats, embosomed among the leaves and branches, the ascent being by a flight of steps.

of Charles James Fox on the other. The road is perfectly embowered, and so close is the foliage that you have no idea of the beautiful view which awaits you, until leaving the statesman's house to the left, you pass through a sort of wicket gate on the right, and follow a foot-path to where two[146] magnificent trees crown the hill ; it is wisest to wait until passing along the level ridge, you arrive at the "view point," and there, spread around you is such a panorama as England only can show, and show against the world for its extreme richness.[147] On the left is Cooper's Hill, which Denham, that high-priest of "Local poetry," long ago made famous ; in the bend just where it meets the plain, you see the towers of Windsor Castle ; there is Harrow Hill, the sun shining brightly on its tall church ; a deep pall hovers over London, but you can see the dome of St. Paul's looming through the mist ; nay, we have heard of those who have told the hour of the day upon its broad-faced clock, with the assistance of a good glass. How beautifully the Thames winds! Ay! there is the grand stand at Epsom, and there Twickenham, delicious soft, balmy Twickenham ; and Richmond Hill—a very queen of beauty!

Yonder, beyond the valley, are Foxes Hills crowned with lofty pines—and that is the church at Staines, and as you turn, there again is Cooper's Hill ; Laleham seems spread as a tribute at your feet, and there is no end to the villages and mansions—the parks, and cottages like snow-drops in a parterre, and church spires more than we can number ; while close behind us are the stones, piled thickly one on the other,—the only relics of the holy Chapel of St. Anne.[148]

---

[146] There were originally four ; we remember three, but two have been lately destroyed.

[147] St. Anne's Hill, anciently called Eldbury or Oldbury Hill, has on its top visible traces of an encampment. There is a group of trees on its summit near which stood a small chapel dedicated to St. Anne, of which a few stones are now all that remains. They are shown in our cut. It is a spot which attracts all lovers of nature by the beauty of the view. Cowley, in a letter dated May 21, 1665, says, "methinks you and I and the Dean (Dean Spratt) might he very merry upon St. Anne's Hill. You might very conveniently come hither by way of Hampton Town, lying there one night." A curious Instance of the badness of roads and inconvenience of travelling in those days, Hampton being but thirteen miles from London, and Chertsey only twenty.

[148] In Chertsey Church is a black marble tablet to Laurence Tomson, buried there, and one of the earliest translators of the New Testament into our language, of which two editions were published in the reign of Queen Elizabeth. He resided during the last twenty years of his life at Laleham, and died in 1608. Antony Wood speaks of his being a great logician and philosopher, and states that a report was then current at Chertsey that he built the house which now stands on the top of St. Anne's hill, out of the ruins of St. Anne's

THE NUN'S WELL.

How grandly the promontory of St. George's Hill stands out—sheltering Weybridge, and forming a beautiful back-ground to Byfleet and the banks of the Way ; not forgetting its ruins—a Roman encampment of two thousand years ago, and its modern ornaments of rare trees, of which a generous nobleman has made common property, to be enjoyed daily by all who choose. At the foot of this richly planted hill, is the beautiful park of Oatlands—on the eve of becoming an assemblage of villa-grounds. How pleasant to feel that we can account, by our own knowledge of that glowing mount, for all the shades formed by the hills and hollows, and different growths of trees in the depths or heights of "the encampment," which forms the delight of many a toilsome antiquary. Beyond are the more distant eminences of the North

Chapel, and on the very spot where that chapel stood, having a prospect into several counties ; if so, these stones are, probably, the relics of St. Anne's Chapel and Laurence Tomson's house.

quary. Beyond are the more distant eminences of the North Downs, and a tract of country extending into Kent. But we have not yet explored the beauties of this our own hill of Chertsey ; truly, to do so would take a day as long as that of its own black cherry fair.

GATE OF FOX'S HOUSE.

A path to the left, among the fern and heather, leads to a well famed for its healing properties it is called the Nun's Well ;[149] even now, the peasants believe that its waters are a cure for diseases of the eye ; the path is steep and dangerous, and it is far pleasanter to walk round the brow of the hill and overlook the dense wood which conceals the well,

---

[149] The spring, called the "Nun's Well," once used medicinally, and which rarely freezes, is lined with stone, and is almost hidden with the vegetation which flourishes thickly around it. It is on the north side of the declivity, and on the east is another spring formerly celebrated for its virtues. It is in a wood called "Monk's Grove."

fringing the meadows of Thorpe, than to seek its tangled hiding-place in the dell. The monks of old would be sorely perplexed if they could arise, to account for the long line of smoke which marks the passage of the different trains along their railroads. But we turn from them to enjoy a ramble round the brow of St. Anne's Hill ; the coppice which clothes the descent into the valley, is so thick, that though it is intersected by many paths, you might lose yourself half-a-dozen times within an hour ; if it be evening, the nightingales in the thickets of Monksgrove have commenced their chorus, and the town of Chertsey, down below, is seen to its full extent, its church tower toned into beauty by the rich light of the setting sun, while through the trees and holly thickets you obtain glimpses of the Guildford and Leatherhead hills, so softly blue, that they meet and mingle with the sky.

Those who feel no interest in monkish chronicles, may reverence St. Anne's Hill, because of its having been the favourite residence of Charles James Fox, the contemporary of Pitt and Burke and Sheridan and Grattan, at a period when men felt strongly and spoke eloquently.

TEMPLE OF FRIENDSHIP.

The site of the house on the south-eastern side of the hill, is extremely beautiful, and it is much regretted in the neighbourhood that it finds so little favour in the heart of its present noble proprietor. The grounds are laid out with much taste ; there is a noble cedar planted by Mrs. Fox, when only the size of a wand. The statesman's widow survived her husband more than thirty-six years, but never outlived her friends or her faculties. There is a temple dedicated to Friendship, which was erected to perpetuate the coming of age of one of the late Lords Holland ; on a pedestal ornamented by a vase, are inscribed some verses by General Fitzpatrick ; another placed by Mrs. Fox to mark a favourite spot where

Mr. Fox loved to muse, is enriched by a quotation from the "Flower and the Leaf," concluded by two graceful stanzas—

> "Cheerful in this sequestered bower,
> From all the storms of life removed
> Here Fox enjoyed his evening hour
> In converse with the friends he loved.
> And here these lines he oft would quote,
> Pleased from his favourite poet's lay,
> When challenged by the warbler's note
> That breathed a song from every spray."

At the bottom of the garden is a grotto, which must have once possessed many attractions, and above it, there is a pretty little quaint chamber that was used as a tea-room, when, according to the custom of the time, the English drank tea by daylight ; it is adorned by painted glass windows ; there are portraits of the Prince of Wales, and Mr. Fox, when both were looking their best, and the balcony in front commands a delicious view of the surrounding country.

The peasantry are still loud in their praise of "Madam Fox ;" and some remember with gratitude the education they received at her school, and love to tell how the old lady was drawn there at "feast times," to see how they all looked in their new dresses. She certainly retained her sympathy with the young, and put away the feeling and habits of old age with a determined hand, for, it is said, when she was eighty she took lessons on the harp. The present generation remember personally nothing of the great statesman ; he has become history to us, and we must look to history, garbled as it always is, and always will be, by the opinions and feelings of its writers, to determine the position of Charles James Fox in the annals of his country. Those who were admitted to his society have written with en-

SUMMER HOUSE IN FOX'S GARDEN.

thusiasm of his social qualities, and bestow equal praise on his brilliant talents, his affability of manner, and the generosity of his disposition. He was the third son of Henry Fox, afterwards Lord Holland, and his mother was the eldest daughter of Charles, second Duke of Richmond, and consequently great-granddaughter to Charles II.; the maternal descent is one of blotted royalty, of which a man like Fox, could not have been proud. His academic course was unmarked by any of those honours of which Oxford men are so ambitious, and yet, like his great rival, William Pitt, he became a statesman before he was of age.

FOX'S ARBOUR.

At St. Anne's Hill he enjoyed as many intervals of repose and tranquillity as could fall to a statesman's lot ; in the time of wars and tumults, how he must have luxuriated in its delicious quiet, surrounded by friends who dearly loved him ; and swayed only for good by the wife who (although it is known that her early intimacy with him was such as prevented her general recognition in society) according to the evidence of all who knew her, was the minister only to his better thoughts and nobler ambitions, and who weaned him from nearly all the follies and vices which stained his youth and earlier manhood. Various causes led to his death, before age had added infirmities to disease. He died at Chiswick House, and his last words addressed to Mrs. Fox were, "I die happy." It is said he wished to be buried at Chertsey, but his remains were interred in Westminster Abbey.

The brilliant Sheridan pronounced so elegant an eulogium on his character, that it is pleasant to think of it in those shades where, as we have said, he so often sought and found repose : "When Mr. Fox ceased to live, the cause of private honour and friendship lost its highest glory, public liberty its most undaunted champion, and general humanity its most active and ardent assertor. In him was united the most amiable disposition with the most firm and resolute spirit ; the mildest manners, with the most exalted mind. With regard to that great man, it might, indeed, be well said, that in him the bravest heart and most exalted mind sat upon the seat of gentleness."

COWLEY'S SEAT.

There is, at all events, an imaginary pleasure in turning from the wearing out turmoil of a statesman's life, to what the world believes the tranquil dreams of a poet's existence. But there are few things the worldling so little understands as literary industry, or so little sympathises with as literary care. We have no inclination to over-rate either its toils or its pleasures, and perhaps no life is more abundantly supplied with both. Its toils must be evident to any who have noted the increasing literary labour, which is necessary to produce the ordinary sources of comforts ; but its high and holy enjoyments are not so apparent ; they are so different from those of almost all others as not to be easily explained or understood ; but above all other gifts, the marvellous gift of poesy is a distinction conferred by the Almighty, and should be acknowledged and treasured as such. We know little of a poet's studies except by their imperishable produce, and it is a common but ill-founded prejudice to imagine regularity or diligence incompatible with high genius. Genius is neither above law, nor opposed to it ; but as many have a poetic taste and temperament *without* the inspiration, the world is apt to mistake the eccentricity of the pretender for the outward and visible sign of genius. Whether or not the poet of the Porch-house of Chertsey had the actual poetic fire we do not venture to determine. Abraham Cowley takes a prominent position amongst the poets of our land, and the eventful times in which he lived, and his participation in their tumults give him additional interest in all the relations of his anxious and not over-happy life. It is recorded of him that he became a poet in consequence

COWLEY'S HOUSE – STREET FRONT.

of reading the Faery Queene, which chance threw in his way, while yet a child. In allusion to this, Dr. Johnson gave his well-known definition of genius—"A mind of large general powers, accidentally determined to some particular direction." We had almost dared to say this is rather the definition of a philosopher than of one who comprehended the spirituality of a marvellous gift. Abraham Cowley—the posthumous son of a London grocer—owed much to his mother. She, by her exertions, procured him a classical education at Westminster School. She lived to see him loved, honoured, and great, and what was better still, and more uncommon, grateful. At the age of fifteen he published a volume called "Poetic Blossoms," which he afterwards described as "commendable extravagancies in a boy." He obtained a scholarship in Trinity College, Cambridge, in 1636, and there took his degree ; but was ejected by the Parliament, and thence removed to Oxford. Shortly after, he followed the Queen Henrietta to Paris, as Secretary to the Earl of St. Albans, and was employed in the court of the exiles in the most confidential capacity. In 1656 he returned to England, and was immediately arrested as a suspected spy. He submitted quietly—the royalists thought too quietly—to the dominion of the Protector, but his whole life proved that he was no traitor. At the Restoration, that great national disappointment, his claims upon the ungrateful monarch were met by a taunt and a false insinuation—he was told that his pardon was his reward! Wood said, "he lost the place by certain enemies of the Muses ;" certain "friends of the Muses," however, procured for him the lease of the Porch-house and farm at Chertsey, held under the Queen, and the great desire of his life—solitude—was obtained.

COWLEY'S HOUSE – GARDEN FRONT.

The place still seems a meet dwelling for a poet, and is, perhaps, even more attractive to strangers than St. Anne's Hill. The porch, which caused his residence to be called "The Porch-house," was taken down during the last century by the father of its present proprietor, the Rev. John Crosby Clarke, and the house is now known as "Cowley House."[150] It is situated near the bridge which crosses a narrow and rapid stream, in a lonely part of Guildford Street ; a latticed window which overhangs the road is the window of the room in which the Poet expired ; on the outside wall Mr. Clarke has recorded his reason for removing the porch. "The porch of this house, which projected ten feet into the highway, was taken down in the year 1786, for the safety and accommodation of the public."

"Here the last accents flowed from Cowley's tongue."

The appearance of the house from Guildford Street, is no index to its size or conveniences.[151] You enter by a sidegate, and the new front of the dwelling is that of a comfortable and gentlemanly home ; the old part it is said was built in the reign of James the First, and what remains is sufficiently quaint to bear out the legend ; the old and new are much mingled, and the modern part consists of one or two bed rooms, a large dining room, and a drawing room, commanding a delicious garden view, the meanderings of the stream, and a long tract of luxuriant meadows, terminated by the high and richly timbered ground of St. Anne's Hill. A portion of the old stairway is preserved, the wood is not as has been stated oak, but sweet chestnut. One of the rooms is panelled with oak, and Cowley's study is a small closet-like chamber, the window looking

---

[150]The large outer porch of Cowley's house had chambers above it, and beneath the window in front a tablet was affixed, upon which was inscribed the epitaph "upon the living author" which Cowley had written for himself whilst living in retirement here, commencing

"Hic, O Viator, sub lare parvulo,

Couleius hic est conditus hic jacet."

It is represented in its original condition in the two views we have engraved.

[151] Some additional rooms have been added to the house by the same occupant, who has, however, religiously preserved all the old rooms, which still exhibit the "fittings" that existed in Cowley's time. The bedchambers are wainscotted with oaken panels. The staircase is a very solid structure, with ornamental balusters, leading toward the small study in which the poet wrote,—a little back room, about five feet wide, looking upon the garden. It may be distinguished in our back view of the house, by a figure placed at the window. Cowley ended his life in this house, at the early age of forty-nine.

STAIRCASE – COWLEY'S HOUSE.

towards St. Anne's Hill.[152] It is never difficult to imagine a poet in a *small chamber,* particularly when his mind may imbibe inspiration from so rich, and lovely a landscape. Beside the group of trees, beneath whose shadow the poet frequently sat, there is a horse chestnut of such exceeding size and beauty, that it is worthy a pilgrimage, and no lover of nature could look upon it without mingled feelings of reverence and affection.[153]

Here then amid such tranquil scenes, and such placid beauty, the "melancholy Cowley," passed the later days of his anxious existence ; here we, may fancy him receiving Evelyn and

---

[152] The father of the present proprietor was Chamberlain of London, and greatly beloved and respected in Chertsey. It is a happiness to be able to record also how much Mr. Clarke deserves the gratitude of the dwellers in our little town. During the late visitation of the cholera, his attention was drawn to the crowded state of the churchyard, and he not only made a grant of a piece of land to the parish as a cemetery, but has been at the sole expense of enclosing it, and erecting the necessary buildings for the purposes of interment.

[153] There is also in the garden a walnut-tree of which the history is curious. When Mr. Clarke was sheriff of London, it was a custom for the out-going sheriff to present to the in-coming sheriff, when he transferred to his custody the prisoners in Newgate, a bag of walnuts ; one of these walnuts Mr. Clarke planted in the garden, of which it is now— more than half a century having passed—the pride.

Denham, the poets and men of letters of his troubled day, who found the disappointments of courtly life, more than their philosophy could endure. Here, his friendly biographer, Doctor Spratt, cheered his lonely hours.

Cowley was one of those fortunate bards who obtain fame and honour during life. His learning was deep, his reading extensive, his acquaintance with mankind large. "To him" says Denham in his famous elegy.—

"To him no author was unknown,
Yet what he wrote was all his own."

TREES ON ST. ANNE'S HILL.

His biographer adds, "There was nothing affected or singular in his habit, or person, or gesture ; *he understood the forms of good breeding enough to practise them without burdening himself or others."* This indeed is the perfection of good breeding and good sense.

Having obtained, as we have said, the Porch-house at Chertsey, his mind dwelt with pleasure—a philosophic pleasure—upon the hereafter, which he hoped for in this life of tranquillity, and the silent labour he so dearly loved ; but he was destined to prove the reality of his own poesy—

> "Oh life, thou *Nothing's* younger brother,
> So *like* that one might take one for the other."

The career of Abraham Cowley was never sullied by vice,[154] he was loyal without being servile, and at once, modest, independent and sincere. His character is eloquently drawn by Doctor Spratt. "He governed his passions with great moderation, his virtues were never troublesome or uneasy to any, whatever he disliked in others he only corrected by the silent reproof of a better practice."

He died at Chertsey on the 28th of July 1667,[155] and was interred in Westminster Abbey. A throng of nobles followed him to his grave, and the worthless king who had deserted him, is reported to have said, that Mr. Cowley had not left a better man behind him in England.

It is said the body of Cowley was removed from Chertsey by water, thus making the Thames he loved so well, the high-way to his grave ; there is something highly poetic in this idea of a funeral, so still and solemn, with the oars dropping noiselessly in the blue water. Pope in allusion to it, says

> "What tears the river shed,
> When the sad pomp along his banks was led ;"

which rather inclines us to the belief that in this, as in many other instances, the poetic reading is not the true one,

> "The muses oft in lands of vision play :"

---

[154] Brayley in his History of Surrey, states that Cowley accompanied by his friend Dean Spratt, having been to see a "friend," did not set out for his walk home until it was too late, and had drunk so deep, that they both lay out in the fields all night ; this gave Cowley the fever that carried him off. Brayley's authority for this slander, (which is not borne out by his poet's previous course of life), is "Spence's Anecdotes."

[155] On comparing dates, it is evident that Cowley could not have enjoyed his retirement more than between two and three years.

but the fact that he died at Chertsey, as much respected as a man, as he was admired as a poet is certain, and his house is often visited by strangers, who are permitted to see his favourite haunts by the kindness of its proprietor who honours the spot so hallowed by memories of "the melancholy Cowley :" —he who considered and described "business" as—

"The contradiction to his fate,"

But we must postpone our farther rambles for the present.

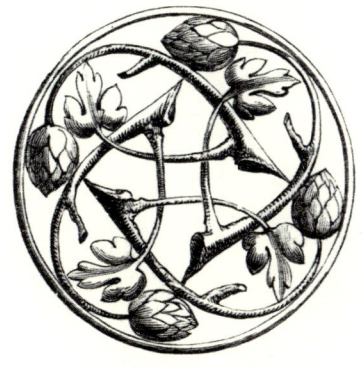